The
Garland Library
of
War and Peace

The
Garland Library
of
War and Peace

Under the General Editorship of

Blanche Wiesen Cook, *John Jay College, C.U.N.Y.*

Sandi E. Cooper, *Richmond College, C.U.N.Y.*

Charles Chatfield, *Wittenberg University*

Sir Randal Cremer
His Life and Work

by

Howard Evans

with a new introduction
for the Garland Edition by
Naomi Churgin Miller

Garland Publishing, Inc., New York & London
1973

The new introduction for this

Garland Library Edition is Copyright © 1973, by

Garland Publishing Inc.

———————

All Rights Reserved

———————

Library of Congress Cataloging in Publication Data

Evans, Howard, 1839–1915.
  Sir Randal Cremer.

  (Garland library of war and peace)
  Reprint of the 1909 ed. published by T. F. Unwin,
London.
    1. Cremer, Sir William Randal, 1828–1908. 2. Peace.
I. Title. II. Series.
JX1962.C8E85 1973   327'.172'0924 [B]
ISBN 0-8240-0250-4   74-147455

Printed in the United States of America

Introduction

Howard Evans's biography of Sir Randal Cremer (1828-1908) is the only complete account we have of an English trade unionist whose qualities of leadership and prodigious energy created two important organizations committed to the achievement of international arbitration of disputes, a world court and general disarmament. Acknowledging the value of his work for peace, the French government conferred upon him the Cross of the Legion of Honor, Norway made him a commander of the Order of St. Olaf and his own government honored him with a knighthood. The climax of his career came in 1903 when he received the Nobel Peace Prize, the greatest recognition that could be accorded him. Since Howard Evans was Cremer's friend and a colleague of forty years standing as well as a participant in many of the events he describes, this book is an important contemporary document of keen interest to students of British working-class history as it must be to those concerned with the late nineteenth-century peace movement.

Cremer's achievement was a triumph of sheer character over adverse circumstances. He was born into a poor working-class family in Fareham, Wiltshire. His father, a coach painter, deserted his family, leaving to the mother the responsibility for the care of three young children. Cremer's mother was probably the most dominant influence in shaping the discipline which marked his own life. She kept a small school and with her meager earnings barely supported the needs of the family. A Methodist, she brought up her children strictly. Cremer recalled the quiet Sabbaths when only religious literature entered the house and all activities reflected the sanctity of the day. Although later he totally rejected organized religion, Cremer's veneration of his mother prevented him from expressing his feelings publicly. His early training encouraged the development of a personal morality which so impressed observers that they preferred to describe him as a "broad-minded Christian." As a child Cremer revealed an inquiring mind and a desire for self-improvement that was to carry him far beyond the meager education he received in the local church school. Instinctively he rejected his teacher's admonition to "order himself lowly and reverently towards his betters" and his warning against attending Chartist meetings advocating manhood suffrage. When he was older and serving his apprenticeship as a carpenter, he seized every opportunity to attend a mechanics' institute and the many public meetings dealing with issues vitally affecting British working classes.

The trade union movement gave him the opportunity to display a capacity for leadership which later served the cause of world peace. Evidences of trust in his judgment occurred early. When he was still a journeyman carpenter and the nine-hour movement was the dominant concern of the building trades, the men selected Cremer as the delegate from their shop to the central council directing the agitation. Soon after, the struggle for the right of unions to organize the men came under fire, and Cremer was chosen as one of the seven-member council which organized the effort for his trade. Cremer himself was one of the chief organizers of the important Amalgamated Society of Carpenters and Joiners, and by the 1860s, a leading figure in the trade union movement.

By then, political issues claimed his attention. British workingmen, almost unanimously, viewed the American Civil War as a contest between slavery and freedom and gave their support to the North. Cremer helped organize one of the most impressive of working-class demonstrations on behalf of the North in St. James's Hall, presided over by John Bright, the distinguished Victorian reformer. When a workmen's committee for the support of the North was organized Cremer became its secretary. A second event which evoked profound working-class feeling was the visit to England in 1864 of Garibaldi, the Italian republican hero. He was greeted everywhere with expressions of popular sympathy and support. Cremer actively participated in these demonstrations and later helped organize the Primrose Hill meeting which protested alleged government pressure for Garibaldi's departure. This event, in turn, contributed to the decision to launch a movement for manhood suffrage. Again Cremer played an important role in organizing the Reform League to direct the agitation. When the Reform Bill of 1867 conferred the vote on urban workingmen, the way was opened for their direct participation in national politics, and Cremer was among the earliest workingmen to seize the new opportunity by standing for election to the House of Commons. He unsuccessfully contested Warwick in 1868 and again in 1874 but not until the general election of 1885 was he successful, elected to a seat from the predominantly working-class metropolitan constituency of Haggerston. As a result of his trade unionist activities, Cremer knew most of the prominent labor leaders of his time: George Howell, secretary to the Trades Union Congress and later a member of Parliament, George Odger, one of the most important of the London trade unionists, Robert Applegarth, secretary of the Amalgamated Society of Carpenters and Joiners and Joseph Arch, the organizer of the agricultural workers. Working together with them, Cremer, in 1864, helped found the International Workingmen's Association, better known as the First International, and became its secretary. He hoped that an international organization of workingmen would devote itself to improving conditions of work for all labor. When he and others of the British delegation found that their pragmatic goals deviated from the increasingly ideological concerns of their European counterparts — when class revolution rather than an improvement of working conditions became the avowed aim of the organization — Cremer and his friends disassociated themselves from the International. But his first foray into international organization brought him into touch with French labor leaders who later helped him with his own organization for arbitration and world peace. This was the only concrete advantage that he gained from the experience.

By the time Cremer adopted the cause of international arbitration as peculiarly his own, he had demonstrated his talent for leadership. He was energetic, selfless, and possessed of a "splendid audacity," and no one could surpass his skill in organization. On short notice, he convoked great public meetings, drew up manifestoes and obtained signed petitions and addresses from prominent figures and also from the rank and file of the trade unionists whom he knew so well. The force of his own conviction and his confidence of success persuaded men to follow his lead. Reserved and self-effacing, Cremer preferred the office of secretary to more prominent positions in the organizations which he founded. As a result, he often remained in the background at the important affairs he organized with other men taking the lead which he had mapped out in advance. He geared his plans not to the modest means at his disposal but rather to the great objectives he had in mind, and so very soon after he took up the cause of international arbitration, he conceived of an international effort embracing workingmen as well as legislators. Primarily

INTRODUCTION

concerned with mobilizing workingmen in his movement for peace, he contributed significantly to the
transformation of the late nineteenth-century peace
movement from a predominantly middle-class endeavor to one that was characterized by significant
working-class participation and leadership. His work
earned him the admiration of many public figures.
Andrew Carnegie regarded him as the best example of
the modern hero — the man who devoted his life to
the achievement of lasting peace and in this way to
the preservation of civilization itself.

Cremer's interest in arbitration awakened early and
was reinforced by the successful application of this
procedure to the settlement of industrial disputes. It
was in his youth that he first felt the appeal of the
cause. One evening, when he was about eighteen years
old and still serving his apprenticeship, he attended a
public meeting addressed by an emissary from the
London Peace Society. The speaker argued for
peaceful methods to resolve international disputes,
and so end forever the danger of war. Cremer was
deeply moved. He recalled later: "I listened with rapt
attention, and the next day I discussed the matter
with two or three shopmates who had been present.
They poohpoohed the idea and declared that the
world had always settled its disputes by force and
would continue to do so. That lecture sowed the
seeds of international arbitration in my mind, though
the word 'arbitration' had hardly been used." Twenty
years later the seeds sown in this unexpected fashion

began to bear their fruit. Because of his activity in the trade union movement, Cremer often heard of arbitration in subsequent years. In the 1860s, trade unions, as eager as their employers to avoid costly strikes, began to refer their grievances to arbitration. Success in this area strengthened Cremer's conviction of its utility for the settlement of international disputes. In 1868, when he began to campaign for a seat in the House of Commons, he had already made his decision, and his platform committed him to work for international arbitration and the establishment of a world court. By then arbitration was no longer a strange and unfamiliar term, and his advocacy could not be dismissed as impractical or visionary.

Cremer enjoyed advantages denied to earlier peace advocates. First, the pioneering work for peace had already been done, and the foundation established for his own undertaking. Second, by concentrating on arbitration, Cremer avoided the issue of nonresistance to all wars, identified with the Quakers, which had divided and weakened the early peace movement. Third, his natural constituency — the workingmen — won the right to vote by the Reform Acts of 1867 and 1884, enabling labor to become politically influential. Fourth, arbitration had been used successfully in Anglo-American relations. The settlement of the Alabama Claims case in 1872 was merely the most recent example of a procedure that had been applied to previous conflicts. In fact, by 1870 Britain had been party to twenty-three arbitration cases and the United States to twenty-four, a unique record which justified the description of arbitration as an Anglo-American invention. Because of its demonstrated utility, the cause of arbitration attracted the support of men in high office on both sides of the Atlantic. Cremer's task, then, was not to argue for a novel procedure but rather to win for it a broader and more regular application to all disputes which diplomacy could not resolve.

To achieve his ends, Cremer founded two organizations: the International Arbitration League around 1871 and the Inter-Parliamentary Union in 1889. Both figured prominently in his agitation. The first originated in the fear of British intervention in the Franco-Prussian War of 1870 and of the possible failure of the Alabama Claims arbitration. To avoid such consequences, Cremer hastily organized his friends with whom he had served in the Reform League into a Workmen's Peace Committee which shortly thereafter adopted the name by which it was to be known. Edmund Beales, the former president of the Reform League, assumed the presidency of the new organization; a Marleybone shoemaker, Benjamin Britten, served as treasurer; and Cremer took the position he favored above all others, the secretaryship. The first public statements of the league called for nonintervention in the Franco-Prussian War and an amicable settlement of the outstanding issues in the Alabama Claims case; the league's first major project was the draft of a scheme for a high court of nations. Believing that arbitration as an international concern required international action on its behalf, Cremer encouraged the formation of a French counterpart of the Arbitration League in 1875. Similar groups appeared in other European countries creating opportunities for a coordinated working-men's international movement for arbitration and a world court.

From its inception, the International Arbitration League was designed to be a workingmen's organization, expressing the views of this class on important issues of war, peace and international morality. Cremer used the league to mobilize workingmen's opposition to British intervention in the Russo-Turkish War of 1876, to British annexation of the Transvaal in 1877, the occupation of Egypt in 1882, and in 1899 to the Boer War. The organization worked for an Anglo-French arbitration treaty and celebrated its achievement in 1903, and in the year before Cremer's death, tried to counteract the growing hostility between Britain and Germany. In all of these protests and demonstrations, Cremer emphasized the working-class character of the league. Most of the officers and the rank and file of its members were workingmen. To insure their control of the organization in the future, Cremer allocated to it his Nobel Prize money and required that workingmen constitute at least two-thirds of the council, the executive committee of the league.

In securing the money required to finance the

league's activities, Cremer proved his ability to win the support of a variety of people. Initially, the British Peace Society provided a modest subsidy, eager to enlist workingmen on behalf of the cause of peace. When this ended, Cremer turned for help to some of the trade unions and to wealthy philanthropists, notably Samuel Morley (1809-86) a successful hosiery manufacturer, later elected to the House of Commons; George Palmer (1808-97), producer of biscuits and also a member of Parliament; Richard and George Cadbury, confectioners; and, most important, from Andrew Carnegie who became acquainted with Cremer and his work while serving as American ambassador to Great Britain. Carnegie supplemented Cremer's gift to the Arbitration League and probably was responsible for many benefactions to the league. The evidence suggests that Cremer's may have been the single, most important influence in shaping Carnegie's decision to devote his energies and resources to the achievement of world peace.

Cremer's second organization, the Inter-Parliamentary Union, was designed to mobilize support for arbitration from a different quarter — elected members of legislative bodies. Themselves committed to the principle of arbitration in international affairs, they acted as pressure groups within their own governments on behalf of their objective. The idea was ingenious. Originally conceived by an Austrian, Albert Fischoff, in 1875, it became a reality only when Cremer directed his energies to implement it.

14

INTRODUCTION

After he was elected to the House of Commons, he was in a position to sound out others on its feasibility, and in 1888, at an Anglo-French meeting of legislators, the foundation was laid for the Inter-Parliamentary Union. Frédéric Passy became the first president, with Cremer as one of the vice presidents as well as secretary for the British section of the organization. Conferences soon followed in regular succession: London, Rome, The Hague, Brussels, Budapest, Christiana, Paris, Vienna and St. Louis. The climax of these meetings, at least for Cremer, came in 1906 when the Inter-Parliamentary Union met in the gallery of the House of Lords. In many ways, the conference was a personal tribute to Cremer and to what he had accomplished. The delegates heard a speech by Campbell-Bannerman, the prime minister, who reiterated his own and his government's commitment to world peace. Other governments also had responded to the work of the Inter-Parliamentary Union. The organization proved its worth and nowhere better than in its efforts to achieve treaties of arbitration between states. In this regard, Anglo-American relations held out the best hope for fruitful action.

Even before he organized the Inter-Parliamentary Union, Cremer used his seat in the House of Commons to initiate action for an Anglo-American treaty of arbitration. In 1887 he drew up a memorial urging such a treaty, addressed to the president and the Congress of the United States and signed by 232 members of Parliament. This was the first time, remarked John Bright, that members of a legislature memorialized a foreign government on behalf of a specific cause. That first visit to the United States was an important event in Cremer's work for arbitration. The way was prepared for him by the intercession of Andrew Carnegie, the sympathy of Sir Julian Pauncefote, the British ambassador to the United States, and by the equally enthusiastic support of Walter Gresham and later of his successor, Richard Olney, secretaries of state in Cleveland's administration. Three years later, Congress passed a joint resolution in favor of treaties of arbitration, and in 1893 the House of Commons, responding to American overtures, passed unanimously Cremer's motion inviting the government to begin negotiations of an Anglo-American treaty of arbitration. Since the interests of both countries favored the peaceful settlement of all disputes, arbitration commanded the support of both political parties. Gladstone, the Liberal, and Salisbury, the Conservative, were prepared to commit their governments to the principle of arbitration in Anglo-American affairs. As a result of Lord Salisbury's initiative in 1896, the Olney-Pauncefote treaty of arbitration was negotiated only to be withdrawn by the president when the Senate's amendments seemed to vitiate the purpose of the treaty. Nevertheless, in the years following the successful conclusion of the Alabama Claims case, both countries resolved peacefully a succession of disputes: the

INTRODUCTION

Bering Sea controversy in 1892, the Venezuela Boundary issue in 1895, the Alaskan Boundary question in 1903 and the conflicting claims to the use of the North Atlantic Fisheries in 1909. Although a permanent Anglo-American arbitration treaty was delayed until 1914, the peaceful settlement of disputes was an important theme in Anglo-American relations in the decades after 1870. Cremer contributed to this achievement. He popularized the principle of arbitration and created public support for it and an atmosphere in which government initiatives met with ready public acceptance. In this rests his own unique accomplishment.

Cremer played no direct role in bringing about the Hague Conferences of 1899 and 1907. They were the result of Russian initiatives which other states found it in their interest to accept. These meetings mark the climax of the nineteenth-century peace movement. But they also reveal the extent to which governments, rather than popular movements, determined the course of events. Sir Julian Pauncefote came to the Hague Conference of 1899 armed with a scheme for a world court and compulsory arbitration. The delegates rejected compulsory arbitration and accepted the plan for a world court only after they excluded from its jurisdiction all cases involving the honor or vital interests of a country. Proposals for arms limitation, offered on both occasions, failed dismally. The second Hague Conference ratified an explicit statement on the obligations of neutral states in time

INTRODUCTION

of war, but the Declaration of London which attempted to define categories of contraband could not secure parliamentary ratification; the bill for this purpose was even denied a second reading. Despite the genuine achievements of Cremer and others like him who labored for world peace before 1914, imperial rivalries, opposing alliance systems and increasing arms budgets established the limits to their endeavor. The world war of 1914 ended a significant chapter in the age-old struggle for peace among nations, but amidst the debacle of their hopes, people who cherished peace renewed their commitment to its achievement.

Naomi Churgin Miller
Hunter College — C.U.N.Y.

SIR RANDAL CREMER

Sir Randal Cremer, M.P.

SIR RANDAL CREMER

HIS LIFE AND WORK

BY

HOWARD EVANS

T. FISHER UNWIN

LONDON
ADELPHI TERRACE

LEIPSIC
INSELSTRASSE 20

1909

CONTENTS

CHAPTER I.

PAGE

FOREWORDS 11

CHAPTER II.

EARLY LIFE 18

CHAPTER III.

THE INTERNATIONAL 31

CHAPTER IV.

GARIBALDI'S VISIT AND THE REFORM LEAGUE . . 40

CHAPTER V.

EARLY ELECTION CONTESTS 49

CHAPTER VI.

THE PIONEERS OF PEACE 56

CHAPTER VII.

THE GENEVA ARBITRATION 74

CHAPTER VIII.

BIRTH OF THE WORKMEN'S PEACE ASSOCIATION . 82

5

CHAPTER IX.

PAGE

PIONEER WORK IN PARIS 88

CHAPTER X.

THE EASTERN CRISIS 97

CHAPTER XI.

SOUTH AFRICA AND EGYPT 105

CHAPTER XII.

IN PARIS AGAIN 109

CHAPTER XIII.

FIRST ELECTION FOR HAGGERSTON . . . 114

CHAPTER XIV.

DE PROFUNDIS 119

CHAPTER XV.

FIRST INVASION OF WASHINGTON . . . 123

CHAPTER XVI.

BIRTH OF THE INTERPARLIAMENTARY UNION . . 134

CHAPTER XVII.

OPPORTUNITY AT LAST 150

CHAPTER XVIII.

SECOND VISIT TO WASHINGTON 158

CONTENTS

CHAPTER XIX.

PAGE

THE INTERPARLIAMENTARY AT THE HAGUE AND BRUS-
SELS—A DEFEAT AND A PETITION . . . 169

CHAPTER XX.

THE INTERPARLIAMENTARY AT BUDA-PESTH . . 176

CHAPTER XXI.

THIRD VISIT TO WASHINGTON 182

CHAPTER XXII.

THE TZAR'S RESCRIPT AND THE FIRST HAGUE CON-
FERENCE 189

CHAPTER XXIII.

INTERPARLIAMENTARY UNION AT PARIS . . 203

CHAPTER XXIV.

THE BOER WAR 216

CHAPTER XXV.

A FRENCH INVASION OF ENGLAND . . . 224

CHAPTER XXVI.

BRITISH INVASION OF FRANCE 235

CHAPTER XXVII.

FOURTH VISIT TO WASHINGTON 260

8 CONTENTS

CHAPTER XXVIII.

PAGE

THE NOBEL DINNER 267

CHAPTER XXIX.

THE INTERPARLIAMENTARY UNION AT WESTMINSTER . 280

CHAPTER XXX.

SECOND HAGUE CONFERENCE 291

CHAPTER XXXI.

THE FINAL EFFORT 298

CHAPTER XXXII.

IN MEMORIAM 304

CHAPTER XXXIII.

" HE BEING DEAD, YET SPEAKETH " . . . 316

CHAPTER XXXIV.

REPORTING PROGRESS 326

CHAPTER XXXV.

CHARACTERISTICS, BENEFACTIONS, HONOURS . . 331

CHAPTER XXXVI.

THE ULTIMATE GOAL 348

INDEX 353

ILLUSTRATIONS

SIR RANDAL CREMER . . . *Frontispiece*

Facing page

CARD OF MEMBERSHIP OF THE INTERNATIONAL . 32

CREMER COTTAGES AT FAREHAM . . . 314

PROGRESS OF COMPULSORY ARBITRATION FROM 1903 TO 1908. (CHART ISSUED BY THE FRENCH FOREIGN OFFICE) 326

SIR RANDAL CREMER

CHAPTER I

FOREWORDS

THIS volume is written with the double purpose of telling the life-story of a man who devoted himself to the service of humanity, and of giving a succinct history of one of the most notable movements of modern times. The cause and the man are inseparable. Though a due meed of honour must be paid to others who have co-operated in the work that has been done, and especially to those early pioneers who, like Immanuel Kant, cherished "the sweet dream of perpetual peace," and sought to realise it, the foremost leader for a whole generation was the man whose history is herein recorded.

His life-story is an amazing chronicle of persistent effort, of indomitable courage, and in the end of splendid success. Seldom did a man start in life with so small a fulcrum to move the world.

11

The only parallel modern instance is that of
William Lloyd Garrison, the great American
abolitionist. As will be seen hereafter, the dominant idea in the mind of Cremer was the fraternity
of the peoples. To realise this idea he became
the first English secretary of the International ; it
finds a prominent place in his first address to the
electors of Warwick ; and when the Franco-
German War broke out he gathered around him,
in his own house, a little band of workmen
comrades enlisted in the apparently hopeless task
of making war against war.

> " Such earnest natures are the fiery pith,
>   The compact nucleus, round which systems grow !
> Mass after mass becomes inspired therewith,
>   And whirls impregnate with the central glow."

Although the International Arbitration League
in its earlier years accomplished much useful propagandist work in this country, more especially
among labour organisations, as well as in Paris,
where it was assisted by Victor Hugo and other
eminent Frenchmen, nothing much could be
effected on a great scale until its leader was able
to find a seat in Parliament. Cremer had to wait
for fifteen long years before he was able to secure
this vantage-ground. When he did enter Parliament he was already fifty-seven years of age, a
time of life when it is difficult for a man to enter
upon a parliamentary career, and when most men
are inclined to put off their armour rather than gird

themselves for any fresh effort. With Cremer it was otherwise. While he took an active part in other progressive movements, especially those in which the industrial classes were more especially concerned, he devoted himself mainly to the great purpose of his life. His strenuous efforts were largely successful, as will be seen hereafter. Though he had to contend with many difficulties and discouragements, both at home and abroad, and, owing to unexpected obstacles, he failed in his immediate purpose with regard to the United States ; his very mission to Washington indirectly resulted in the establishment of arbitration between all the American republics, and led ultimately to the creation of the Inter-Parliamentary Union, which in recent years has grown to proportions far beyond his most sanguine hopes. These successes were mainly due to the indefatigable energy of Cremer himself, and were attained by an expenditure of money which would have been utterly inadequate had it not been for his unbounded faith and his inexhaustible energy. His work, of course, remains uncompleted, and must remain incomplete so long as the peoples of Europe continue to allow themselves to be cursed with the ruinous expenditure on bloated armaments which press so heavily on all the wage-earners. But the triumphs of arbitration are already so great that the man who laboured in the cause till the ripe old age of eighty might be amply satisfied with the progress made in his own lifetime.

" For he saw ere his eye was darkened
  The sheaves of the harvest-bringing,
And heard while his ear yet harkened
  The voice of the reapers singing.

Ah, well ! the world is discreet ;
  There are plenty to pause and wait ;
But here was a man who set his feet
  Some time in advance of fate."

The International Arbitration League, of which
Cremer was the founder, and for many years the
leader, in two important respects had its own dis-
tinct and separate lines of action. It was originally
a purely labour organisation, and in the main it
continues to be so, for it is provided even now in
the Cremer Trust that a majority of two-thirds
of its Council must belong to the ranks of labour.
Consequently throughout its history it has been in
close touch with working men's organisations at
home and abroad, as will be seen hereafter. Yet,
further, its action has been developed on interparliamentary lines, Cremer having acquired a
vantage-ground in this direction which other men,
equally earnest, were not able to obtain.

As this book is biographical it is necessarily
limited in its scope to that large part of the
pacific movement with which Cremer was more
directly connected. It is only right, however, that
acknowledgment should be made of the important
services rendered to the cause, not only by the
early pioneers, but by later comrades connected
with other bodies. In particular due honour should

be paid to Dr. Darby, Miss Peckover, and Miss Ellen Robinson, of the Peace Society ; to Mr. Felix Moscheles and Mr. J. F. Green, of the International Arbitration and Peace Association ; and to Mr. T. P. Newman and Mr. Perris, of the National Peace Council.

Cremer in his later years conceived the idea of writing the story of his own life, but the memoranda which he left were of the most fragmentary character, whose only value was to refresh my own recollections. Throughout this book, as far as possible, I have endeavoured to tell the story as he would have told it himself. I knew the mind of my friend better than any other living man, have constantly shared his disappointments and his triumphs, and, above all, his unfaltering faith in the future. The story in its main features may seem somewhat prosaic to those who delight in sensationalism, but this man had no thought for dramatic effect ; his ruling passion was to serve humanity, and in that service he was always ready to deny himself, and even to abase himself. When he had once obtained the means whereby he could work the man was absorbed in the cause, and with his dominant idea in view the present biography has been written.

The reason why I have been selected to tell the story of Cremer's life is that from the first hour I have been associated with him in the work of the League ; that for thirty years I have been chairman of its Council ; that when Cremer devoted the Nobel Prize to the cause I became, at his request, the secretary of his trustees ; and that by his Will I became one of his executors.

I have to tell the story of a life that was comparatively uneventful, except in relation to the one grand purpose to which he was devoted. For nearly forty years Cremer set before himself a task which might have daunted the greatest statesmen in Europe, and for the greater part of the time he had but a languid support from most of those who theoretically accepted the principle of arbitration. He said, " This one thing I do " ; and to this one thing every other consideration was subordinate. Yet he was by no means a man of one idea. Compulsory and free education, public libraries, commons preservation, registration reform, taxation of ground values, nationalisation of the land, religious equality, the right of free speech, the deliverance of trade unions from judge-made law, the protection of weaker races, the emancipation of oppressed nationalities were all causes dear to his heart in which he took a keen interest ; but he felt the necessity of concentrating his whole strength on the tremendous task before him, on which the future of humanity so largely depended.

Other and greater men had failed before him. He had seen with his own eyes how the high hopes and laborious efforts of men like Bright, Cobden, and Henry Richard had been cruelly blasted ; that in this country Christian men too often accepted the principle of human brotherhood with a lazy acquiescence which frequently broke down under the strain of a spurious patriotism, and that abroad the democracy was deluded by the dream of one more war that should establish a socialist millennium. But none of these things moved him, neither did he count his life dear unto himself if only he could advance the great cause to which that life was consecrated. Of this man's disinterestedness it is superfluous to say a single word. His life story is the best testimony.

My thanks are due to my sons, A. H. Evans and F. Evans (Amalgamated Society of Engineers), without whose material assistance this book could not have been written.

CHAPTER II

EARLY LIFE

WHEN Cremer was born, in 1828, George IV. was King. It was a time of intense misery for the labouring classes. Working men while in work to-day have no conception of the poverty of the actual workers of that period. Only about a dozen years before the maddened farm labourers of the eastern counties had risen in revolt, inscribing on their banner "Bread or Blood." When Cremer was a small child, in 1834, a body of Dorset labourers who had the audacity to form a trades union were transported with burglars and highwaymen to the Antipodes. It was in such a world as this that Cremer began his life.

There were two causes for the distress—the great war, and the Corn Law which was passed at its close. As to the war, Thorold Rogers writes in his "Work and Wages": "Thousands of homes were starved in order to find the means for the great war, the cost of which was really supported by the labour of those who toiled on and earned the wealth which was lavished freely, and at good interest for the lenders, by the Government. The enormous taxation and the gigantic loans came from the store of accumulated capital, which the employers wrung from the poor wages of labour, or the landlords extracted from the growing gains of their tenants. To outward appearance the strife was waged by armies and generals ; in reality the resources on which the struggle was based, and without which it would have speedily collapsed, were the stint and starvation of labour, the over-taxed and underfed toils of childhood, the under-paid and uncertain employment of men. Wages were mulcted in order to provide the waste of war, and the profits of commerce and manufacture."

As soon as the war had ended the misery of the working classes was prolonged by the passing of the Corn Law of 1815, which prohibited the importation of corn until the price rose to eighty shillings a quarter.

William Randal Cremer was born on March 18, 1828, and was baptized in the Wesleyan chapel at Fareham shortly afterwards. His father, George Cremer, originally came from Warminster, in Wilts ; his mother, Harriet, whose maiden name was Tutte, was the daughter of a local builder. The child was named Randal after his maternal grandfather, Randal Tutte.

To his father, who was a working coach-painter, Cremer owed nothing, for he deserted his family when the child was little more than an infant. To his mother he owed much, and he always had a warm corner in his heart for her memory. At one time Cremer contemplated setting up a memorial tablet in the interior of the Wesleyan chapel at Fareham, of which she was for many years a member ; but ultimately he conceived the more utilitarian design of erecting a few almshouses in his mother's memory, of which I shall have more to say hereafter.

Fareham, in the south of Hants, is a straggling little town of small importance. The Romans found its soil good for brickmaking, afterwards a tribe of West Saxons settled there, and ultimately most of the land became part of the royal endowment of the See of Winchester. Once, and apparently once only, some centuries ago, Fareham sent representatives to Parliament, but the burgesses found the honour too burdensome. An arm of the sea stretches up from Portsmouth to Fareham, and thus affords it the advantage of a small shipbuilding trade.

Cremer once gave the House of Commons some graphic reminiscences of the home of poverty in which he was brought up, when he opposed the proposal of Sir Michael Hicks-Beach to levy a shilling duty on corn. He said that when his mother, who kept a dame school, had only five or six shillings a week on which to keep herself, him, and his two sisters, a two-pound loaf cost eightpence. For breakfast the children had three thin slices of bread with a very thin scraping of butter, and a cup of weak tea without milk or sugar. Dinner consisted of boiled duff—flour and water stewed together and boiled like a pudding—with potatoes, and perhaps once a week an ounce or two of meat. The tea was like the breakfast, and usually the children had to go to bed without supper, hungry as wolves. Naturally, the boy grew wan and pinched, and the old grandmother used to say, " Ah, Harriet, I am afraid you will never save that poor boy." A kindly gift of flannel shirts from the parson, as Cremer believed, really saved the boy's life.

As Cremer grew older, he was sent to a Church school, where he was, of course, taught to order himself lowly and reverently towards his betters, a rule of which in after-life he was very often oblivious. The Church Socialists nowadays put a convenient gloss on these awkward words, but at that time they were taken in their obvious and literal meaning. Cremer, in his brief reminiscences says : " In those days the Chartists were attracting a great deal of attention by their meetings, and by what was considered their treasonable utterances. One day at school the old schoolmaster tried to explain to us gaping boys what dangerous people the Chartists were, and ended by saying that the magistrates of the town had given orders that if they came there, anybody who listened to them would be arrested. Although I was only ten or eleven, it struck me as very odd that the people who went to listen to the Chartists

should be arrested, and I could not help asking
myself why the magistrates did not arrest the
Chartists themselves."

Cremer was not only a scholar in the Church
school, but also a chorister in the church ; in fact,
he was rather a favourite of the vicar, the Rev.
Sir Henry Thompson, who presented him with a
Bible when he left the choir.

Cremer's mother was a strong Methodist. In
the few fragmentary notes of his early days which
he left behind him he says : " My mother's notions
concerning the way in which the Sabbath should
be kept were so severe that we were not allowed
to read the newspaper or anything of a secular
character, so whatever reading was done was confined to the Bible or religious books and tracts.
We were not allowed even to go for a walk on a
Sunday."

As the lad grew older, of course, this discipline
was somewhat relaxed. There were Radicals even
in Fareham, one of whom lent him *Lloyd's News*,
and another the *Weekly Dispatch*, the result being
that young Cremer himself became a Radical.
Here is a fragmentary note of Cremer's discussion
with the Rev. Mr. Dawson, who had preached from
the text, " In the sweat of thy face shalt thou
eat bread." " I asked him if he considered that
curse to apply to the whole human race. He
answered, ' Yes, certainly.' I then asked him how
it happened that so many people were allowed to
evade this curse by not working at all, and yet

living in luxury. This he appeared quite unable to answer. Not long after he preached a sermon rebuking those who meddled with politics, and asserted that the best politics were to be found in the Bible."

At twelve years of age the poverty of the family made it necessary that young Cremer should leave school and begin to earn his own living. Cremer's own account of his first start in life is as follows :

" My first job was as a pitch-boy in a shipyard. My duties were not confined to heating pitch, for I had to make myself generally useful. If, for instance, pieces of timber or wooden wedges used in building were caught by the rising tide, I had to go into the water and bring them back again. It was a rough-and-tumble life, but it was in the open air ; and to it I attribute the change in my constitution which has resulted in my living until now, though the effect of the early privation and the improper feeding is a legacy of dyspepsia, which makes it imperative for me to consider my diet carefully, taking very small mouthfuls and chewing them for a long time. My day's work began at six in the morning and finished at six in the evening, six days a week, for the Saturday half-holiday was unknown in those days. My wage was two shillings a week."

At the end of three years Cremer's employer failed in business, and he was then fortunate enough to be apprenticed for six years to an uncle who was in the building trade, and who took him without a premium. His cousin and fellow-apprentice says that he was at this period of an inquiring mind and fond of discussion, so that sometimes their master had to tell them to drop argument and get on with their work. Young Cremer eagerly availed himself of opportunities for self-improvement, and used frequently to attend lectures and public meetings. In his scanty reminiscences of youthful days Cremer says : " One evening there was a lecture on ' Peace,' probably given by a lecturer of the original Peace Society. The speaker advocated the settlement of international disputes by peaceful means instead of war. I listened with rapt attention, and next day I discussed the matter with two or three shopmates who had been present. They pooh-poohed the idea, and declared that the world had always settled its disputes by force and would continue to do so. That lecture sowed the seed of International Arbitration in my mind, though the word ' arbitration ' had hardly been heard." When his apprenticeship had ended, he for a time was employed at a coach-builder's in Fareham, but not long afterwards he removed to Brighton, where he became attached to a workmen's institute in which the Rev. Frederick Robertson took a warm interest, and he frequently attended the church in which that brilliant clergyman preached. It was at Brighton during an election that he made his first political speech.

In 1852 Cremer migrated to London, and being

a skilled workman, he immediately found work at the West End. At that time a carpenter's wages in London were only sixpence an hour ; they are now tenpence. Shortly afterwards an agitation arose in favour of shorter hours, and the men succeeded in leaving off work at four o'clock on Saturdays.

In 1858 the nine hours' movement was started, the object of which was to obtain a reduction of the hours in the building trade from ten hours to nine per day. Cremer says : " It was during this agitation that I made my first speech in London in favour of the objects of the movement. I was then working as a journeyman, and some time after I was appointed a delegate from the shop where I was working to the council of the movement. It will hardly be believed, but when the fact became known to my employer he discharged me, and threatened to shoot me if he ever found me again on his premises." All employers were not of the same kind. Another builder was proud of the fact that Cremer had been one of his workmen, and for many years sent a liberal subscription to the League as a proof of his sympathy with the cause of Peace ; he also contributed to the expenses of Cremer's first election to Parliament.

Ultimately Cremer became a member of the " Conference," which consisted of seven men from each branch of the building trade. The master builders locked out seventy thousand men. It was essentially a struggle for the right of combination.

A document was drawn up, which the workmen were called upon to sign, in which they promised not to join any trade union. Cremer was sent into the country, and during the campaign made more than a hundred speeches. This dispute resulted in a drawn battle. This attempt to crush Trade Unionism failed, for the employers had to withdraw their odious document; but, for the time being, the men failed to secure the nine hours' day.

In 1860 Cremer married Charlotte, daughter of Mr. J. Wilson, of Spalding, who was devotedly attached to him.

At this period Cremer was a member of a small society of carpenters called the Progressive, but he as well as others, saw the necessity of uniting the men of his trade in one body, and accordingly they formed the Amalgamated Society of Carpenters and Joiners. Subsequently, when an unfortunate dispute broke out in that Society he became a member of the General Union of Carpenters, of which he remained a contributing member to his death. Such was his sturdy independence that when this Union became contributory to the Independent Labour Party he objected to such a step, and his payments consequently fell so far in arrear that he was declared out of benefit when his executors applied for his funeral money. He certainly never intended to withdraw his membership, but his protest against the action of the Society was cut short by his death.

When the American Civil War broke out in

1861, most of the political leaders on both sides sympathised with the South rather than with the North. The majority of the working classes, however, with a clear instinct of the solidarity of labour interests, sided with freedom against slavery. This was especially the case in Lancashire, where the war produced a veritable cotton famine. The mills were almost entirely closed, and the operatives were well-nigh starved, but they would not join in any demand for British intervention. There is no doubt that the Southern States hoped to force Great Britain to interfere on their behalf.

Early in 1863 Cremer, in conjunction with other working-class leaders, convened a great meeting of London working men in St. James's Hall, which was presided over by John Bright, who at the close of his speech uttered these memorable words : " Impartial history will tell that when your statesmen were hostile or coldly neutral, when many of your rich men were corrupt, when your Press, that should have instructed and defended, wrote mainly to betray the fate of the Continent, and its vast populations being in peril, you clung to freedom with an unfaltering trust that God in His mercy will yet make it the heritage of all His children."

The chief resolution, which was unanimously adopted, ran as follows :

"That the Government of this country in permitting the pirate ship *Alabama* to leave Liverpool was guilty of negligence and has failed in its duty to a friendly nation."

The Workmen's Committee, which was interested in the cause of the Northern States of America, had further communication with John Bright, and Cremer, as its secretary, received the following communication from him, which, as will be seen, was a direct encouragement to working-class leaders to organise their followers in favour of parliamentary reform :

4, HANOVER STREET, LONDON.
June 6, 1863.

" DEAR SIR,—I have to thank your Committee for the kind expression of their feelings towards me conveyed in the copy of the resolution you have forwarded to me. I hope the course we have taken together on the great American question has been of some use.

" With regard to the future, and to other questions, I look forward to the time when the artisans of this kingdom will make some powerful movement to obtain and secure political influence.

" I believe it to be impossible in any country to raise the condition of the great body of the people whilst they are shut out from political power. Excluded from their just place in the nation, they can never have that self-respect and that hope of a better time without which their progress upward is impossible.

" At this moment there is little political action in England, and all eyes and hearts turn naturally to the scene of the American contest—but a change

will come, and it may come soon ; and when it does
come, I hope you and your friends will be ready to
make an effort for the extension of political rights
to the people of the United Kingdom.

" For this great object my services will be
always at your disposal.

" I am, with much respect, yours,

" JOHN BRIGHT."

When the Workmen's Peace Association was
formed, nearly ten years later, one of its first acts
was to issue an address to the working men of
the United States urging them to press upon their
Government the desirability of withdrawing the
indirect or consequential claims which at one time
threatened to imperil the settlement of the *Alabama*
dispute by arbitration.   This address recalled the
fact that during the American Civil War, while
the rulers of this country favoured the cause of
the South and slavery, the working classes stood
staunchly for the North and freedom.   The
address stated the case thus :

" The working classes of this country in all our
great towns declared in emphatic language their
sympathy with your cause, and their determination
that Britain should not interfere in your struggle.
Semi-starvation in our cotton districts, and the
lavish expenditure of gold raised by the Con-
federates were not powerful enough to compel
or bribe the masses or their leaders to desert the
cause.   Many of those who now address you took

an active part in organising the demonstrations of that period. At that time but a fraction of us possessed the franchise, and therefore had no direct power of controlling the actions of our Government. But we stood resolutely by you in the hour of danger, and counterbalanced the efforts of aristocratic supporters of the slave power— protesting against the remissness of our Government in allowing the *Alabama* to escape. We are therefore not morally responsible for the damage done by that vessel." The address concluded by urging the necessity of a code of International Law, and the establishment of an International Tribunal where such laws shall be administered, and the reference of any future disputes to the arbitrament of reason and law. This address thus clearly indicated the great object which Cremer had in view from the first, and to which his life was henceforth devoted. The very fact that Cremer had organised the great gathering at St. James's Hall in the dark days of the American Civil War made him in after-years a welcome guest at Washington and the great cities of the Northern States.

CHAPTER III

EARLY in the sixties Tolain, a French workman who subsequently became a Senator, came over to this country with a comrade, Fribourg, to study English labour organisations. They were introduced by certain foreign workmen to Odger, Cremer, Potter, Lucraft, and other labour leaders, who showed them that the main reason why English workmen obtained better wages and worked shorter hours than the French was the activity of the trade unions. At that period it was difficult in France to organise trade unions at all or to induce the workers to make the necessary pecuniary sacrifice. The result of these conferences was the formation of the International Working Men's Association, prominent members of the London Trades Council taking an active part.

The first conference of the new association was held September 25-28, 1865, at 18, Greek Street, Soho, and was followed by a soirée at St. Martin's Hall, Long Acre. Probably the only survivors of the first central council are Howell, Applegarth,

Lasassie, and Stainsby. George Odger was president of this council and Cremer was hon. secretary. The association published a lengthy address to the workmen of Europe which certainly did not appear to be of a revolutionary character. It declared that " this International Association and all societies and individuals adhering to it will acknowledge truth, justice, and morality as the basis of their conduct towards each other and towards all men, without regard to colour, creed, or nationality. They hold it the duty of a man to claim the rights of a man and a citizen, not only for himself but for every man who does his duty. No rights without duties, no duties without rights." The men who framed this address were evidently steeped in the writings of Mazzini.

The first rule indicated the general objects of the association as follows : " This association is established to afford a central medium of communication and co-operation between working men's societies existing in different countries and aiming at the same end ; viz., the protection, advancement, and complete emancipation of the working classes." The governing council of the association was to consist entirely of working men.

The main idea of the founders of the International was the solidarity of labour. They had discovered that labour questions are essentially international, and that the advance of the workmen of the most progressive nations is necessarily retarded by those who are less intelligent and badly

CARD OF MEMBERSHIP OF THE INTERNATIONAL.

To face p. 32.]

organised. Their intention was to create an Intelligence Department whereby the workmen of the most backward nations should be encouraged to emulate the example of their more forward brethren. In recent years the original idea has been partially carried out by periodical international conferences of representatives of the miners, and with more or less success a few other trades have attempted to follow their example. Governments have also to a large extent recognised that labour questions are international. In 1890 the German Emperor convened a conference at Berlin.

Cremer regarded with great satisfaction this new departure, more especially as some of the principal delegates were our own men. In the editorial columns of the *Arbitrator* of this period occurs the following paragraph : " And now we find M. Tolain, Senator, president of the vast meeting we held in the Chateau d'Eau Theatre at Paris, M. Jules Simon, the president of last year's Interparliamentary Conference, and Mr. Burt, the president of our League, sitting as delegates in the conference of the New International at the Radziwill Palace in Berlin. We are quite aware that the members of the conference are strictly confined to the programme which was submitted beforehand to their respective Governments, but in such gatherings the informal proceedings are often as important in their ultimate results as the formal sittings. It is impossible for direct or indirect representatives of labour from various countries to keep out of sight the misery inflicted by the war system of Europe upon the industrial classes. Out of the present conference may grow greater results than its convener dreamed. Germany has hitherto been closed against us. Our president now enters it through the door of a palace, and it will not be our fault if the door is not kept open."

Other conferences of an official character, dealing chiefly with the work of women and children, the hours of labour, and the regulation of unhealthy trades, have also been held at Berne and elsewhere. It will thus be seen that the idea of the International at its formation has to some extent been carried out by the action of the Governments.

The leading English representatives at the first conference of the International were content to move cautiously, but most of the Continentals were far more advanced in their views, and, as will be seen hereafter, the moderate policy of the Englishmen was ultimately overborne by their continental comrades.

Gustav Jaeckh, in his " History of the International," says : " Odger, president of the General Council, directed the proceedings on each of the three days with conspicuous skill. Cremer, who was secretary of the council, first read a report on the general situation of the movement, and expounded in it the International programme ; he also drew attention to the fact that the leading unions had taken a very active part in politics, and he attributed this new attitude to the influence

which had been a consequence of the new movement ; he hoped that these ardent spirits would
be able to induce the great mass of their comrades to follow a similar policy. Owing to the
energetic action of the English delegates a strongly
worded resolution in favour of an independent
Poland was carried."[1]

The International soon began to make much
noise in the world, and on a very small expenditure. Among the papers which Cremer preserved
was the balance-sheet for the first two years which
he presented to the Geneva conference in 1866.
The receipts of the British section were £83 2s.
4½d., while the expenditure amounted to £108 18s.
8d., most of the adverse balance having been
loaned by two or three trade unions. The continental income was only £17 2s. 4d. The wonder
is that with such absurdly small means the
International contrived to live at all, but in those
days labour leaders had to do their best with very
limited resources. Not a few of them had to
work without any pay. At one time when Odger
was secretary of the London Trades Council he
used to deliver notice of the meetings to its
members at their own houses in order to save
postage.

At Geneva differences between the British and
Continental delegates soon appeared. The British
delegates were bent upon a practical prosaic programme—a Nine Hours' Bill, in time an Eight
Hours' Bill, and higher wages for their work.

They urged that if the International Association was to thrive in England it must show that it can help the workman in his need. No success could be expected in this country without proofs of practical utility. Mr. Onslow Yorke, in his " Secret History of the International," says that " the brethren in Paris bitterly complained of Odger, Cremer, and their friends as not being Radical enough for them. They [the English] wished to have the help of all good men in bringing to an issue some of the high social problems which engaged their mind."

Some sixty English delegates attended. Cremer, Odger, Dupont, Lucraft, and Eccarius represented the General Council of London. As the discussion proceeded the differences between the English delegates and the Continentals became more marked, apparently irreconcilable. Mr. Yorke says in his book that Odger and Cremer were arrested on their return through France and their papers seized ; but Cremer always asserted that this statement was incorrect. From this time forward Cremer's name disappears from the record of the International, and Eccarius, a German tailor, became secretary. This man was afterwards falsely accused of selling the secrets of the International, but those who knew him best protested that a more honest fellow never lived.

From the time of the Geneva conference the International became more and more revolutionary in its aims and objects. Rightly or wrongly it was reckoned largely responsible for the insurrection of the Commune of Paris at the close of the Franco-German War, but its share in that bloody and futile struggle was probably much exaggerated. In 1872 it held a congress at Basle, where Bakounine, the Russian nihilist, became the leading spirit. Mr. Yorke sums up the proceedings as follows : " With Odger fell the founders of the International—Tolain, Friburg, all the men of peace and study. The old society of thoughtful working men was gone ; a new society of doctors, journalists, and professors had usurped its place. New men, new methods, and new purposes amazed the world. The men of study yielded to the men of strife. As Tolain fell, Bakounine grows ; as Odger passed into the shadow, Marx rose into the light. Some English names were kept upon the *rôle* as blinds ; but power was not now with them, even in that small degree to which they had been used. The people and the purposes had been changed.'¹

Cremer's brief connection with the International proved highly useful to him in his later years. He was thus brought into contact with a number of labour leaders in France who rendered him effective assistance in organising peace demonstrations in Paris, when memories of the Commune had largely faded away. Among these in particular were Tolain, a member of the French Senate ; Limousin, a workman who afterwards became a journalist ; Longuet, sub-editor of

Justice, at one time the organ of M. Clemenceau ; Camelinat, who was Master of the Mint in the days of the Commune ; and Herman Jung, a Swiss watchmaker, who subsequently settled in Clerkenwell, and whose cruel murder was a terrible blow to his lifelong friend.

Looking back at a distance of forty years, it may be confidently affirmed that Cremer was amply justified in withdrawing from the International when it embarked on revolutionary courses. I need not point to the lurid episode of the Paris Commune—for which, indeed, the International was only indirectly responsible ; the present attitude of the Socialist party in all the countries of Europe is his justification.

In the earlier efforts of the League to secure the co-operation of labour leaders on the Continent the most formidable difficulty was the prevalence of the idea that a bloody revolution must precede an era of universal peace. It has only been by slow degrees that this difficulty has been surmounted. Happily of late the great majority of Socialists in every European country have reached the conclusion that progress must be evolutionary rather than revolutionary.

The International lingered on till 1874. In the autumn of that year it held a small conference at Brussels, and Cremer expressed his disappointment at its failure as follows : " The revolution in the objects of the association naturally brought about divisions and secessions, which continued until its forces became powerless, and that which had bid fair to become the most powerful and useful association which the world has seen is to-day represented by the fourteen delegates meeting at Brussels and calling themselves a congress. The men who now occupy the stage are only minor actors ; every one of the originals have long ago disappeared. Probably this is the last congress of the once dreaded organisation, although a few of its sections may still linger on. The idea of an International Working Men's Association is, however, too good to be utterly abandoned, and when the last act of the present one has been played, and the curtain has descended, let us hope that another will take its place, with pilots to direct its course possessing, if not greater brains, cooler judgments and more practical capabilities than those who have made shipwreck of the present. Whether the Workmen's Peace Association contains the nucleus of the future International Working Men's Association time will reveal."

CHAPTER IV

GARIBALDI'S VISIT AND THE REFORM
LEAGUE

THE visit of Garibaldi to England in April, 1864,
was an epoch-making event in the history of
English democracy ; men then came together who
never separated until they had won household
suffrage in the borough constituencies. By all
classes in this country Garibaldi was regarded with
enthusiastic admiration—of course with the exception of the Roman Catholics, who desired the con-
tinuation of the temporal power of the Pope.

The story of the Italian hero cannot be told
in detail here. Suffice it to say that his splendid
defence of Rome against the French army in 1849
had already won for him boundless popularity in
this country, and he still further excited the enthusiasm of the British people in 1860 by his
embarkation from Genoa to Sicily with a thousand
volunteers, among whom was a British contingent.
After defeating the troops of the King of Naples
in several engagements, he passed over from Sicily
to the mainland at Reggio, and entered Naples

without firing a shot, the Bourbons flying before
him. For the moment he was appointed dictator
of the Kingdom of Naples, but was well content,
though a Republican in theory, to hand over that
kingdom to Victor Emmanuel. Two years later
Garibaldi appeared in the Romagna and endeavoured by force of arms to deliver the Papal
State from clerical misrule ; but at Aspromonte
he was defeated, wounded, and taken prisoner by
the troops of the King of Italy.

In the spring of 1864 Garibaldi visited London
and had more than a royal reception. Vast
multitudes thronged the streets to greet him. An
immense procession, gathered from all parts of
London, filed past him at the station gates. So
great was the crush that it took four hours for him
to proceed from Nine Elms to Stafford House, Pall
Mall, where he was the guest of the late Duke of
Sutherland. In this reception Cremer, who was
already on terms of intimacy with Mazzini, took
a prominent part ; and he delighted to speak of
his intercourse with Garibaldi in spite of the
difficulties of language. From all the principal
towns in England came pressing invitations to
Garibaldi that he would honour them with a visit,
but his sojourn in this country suddenly came to
an end. He remained in England only two or
three weeks, the greater part of the time in com-
parative seclusion, and then he was conveyed to
his island home at Caprera in the yacht of the
Duke of Sutherland.

It was given out at the time that Garibaldi's constitution had become enfeebled, and that he had not fully recovered from the wound which he received at Aspromonte ; but the fact was that the Court and the Government took the alarm, and accordingly the Italian hero was hurried out of the country. His admirers were naturally indignant, and convened an open-air demonstration on Primrose Hill, which was forcibly broken up by the police. Cremer was one of the organisers of this gathering. The committee at once adjourned to a tavern at the foot of the hill, and determined to start a Reform League. At that time the great majority of working men in London were unenfranchised. Lodgers possessed no votes, and thousands of compound householders were left off the register because they only paid rates through their landlords.

The Reform League grew rapidly ; branches were started all over London and offices were taken in Adelphi Terrace. The present writer speaks from personal recollection, he having been probably the youngest member of the council. Happily for the League and for the peace of London, Edmond Beales was elected president, he having been previously associated with some of the labour leaders in a movement on behalf of the insurgents in Poland. Strange to say, he was a devout Evangelical Churchman, more at home in a prayer-meeting than in a march upon Hyde Park. At Adelphi Terrace he had a very difficult team to drive, but he held his office with firmness and dignity. He was savagely attacked by the Tory press, especially when he was appointed a County Court Judge some time after the dissolution of the League. This appointment, however, was but a poor compensation for his loss of business as a Chancery barrister during the time of his political activity. The secretary of the League was George Howell, a bricklayer, who was afterwards secretary of the Trades Union Congress, author of several standard works on labour questions, and subsequently M.P. for North-East Bethnal Green, who is still living at a ripe old age. Charles Bradlaugh was of course prominent, more especially at great open-air gatherings ; so also was George Odger, secretary of the London Trades Council. Cremer, too, had a very active part in the work of organisation.

The Reform League was at first rather shy of outdoor demonstrations at the West End ; but Lucraft, an artistic chairmaker of Islington, who afterwards sat for many years on the London School Board, forced the situation. He had been accustomed to hold meetings in Hoxton Square, but one day he announced that Trafalgar Square would be the next meeting-place. Then the League resolved to take charge of the meeting, with Edmond Beales as Chairman. An immense crowd assembled, and at the close a procession was formed and proceeded to Carlton House Terrace, where Mr. Gladstone then resided. As he was not at home we

marched up through Pall Mall to St. James's
Square, where old Lord Derby came out on his
balcony to look at us. Thence we marched to
John Bright's lodgings in Hanover Street. He
happened to be away in the country, but Cremer
climbed a lamp-post, clinging to the crossbar, and
harangued the crowd from that inconvenient
position.

The next advance was to Hyde Park. Cremer
always claimed that it was on his motion that the
council of the League resolved that it would be for
the health of reformers that they should take an
airing in Hyde Park on July 23, 1866. In spite
of the prohibition of the Tory Government the
League determined to persevere. The programme
was that if the gates were closed the various
sections should march to Trafalgar Square. The
South London men did so ; and Edmond Beales
on being refused admission at the Marble Arch
drove off in the same direction.

Cremer's account of what afterwards occurred
near the Marble Arch was as follows : " The
pressure of the crowd on those who were close to
the railings was so great that they had to grasp
the railings to save themselves from being crushed
against them. Then the police inside the Park
began to hammer men's knuckles with their
truncheons, and very soon the old railings, which
were not very firmly fixed, gave way and the
people rushed in." As Cremer was in the thick of
this affair the account is probably correct ; and as

I happened to enter without molestation by the gate at Hyde Park Corner, I can testify that several meetings of an impromptu character were held that evening in spite of the police, the footguards, and the cavalry. A large number of people were arrested and locked up in the Marble Arch, and afterwards were sentenced by Mr. Knox, the police magistrate, to a fine of forty shillings or a month's imprisonment—a shameful travesty of justice. The excitement was prolonged for some time. Crowds went to the Park night after night, and in the end Mr. Walpole, the Home Secretary, a really amiable Conservative, asked the leaders of the League to help in securing order. For this he was blamed by some of the Tory newspapers, but he was amply justified in assuming that reformers were not revolutionists.

About this time General Cluseret, a stormy petrel of revolution, approached Cremer, Odger, and one or two others with an absurd proposal to start an armed insurrection in London. His overtures were, of course, rejected. Cluseret, who afterwards for a time commanded the forces of the Paris Commune, had seen military service in various parts of the world. He had fought as an officer in the French Army both in the Crimea and Africa, then he joined the Garibaldians, and ultimately took service with the Northern Army in the American Civil War. One day he brought a brief note of introduction from Mazzini to Cremer and Odger, which ran as follows : " The bearer,

General Cluseret of the United States, entrusted
with a mission by the State of New York, wishes to
form a correct idea of the tendencies and aspirations of the English popular element and of the
prospects of reform. Will you allow me to introduce him to you? " Apparently from this letter
Mazzini had no idea of Cluseret's real object.
The interview with Cremer and Odger took place
at Cremer's lodgings. The real purpose of this
man may be gathered from the *dossier*, afterwards in the possession of the French Government. There it is stated that Cluseret " visited
England on a double mission to establish an understanding between the Reform League and the
trades unions in order to bring about a revolution, nominally for the profit of the Republican
party, but in reality for the detriment of England.
Mr. Seward is stated to have authorised him to
promise aid in ships, arms, and men. He was
put into communication by Signor Mazzini with
Mr. Peter Taylor, with Mr. Cremer, Mr. Odger,
and Mr. John Bright. He is described as having
been explicit with Odger and Cremer, but extremely prudent with Taylor and Bright. Subsequently General Cluseret was charged by the
Central Section of New York Fenians to make
a repetition of his overtures and provoke a conflict. Cluseret is said to have told Odger,
Cremer, and Hartwell that if they could effect
this he would put at their disposal 2,000
Fenians, armed and equipped with revolvers,

with knives, and *bâtons ferrés*, 500 of them being also armed with carbines. Cremer, Odger, and Hartwell declined, as in case the Government granted an electoral law acceptable to the majority of English workmen, the insurrection would consist of only the Fenians and a few hundred workmen. If the electoral law was, however, distasteful to the people, Messrs. Cremer, Odger, and Hartwell would gladly accept General Cluseret's offer."

This information is given exactly as it appears in the *dossier*. It is in the last degree improbable that such a man as Mr. Seward ever made such an offer through General Cluseret ; it is certain that the overtures of Cluseret were promptly and finally rejected by the English reform leaders. The present writer, long afterwards, had a detailed account of what passed from Cremer's own lips. He indignantly denied that he at any time encouraged Cluseret's mad design. Not only was Cremer essentially a man of peace, but he was of such clear judgment that he was most unlikely to entertain so insane a project.

On a second occasion the Tory Government made another ineffectual attempt to prohibit a Hyde Park demonstration. Three police superintendents appeared and served notices on each member of the council, threatening us with divers pains and penalties if we attempted to hold the meeting ; but these notices were ignored. I had the honour of carrying the banner of the Shoreditch branch of the League into the park on the appointed evening, when we were happily, unmolested.

Although the demand of the Reform League had been for manhood suffrage and vote by ballot, it was considered desirable to dissolve when the second Reform Bill was passed. Cremer returned to work, this time on his own account. He had purchased through a building society the lease of a house in St. Pancras, which he almost doubled in size. The present writer saw him at work on the job. This made him, for a man of small wants, virtually independent. A few years ago he sold the tail end of this lease to his advantage. I mention this fact to explain in part how it came about that Cremer was able to do so much more for the cause beyond the donation of the Nobel Prize. Yet not altogether. Although Cremer was not parsimonious, rather affected good living in continental style, and sometimes entertained his friends to dinner at the House of Commons, he was essentially a man of frugal habits. In spite of the remonstrances of friends on account of his age, he lived alone at his office almost to the last. Some of those who knew him best thought that his life might have been still prolonged by constant womanly care and solicitude.

CHAPTER V

IN the autumn of 1868, on the eve of the General Election, Cremer went on a missionary expedition to various towns in the interest of the Radical wing of the Liberal Party, and at last he came to Warwick, which certainly was not congenial ground. It had an evil reputation as one of the most corrupt constituencies in England. In 1834-35 charges of gross bribery and intimidation at this borough were investigated by the House of Commons. A brother of the Earl of Warwick was one of the candidates. The Earl was not only Lord Lieutenant of the county, but also Recorder of the borough ; and the Town Clerk, who had been the agent in all the corrupt trans-actions, was his nominee. A system of fraudulent voting had been recently commenced by the land agent of the Earl, who had created a number of fagot-voters and supplied them with fictitious receipts for rent. A cheque for £8,000 was signed by Lord Warwick's agent just before the election and presented at the bank ; this money had found its way into the hands of the persons who distributed the bribes. As if this was not enough bands of rioters, armed with bludgeons, were imported into the town to overawe the honest electors. When the virus of corruption once makes its appearance in a constituency its eradication is slow and difficult.

In 1865 the honest electors of Warwick, in spite of the dominant Castle influence, succeeded in returning Mr. Arthur Peel, a Liberal, who won the second seat by a small majority. In 1868 an understanding had been reached by the local leaders on both sides that the Liberal and the Conservative should have a walk over, which meant the virtual disfranchisement of the borough for the time. The Radicals of Warwick strongly desired to upset this pleasant arrangement ; but the Whig section of the Liberals obstinately refused to accept a second Liberal candidate, fearing, no doubt, that the Tories would win both seats. Of course, in a borough like Warwick, under such circumstances, any Radical candidate would be well aware that he was leading a forlorn hope. The Ballot Act was not yet passed, and as a matter of fact an authenticated copy of the poll, showing how each elector voted, was printed and published at the price of sixpence, a sure way of terrorising poor voters at subsequent elections in such a place. Cremer addressed a large meeting at Warwick on the duties of working men at the ensuing election ; and at the close a resolution was carried, almost unanimously, urging him to stand for the borough in the Liberal and industrial interest. That invitation was ratified at four other meetings, and accordingly Cremer issued an address to the electors.

While promising to give a loyal support to Mr. Gladstone, Cremer as an advanced Liberal expressed his desire for further electoral reforms, including vote by ballot and equal electoral districts, secular and compulsory education, Irish disestablishment, direct taxation, Land Law reform, amendment of the law in regard to trade unions, and the establishment of Courts of Conciliation to settle labour disputes. His future lifework was shadowed forth in the following passage : " Peace on earth and goodwill toward men has for eighteen hundred years been preached to the people ; I shall be glad to work for its practical realisation, and to that end shall support the establishment of international Boards of Arbitration to settle disputes among nations, so as to lead to a general disarmament of standing forces, and the establishment of an era of peace."

Letters warmly commending Cremer's candidature were sent by several Radical Members of Parliament, including Henry Fawcett, John Stuart Mill, Peter Alfred Taylor, Charles Gilpin, Walter Morrison, and Sir Andrew Lusk.

Although the Radicals were greatly annoyed at the timidity or selfishness of the local Whig leaders, they were so loyal to Mr. Gladstone that

nearly all of them divided their votes between Peel
and Cremer. The polling was as follows :

PEEL	...	...	...	...	...	...	... 873
GREAVES	...	...	...	...	...	...	... 863
CREMER	...	...	...	...	...	...	... 260

Cremer showed how cheaply an election could be
fought in a small borough. While Mr. Greaves
spent £463 and Mr. Peel £312, Cremer spent
only £135. The supporters of Cremer were so
well pleased at the manner in which he conducted
his campaign that, at a meeting addressed by Mr.
and Mrs. Henry Fawcett, they presented him with
a marble timepiece, which has now become, with
other heirlooms, the property of the League.

In 1874 Cremer was again induced to contest
Warwick, and issued an address very much on the
same lines as the first. In that address occurred
the following passage : " The framing of a code
of international law, and the establishment of an
international tribunal for the peaceful settlement
of disputes between nations, would, by diminishing
the chances of war, enable the Governments of
Europe to reduce their armed forces, save millions
of money for the reduction of national debts, and
the relief of industries now so heavily weighted
with taxation."

I went down to Warwick to assist Cremer in
this contest, and from the first saw how hopeless
it was. This time the Conservatives ran two candidates ; nevertheless, the supporters of Mr. Peel

refused to coalesce with the Radical. The result of the poll was as follows :

REPTON (Tory) ...	...	...	...	...	...	836
PEEL (Liberal) ...	...	...	...	...	...	783
GODSON (Tory) ...	...	...	...	...	...	740
CREMER (Radical)	...	...	...	...	...	183

Some years afterwards, when Mr. Arthur Peel had become Speaker of the House of Commons, Cremer was returned for Haggerston, and was cordially congratulated by the Speaker on his election.

When the National Education League was formed at Birmingham, under the chairmanship of Mr. Joseph Chamberlain, Cremer became one of its earliest members. At the first London School Board election he stood, in conjunction with Professor Huxley, as a candidate for the Marylebone Division, which included Marylebone, Paddington, and St. Pancras. Professor Huxley was elected, but Cremer failed, polling 4,002 votes. His want of success was mainly due to the operation of the Cumulative Vote, under which electors were allowed to concentrate their votes on a single candidate. Mrs. Garrett Anderson, who headed the poll, secured 48,000. In 1872 Cremer again stood for the London School Board—this time for the Tower Hamlets—but was unsuccessful.

Cremer's view of this early contest is of some little interest. He wrote to his sister : " I do not expect to win, but shall poll a considerable

number of votes. The worship of the golden calf
still prevails, but every such candidature as mine,
fought out on economical and honourable lines,
tends to educate constituencies up to the idea of
having other than rich people to represent them.
In this world it is seldom those who sow that reap ;
my vocation is the former, at least so it appears.
Of the other candidates in the Tower Hamlets,
two are brewers, and one is a distiller. My
address is admitted to be far better than that of
either of the other nine candidates. As speakers
they are simply nowhere, but they are wealthy
and so they will probably win. Still, we are
making progress. Who would have thought when
I was a boy that a number of working men would
be bold enough and capable enough to come
forward as candidates for representatives on School
Boards and in Parliament? But it has been done,
and in some instances they have been successful.
In the next generation they will be more so ; we
are now pioneering the way for future triumphs."

In 1884 Cremer was elected a member of the
St. Pancras Vestry, of which he remained a
member till 1887. He took an active part in the
special committee which was appointed to deal
with questions affecting the Sanitary Department.
He also vainly attempted to persuade the Vestry
to memorialise the Government in favour of appro-
priating the funds of the City guilds for educational purposes. He closely interested himself in
the unemployment question, and on one occasion

obtained the issue of an instruction to put in hand relief works.   He also seconded a motion by Mr. Howell Williams, now Mr. Idris, M.P., to take a plebiscite of the ratepayers with reference to the adoption of the Public Libraries Act, but in this he was defeated.

CHAPTER VI

THE PIONEERS OF PEACE

THE Peace Society, whose full title is " The Society
for Promoting Universal Peace,": was founded in
1816, mainly by members of the Society of Friends,
among whom Thomas Clarkson, the friend of the
negro, was the most conspicuous. It was based
upon the principle of absolute non-resistance, so
far at least as its officers were concerned. Probably on that account it did not command much
popular support or attract much public attention
until Henry Richard became its secretary in 1848.
Like his two immediate predecessors in office,
Henry Richard was a Congregational minister.
While personally accepting the Quaker view as
to the unlawfulness of all war from a Christian
standpoint, he saw from the first the necessity
of enlisting the sympathy and support of good
men who, while unable to go so far, were ready
and willing to work for practical and peaceful
methods of settling international disputes. From
1848 to his death, in 1888, Henry Richard was
the central figure of the movement.

A happier choice of a secretary could not possibly
have been made, for he possessed all the qualities of leadership. He had a lofty faith in the
righteousness and reasonableness of the cause, and
in its ultimate triumph—a faith which was never
daunted by difficulty nor discouraged by defeat,
because it had its roots in religious conviction.
Unlike many Christians, he really believed in the
kingdom of God, and that as a citizen thereof it was
his primary duty to promote its extension. He was
singularly modest and unselfish, always seeking
the co-operation of all sorts and conditions of
men, always ready to accept the services of those
who were in only partial agreement with him. He
never feared the face of man, never shrank from
risking and enduring the rebuffs of the great and
powerful, if only the cause could be advanced.
While cherishing the loftiest ideals, he was quite
ready to encounter on their own ground those who
confined themselves to considerations of practical
politics. His Annual Reports at the meetings of
the Peace Society were forceful, logical, and even
brilliant. His speeches, both in and out of
Parliament, were touched with that fervour of
conviction which is so characteristic of Welsh
oratory, and he had a vein of playful satire and
dry humour which was used with telling effect.
He was a man of many battles, and repeatedly he
had to champion the cause of the Welsh people
against academic priggishness, sacerdotal calumny,
and landlord oppression ; but even when his in-

dignation was roused he was free from bitterness and absolutely destitute of personal enmity. For some years he was the foremost spokesman of Nonconformity in the House of Commons, where he commanded the respect and attention of men of all parties.

When Henry Richard became secretary of the Peace Society its President was Charles Hindley, M.P., who once or twice accompanied him on his continental missions ; but the most indefatigable worker in the cause was Joseph Sturge, of Birmingham, a member of the Society of Friends. A braver, truer, kindlier soul never lived. In days when the violence of the physical force Chartists was calculated to alienate a man of peace, Joseph Sturge became the leader of a " complete suffrage " movement, for he was not only a philanthropist but a democrat who loved and trusted the common people. Every good cause commanded his sympathy and active co-operation. He believed in the equality of opportunity long before the phrase was coined and he possessed an unfaltering faith in the kingdom of God. He was a fellow-citizen of every man, irrespective of race, or colour, or creed. Until his death, in 1859, when he was president of the Peace Society, his labours on its behalf were incessant. In Birmingham, which has raised a statue to his memory, he was universally beloved. It was of Joseph Sturge that Whittier sang :

" For him no minster-chant of the immortals
  Rose from the lips of sin ;
No mitred priest swung back the heavenly portals
  To let the white soul in.

But Age and Sickness framed their tearful faces
  In the low hovel's door,
And prayers went up from all the dark by-places
  And Ghettos of the poor.

Not his the golden pen's or lip's persuasion,
  But a fine sense of right,
And Truth's directness, meeting each occasion
  Straight as a line of light.

The very gentlest of all human natures
  He joined to courage strong,
And love out-reaching unto all God's creatures
  With sturdy hate of wrong.

Men failed, betrayed him, but his zeal seemed nourished
  By failure and by fall ;
Still a large faith in human kind he cherished,
  And in God's love for all."

Closely associated with Richard and Sturge in these earlier years was Elihu Burritt, a New Englander, who while working as a blacksmith had acquired such a wide knowledge of ancient and modern languages that he attracted the notice of Governor Everett. For a time Burritt devoted himself to literature and journalism, but he was a born apostle of progress. Temperance, peace, and the abolition of slavery, were causes alike dear to his heart, which he advocated with intense earnestness. He founded in America an international peace society called "The Bond of Brotherhood," and in 1845 he paid a first visit to England. It was Burritt who first conceived the idea of holding a series of international peace congresses in the chief cities of Europe, and Henry Richard and his fellow-workers in the Peace Society warmly welcomed his proposal.

To those who did not look below the surface the time seemed singularly unpropitious, for early in 1848 Louis Philippe of France had been forced to abdicate, and half the thrones of Europe seemed tottering to their foundations; but the leaders of the peace movement had strong faith in the people; they saw that while the leaders of the democracy were ready to draw the sword against monarchs they were animated by common sympathies; though they spoke different languages, *Liberté, Egalité, Fraternité* was not an empty formula. The more sanguine spirits cherished the hope that 1848 was the crimson dawn of a new and happier era; and though they had to suffer cruel disappointment, they never doubted the ultimate triumph of the movement of which they were the pioneers.

The original idea was to hold a first congress in Paris in the summer of 1848, but France was in so disturbed a condition that this project had to be abandoned. The warning given was timely, for in June of that year a fierce Red Republican insurrection broke out, and the streets of Paris were

deluged with blood. Nevertheless in the autumn
a first European Peace Congress was held at
Brussels, attended by hundreds of representatives
of various nationalities, under the presidency of
M. Auguste Visschers, a distinguished Belgian
Jurist.

In the spring of 1849 Richard and Burritt went
to Paris to arrange a second congress. They were
cordially received by de Tocqueville, Carnot,
Arago, Bastiat, Lamartine, and other prominent
public men, and had the active co-operation of
Frederick Passy, who for many years continued to
be the leader of the peace party in France, and
who still survives at a ripe old age. A host of
difficulties had to be surmounted, but the congress
proved a brilliant success, and was attended by no
less than seven hundred British and American
citizens. Among the English delegates were
Richard Cobden, Edward Miall, and Henry
Vincent. Victor Hugo, who presided, delivered an
impassioned speech, in which he thus prophesied
of the future of Europe :

" A day will come when you, France—you,
Russia—you, Italy—you, England—you, Germany
—all of you, nations of the Continent, will, without
losing your distinctive qualities and your glorious
individuality, be blended into a superior unity, and
constitute a European fraternity, just as Normandy,
Brittany, Burgundy, Lorraine have been blended
into France. A day will come when the only battle-
field will be the market opened to commerce, and

the mind opening the new ideas. A day will come
when bullets and bombshells will be replaced by
votes, by the universal suffrage of nations, by the
venerable arbitration of a great sovereign senate,
which will be to Europe what the Parliament is
to England, what the Diet is to Germany, what
the Legislative Assembly is to France ! "

Louis Napoleon was then President of the
French Republic.   His Government showed a
friendly attitude toward the congress, readily
allowing it to be held although Paris was still
legally in a state of siege, permitting delegates
to enter France without passports, and opening the
Hotel of the Minister of Foreign Affairs for a
grand reception.

In 1850 Frankfort was selected as a place of
meeting. In Germany even greater difficulties had
to be surmounted, but Henry Richard by per-
severing effort succeeded in making the Frankfort
congress equal to that of Paris. Counsellor Jaup
presided, and among the speakers were M. Giradin,
editor of *La Presse*, and our own Richard
Cobden. In the previous year (1849) Cobden
had moved a resolution in the House of Commons
inviting the Powers to concur in treaties binding
the parties to refer matters in dispute to arbitration. This was the first attempt to commit the
British Legislature to arbitration as a policy, and
was, of course, unsuccessful. Cobden's proposal
was, however, warmly applauded at the Frankfort
Congress, though the question of international

disarmament then occupied the most prominent place.

The first great International Exhibition was held in London in 1851, and the next Peace Congress was accordingly held in that city. Exeter Hall was the place of meeting and Sir David Brewster presided. Among those who took part therein were Richard Cobden, Horace Greeley, and John Angell James, of Birmingham. Delegates were present from most European countries, including fifteen French workmen—the first attempt to enlist labour in the cause. As a child the present writer was taken by his father to this gathering, and has a vivid recollection of its numbers and enthusiasm.

Similar congresses were held at Manchester in 1852, and at Edinburgh in 1853, but by the latter year a disastrous war was already impending.

When once a nation is inflamed by the war-spirit, as Tennyson has well said :

> "To cast wise words among the multitude
> Is flinging fruit to lions."

A wave of patriotic madness swept over the land. The maintenance of the Turkish power in Europe was held to be absolutely necessary to the existence of the British Empire ; and the occupation of Moldavia and Wallachia by Russian troops was regarded as a menace to liberty and civilisation. Even the great majority of honest Liberals clamoured for war. It may be pleaded in their excuse that they had a hearty hatred of that Russian despotism which had crushed Hungary, and they cherished the vain hope that war would bring deliverance to the oppressed nationalities. The Crimean War has few defenders now ; even Lord Salisbury, in his later years, admitted that " we put our money on the wrong horse." The only gainer by the war was Napoleon III., who had his own ends to serve in promoting it.

Bright, Cobden, and others, who bravely protested against the war, lost their seats in Parliament as a consequence. That, however, was but a momentary evil ; the permanent mischief was that from that time our war expenditure went up by leaps and bounds, and that the work of the Peace Party, so ably planned, and so successfully conducted thus far, was undermined and shattered.

When the Crimean War was brought to an end, it had to be followed by a treaty, like most other wars. No matter how great the hecatomb of victims that have fallen, unless the defeated Power is actually wiped out of existence, the differences in the end have to be arranged by diplomacy. The Plenipotentiaries of the Powers concerned met at Paris. The Peace Congress Committee seized the opportunity, and organised a deputation to Lord Palmerston urging " the importance of proposing at the conference, then sitting, some system of international arbitration which may bring the great interests of nations within the cognisance of certain fixed rules of justice and

right." From such a statesman they had little
to hope, and they were not disappointed. As is
usual on occasions when an unsympathetic Minister
is encountered, they had to listen to all kinds of
objections with hardly any opportunity of reply
But they were not daunted by the rebuff they
received ; on the contrary, they resolved to make
a yet bolder effort, dealing directly with the
diplomatists. Richard, Hindley, and Sturge went
over to Paris and sought interviews with the representatives of the Powers. They were graciously
received, especially by Lord Clarendon, who, while
necessarily guarded in his language, said at the
close of the interview, " I will do what I can."
That promise was fulfilled, for it was at the
instance of Lord Clarendon that the following
Protocol was drawn up :

" The Plenipotentiaries do not hesitate to express, in the name
of their Governments, the desire that States between which any
serious misunderstanding may arise should, before appealing
to arms, have recourse, so far as circumstances might allow,
to the good offices of a friendly Power. The Plenipotentiaries
hope that the Governments not represented at the Congress
will unite in the sentiment which has inspired the desire
recorded in the present Protocol."

To those who have lately seen a number of
international treaties of arbitration drawn up and
signed within a single year, the language of the
Protocol may appear far too cautious ; but the
friends of peace, who were well aware that they
could only expect to succeed step by step, rightly

regarded the Protocol as a substantial gain. Lord Clarendon himself spoke of it as " this happy innovation." Lord Malmesbury approved the Protocol as recognising " the immortal truth that time, by allowing reason to operate, is as much a preventive as a healer of hostilities." Lord Derby equally expressed approval ; as also did Mr. Gladstone, because it was the first time that " the representatives of the principal nations of Europe have given an emphatic utterance to sentiments which contain at least a qualified disapproval of the results of war, and asserted the supremacy of reason, of justice, humanity, and religion."

In all human probability that first step would not have been taken but for the courageous efforts of Henry Richard and his colleagues—men who had very recently been reviled by the War Press as mischievous busybodies, and even as traitors to their own country. It only remains to be said that the desire of the Plenipotentiaries that the Governments not represented at the congress at Paris should accept the view set forth in the Protocol was fully gratified.

Not long afterwards the cause of international peace suffered another serious reverse, this time not from war, but from political conspiracy. Napoleon III. in his youth had espoused the cause of Italian unity ; as he maintained the Papal power in Rome by a French army of occupation, ardent Italian patriots regarded him as a traitor to their cause, and on two occasions sought to assassinate him. On the second attempt, when bombs were thrown by Orsini at his carriage, he had a narrow escape, some persons being actually killed. Simon Bernard, charged with being an accessory to the attempt, was tried in London and acquitted. The result provoked an outburst of ill-feeling in France, more especially on the part of officers of the army. A war panic speedily spread through this country, and it was widely believed that a French invasion was at hand. A call was made for volunteers, put into verse by our own Laureate in the well-known lyric, " Form ! Form ! Riflemen form ! " wherein occurred the insulting lines :

> " True that we have a faithful ally,
> But only the devil knows what he means."

An immense number of volunteers were at once enrolled, and early in 1860 Queen Victoria reviewed twenty thousand of them in Hyde Park. There were no substantial reasons for this scare. Great as was the personal provocation Napoleon III. had received, he still remained our faithful ally ; it was the one redeeming feature in his later lurid career. The friends of peace were equal to the occasion. At the time when the fire-eaters on both sides of the Channel were clamouring for war they were taking the most effective measures to avert it. In the very year (1860) when the volunteers were reviewed in Hyde Park, Richard Cobden for this country and Michael Chevalier

for France, assisted, of course, by the official representatives of both countries, negotiated the Anglo-
French Commercial Treaty.   They had a profound
faith in what Elihu Burritt used to call " the
Higher Law and Mission of Commerce," the
negation of which faith is now represented by some
of our prominent politicians.

For twenty years Henry Richard had to carry
on his work outside the House of Commons.   At
last the Reform Act of 1867, which conferred
the franchise on all borough householders, gave
him his opportunity.   He had often championed
the cause of Welshmen in the London Press, and
at the General Election of 1868 the borough of
Merthyr returned him by a majority of 6,000.
and he continued to hold the seat till his death.
In 1869 he visited most of the countries of Europe
with the object of inducing members of the various
Parliaments to bring the question of international
arbitration to the front.   This effort, which at
first appeared hopeful, was rendered abortive by
the outbreak of war between France and Germany.
During that struggle the friends of peace in this
country had to exert all their strength on behalf
of British neutrality, which was at first endangered
by eager partisans of Germany, and subsequently
by equally eager partisans of France.

In 1873 Henry Richard secured an opportunity
of bringing the question of International Arbitration before the British House of Commons.
Richard Cobden had introduced a similar motion

in 1849, when he was defeated by 176 to 79. So far as the House of Commons was concerned, the question remained in abeyance for twenty-four years. On July 9, 1873, Henry Richard moved the following resolution :

" That an humble address be presented to her Majesty praying that she will be graciously pleased to enter into communication with foreign powers with a view to further improvement in International Law, and the establishment of a general and permanent system of arbitration."

The motion was necessarily couched in general terms, but the phrase " general and permanent system " was sufficiently explicit to show what was in the mind of the man who brought it forward. In a lucid and argumentative speech Henry Richard reminded the House that his proposal had been advocated by such men as Lord Derby and John Stuart Mill ; and though he did not expect that such an international tribunal as he suggested would be immediately constituted, he urged the Government to take some steps in that direction. Mr. Gladstone's reply was mainly sympathetic. He declared that his only motive in opposing the motion was that its adoption would tend to put in jeopardy the cause which the mover had at heart. There was some plausibility in this contention, considering that Germany was flushed with her recent triumph, while France was smarting under the humiliation of the loss of Alsace-Lorraine, and the last instalment of the war indemnity had not yet been paid. Bismarck, the man of blood and iron, was then the strongest force in Europe, and his only idea of the preservation of peace was to hold France down by the Triple Alliance of Germany, Austria, and Italy. The debate on Henry Richard's motion was somewhat languid, but in the end the Previous Question was rejected by 98 to 88, which was then the parliamentary method of carrying the motion.

During his later years Henry Richard was troubled with an affection of the heart, and knew that his life hung by a thread. It was a great satisfaction to him when Cremer entered the House of Commons and began to take up the work which he himself was being forced to relinquish. One of the last votes that Richard gave was in support of Cremer's motion in favour of arbitration, and he expressed his gladness at having the opportunity.

The Peace Society was not the only body which was working in the same direction. Full credit should also be given to the labours of the International Law Association.

This body, whose original title was the " Association for the Reform and Codification of the Law of Nations," rendered valuable service to the cause of peace. It was American in its origin. Shortly after the settlement of the *Alabama* claims by the Geneva Court of Arbitration, Dr. James B. Miles, secretary of the American Peace Society, paid a visit to Europe to prepare the way for an international conference of a semi-private character, and an "International Code Committee" was formed in the United States, with a distinguished jurist, David Dudley Field, as its president. Among the twenty-six persons who composed the committee were Dr. Theodore Woolsey, Dr. Mark Hopkins, Dr. William Sterns, Dr. Howard Crosby, Charles Sumner, Reverdy Johnson, William Cullen Bryant, John G. Whittier, and Elihu Burritt. An International Conference was held at Brussels in October, 1873, the chief subjects of discussion being the codification of the Law of Nations, and the principle of international arbitration. The conference met at the Hôtel de Ville, Brussels, and was attended by men of nine nationalities, Emile de Laveleye being secretary. The British members were Sir Travers Twiss, Professor Mountague Bernard, of Oxford, Professor Sheldon Amos, Lord Sandford, Henry Richard, C. H. Carmichael, H. D. Jenkins, and Sir Henry Barron (British Charge d'Affaires).

When the principle of international arbitration was considered, Dr. Bluntschli (Germany) urged that nations would not accept it where their "vital interests" were concerned. Frederic Passy and Henry Richard urged that it would be impolitic to expressly admit any exception in the resolution. Ultimately the following resolution was unanimously adopted :

"This conference declares that it regards arbitration as a means essentially just, reasonable, and even obligatory for all nations of terminating international differences which cannot be settled by negotiation. It abstains from affirming that in all cases, without exception, this mode of solution is applicable, but it believes that the exceptions are rare, and it is convinced that no difference ought to be considered insoluble until after a clear statement of complaints and reasonable delay, and the exhaustion of all pacific methods of accommodation."

The words " and even obligatory " were inserted on the suggestion of Signor Mancini (Italy), some of those present explaining that they meant moral obligation only.

Subsequently Mr. Thomas Webster, Q.C. (father of Lord Alverstone), moved a series of resolutions formally constituting the association. In one of these resolutions occurs a passage which should here be reproduced, because it points to the work of an earlier society which laboured in the same field. It ran thus : " That the services rendered by the Hon. David Dudley Field in the year 1866 at the Social Science Congress, at which he first mooted this question, be formally acknowledged by this meeting." A final resolution expressed the gratitude of those present to Henry Richard for his long services in the cause, and congratulated him on the success of his motion in favour of international arbitration which had been recently carried in the British House of Commons.

The following year, 1874, the second conference of the association was held at Geneva, in the very room where the Geneva Court of Arbitration had sat two years before, and which bore the name of the Salon d'Alabama. This conference was presided over by David Dudley Field.

From time to time the International Law Association has held representative meetings in various European cities. A few years ago Cremer and the present writer attended as delegates from the International Arbitration League at Brussels, where Lord Alverstone and Mr. Justice Phillimore took a prominent part. The Association has done very useful work, mainly in a legal direction, but space will not allow us to follow its history any farther.

In more recent years other associations have taken an honourable part in the peace movement, more especially the International Arbitration and Peace Association, whose first president, Hodgson Pratt, was indefatigable in his work, and who is now succeeded by Mr. Felix Moscheles, its secretary being Mr. J. Frederick Green. It should be added that for some years past Dr. Evans Darby has ably continued the work of the late Henry Richard as secretary of the original Peace Society. Mr. Walter Hazell, J.P., has for many years been its treasurer, and is now its chairman.

CHAPTER VII

THE GENEVA ARBITRATION

A CASUAL reference has been made in the previous chapter to the Geneva Arbitration, but this event in the end gave such immense impetus to the cause that it is desirable to treat it separately. It was a new departure in the history of nations fraught with beneficent result ; and happily in this country both political parties were so fully involved that the honours may be fairly divided. In such a biography as the present it is necessary not only to record the work of the man who made arbitration easy, but to speak also of the labours of those who prepared the way before him and helped to make his path straight.

At the outbreak of the great American Civil War public opinion in this country was sharply divided. The aristocracy and the upper classes, with a few honourable exceptions, sympathised with the South ; the majority of the lower middle class and of the working class held with the North. Even in Lancashire, where the cotton famine pressed severely on the workers, popular opinion was largely in favour of the Free States as against the Slave States. The former had not yet declared for negro emancipation, but those who were not blinded by passionate prejudice saw that if the North triumphed the abolition of slavery was inevitable.

Unhappily, as is usually the case when a war breaks out, the belligerents speedily became a danger to neutrals. In the very first year of the war the Southern or Confederate States despatched Messrs. Mason and Slidell and two other emissaries on a mission to Europe. They were seized on a steamer flying the British flag by a United States war vessel, an outrage which excited great indignation in this country. The British Government peremptorily demanded the release of the Southern envoys, and ordered immediate preparations for war. Although the United States Government defended the action of the Captain who seized the envoys, it complied with the demand. The incident left sore feelings on both sides, a fact which must be kept in view in considering subsequent events.

The Southern States had no navy, and the Northern States had therefore absolute command of the sea. Accordingly the Confederate Government endeavoured to buy and arm privateers with the object of preying upon the mercantile marine of the United States. The most notable of these vessels was the *Alabama*, which was built by Messrs. Laird in their shipyard at Birkenhead. The United States Ambassador in this country had called the attention of the British Government to the *Alabama* before it started upon its career, and as a matter of fact orders were issued by our Government to prevent its departure the very day after it had started. For two years the *Alabama* did enormous damage to the United States shipping, until at last it was sunk by the *Kersarge* in a sea fight off Cherbourg. Six other vessels were also the subjects of complaint ; but, in the end, the Geneva Court of Arbitration found that in the case of five of these the British Government had not been wanting in its duty towards a friendly Power.

The United States Government was for a time too absorbed in the civil war to deal seriously with the grievance, but no sooner had the resistance of the Southern States collapsed, in 1865, than the British Government was called upon to make reparation, a Liberal administration being then in office. Shortly afterwards the Conservatives came into power, but the discussion continued, and in November, 1868, a Convention, with a view to settlement, was agreed upon. This Convention proved abortive, but negotiations proceeded with the Liberal Government which came into office at the end of 1868, and in 1869 another Convention was signed by Mr. Reverdy Johnson, the American Minister in London, and the Earl of Clarendon, but it was rejected by the United States Senate. In February, 1871, a Joint-Commission was appointed to meet at Washington to

settle the *Alabama* dispute and certain other disputes about the fisheries. The Commissioners
appointed by the British Government were Earl
de Grey (now Marquis of Ripon) and Sir Stafford
Northcote (afterwards Earl of Iddesleigh). It is
desirable to bear in mind that, on either side, no
mere party question was at issue. Mr. Reverdy
Johnson, who conducted the earlier negotiations on
the part of the United States, was, in the American
sense, a Democrat, and had to deal with a British
Conservative Government. Later on one of the
British Commissioners was Sir Stafford Northcote,
a prominent leader of the Conservative party in
this country. The Joint-Commission resulted in
a reference of the whole dispute to the decision
of an International Court of Arbitration sitting at
Geneva. Speedily a difficulty arose through the
American claim for " consequential damages."

Senator Sumner, the author of the claim for
" consequential damages," was a man of such high
character and such lofty ideals that his sincerity
cannot be doubted ; perhaps the best excuse that
can be urged on his behalf is that in the strain
and stress of a prolonged and cruel war his judgment had lost its balance, more especially as the
sympathy of the governing classes in this country
with the slaveowners had stung to the quick his
righteous soul. He could not, or would not, see
that any attempt to enforce such exorbitant demands must necessarily have destroyed all hope
of a peaceful settlement of the quarrel. No high-

spirited, powerful nation would ever concede such a demand until its material resources were exhausted and it was prostrated beneath the heel of a conqueror. Happily for the future of the world, wiser and better counsels prevailed, and the two great branches of the Anglo-Saxon race were spared a fratricidal struggle which would have been the direst calamity to civilisation.

The Commissioners at Washington had paved a way for a settlement by agreeing that the arbitrators should be guided by certain rules of international duty, as follows :

" 1. That a neutral Government is bound, first, to use due diligence to prevent the fitting out, arming, or equipping within its jurisdiction of any vessel which it has reasonable ground to believe is intended to cruise or carry on war against a Power with which it is at peace ; and also to use like diligence to prevent the departure from its jurisdiction of any vessel intended to cruise or carry on a war as above, such vessel having been specially adapted, in whole or in part, within such jurisdiction to warlike use.

" 2. Not to permit or suffer either belligerent to make use of its ports or waters as the base of naval operations against the other, or for the purposes of the renewal or augmentation of military supplies or arms, or the recruitment of men.

" 3. To exercise due diligence in its own ports and waters and as to all persons within its jurisdiction to prevent any violation of the foregoing obligations and duties. It being a condition that those obligations should in future be held to be binding internationally between the two countries."

It was only after these rules had been agreed upon that what were called the indirect or consequential claims were urged and pressed. These claims were on account of (*a*) losses incurred in the transfer of the carrying trade to the British flag, (*b*) the increased cost of assurances of goods carried in American ships, (*c*) the cost involved in the prolongation of war. Naturally such demands excited much irritation in this country. For nearly six months the two Governments were engaged in diplomatic correspondence on the subject, and the Arbitration Commission, which held a first formal meeting in December, 1871, adjourned for six months. It seemed at one time probable that the whole work would collapse. On June 15, 1872, the members of the Tribunal assembled at Geneva. Count Sclopis, who presided, represented Italy ; Baron Staempfl, Switzerland ; Vicompte d'Itajuba, Brazil ; while the United States were represented by Mr. George Francis Adams and Great Britain by Sir Alexander Cockburn. The arbitrators declared the indirect claims to be invalid and contrary to International Law ; President Grant then consented to withdraw them.

Judgment was given on September 14th of the same year. All the arbitrators found that Great Britain was liable for the damages caused by the *Alabama;* four out of the five also decided against Great Britain in the case of the *Florida.* Sir Alexander Cockburn declined to sign the award, but published a justification of his consent to liability in the *Alabama* case.

The claim of the United States was for

£9,500,000 sterling ; the arbitrators awarded
£3,237,000. The amount was certainly excessive.
After all the claims had been satisfied it was said
that there remained a large balance, but this has
been categorically denied by American politicians.

The first act of the Workmen's Peace Association was to formulate a plan for the constitution
of a High Court of Nations ; the second was to
issue an address to working men on the *Alabama*
difficulty. The hitch that had arisen over the indirect or consequential claims put forward by the
Government of the United States was eagerly seized
on by the opponents of arbitration to declare it to
be utterly impracticable. The answer was obvious,
and, in our judgment, conclusive. In the address
which Cremer drew up we said : " If nations had
laws to govern their actions towards each other and
a properly constituted High Court of Nations where
such laws should be interpreted and administered,
we should not have been troubled by the *Alabama*
case at all. Either the departure of that vessel
from our ports would have been legal, in which case
the United States would have had no claim upon
us, or it would have been illegal, in which case the
British Government would not have permitted it to
escape, or if it had done so its liability would have
been clear and unmistakable." This address ended
by urging that the inclusion of indirect or consequential claims should be submitted to the
arbitrators. In the end the course thus suggested
was actually taken.

The main point, however, raised in the address was the establishment of a Permanent High Court of Nations. In the case of the *Alabama* dispute Christian sentiment, latent ties of racial brotherhood, and close commercial relationships forbade a crime which would have been a disgrace to civilisation ; but from the first we recognised the danger of delay when once evil passions are excited by false and narrow ideas of patriotism. The stupid cry of " The British Empire against the world " is only too well calculated to unite the world against the British Empire, and rightly so if its policy is not based on the eternal principles of justice. A nation no more than a man can expect to be a judge in its own cause, and history demonstrates that in the past British statesmen have not always been guided by equity and righteousness. Our demand for a High Court was at the time ridiculed as an impossible dream of unpractical theorists, but now that the Permanent Court at The Hague has been established the laughter has entirely ceased.

CHAPTER VIII

BIRTH OF THE WORKMEN'S PEACE ASSOCIATION

THE British nation was profoundly stirred by the outbreak of the Franco-German War in 1870. At first strong sympathy was expressed in aristocratic circles on the side of Germany. A Workmen's Peace Committee was formed by Cremer, consisting of about fifty men, most of them his old comrades in the Reform League, and an appeal to the working classes in favour of neutrality was drawn up. In that document occurred this passage :

"Let it be at least as regards our own country our firm and unanimous resolve, while we thank our Government for their endeavours hitherto to preserve Europe from the fruitful calamities of the present war, not to allow England to be drawn into it upon any ground or pretext whatever. What we claim and demand—what we would implore the peoples of Europe to do, without regard to Courts, Cabinets, or Dynasties— is to insist upon arbitration as a substitute for war, with peace and its blessings for them, for us, for the whole civilised world."

So humble was the origin of the International Arbitration League that it had no office except

Cremer's private house. As will be seen hereafter, the committee grew into an association, and subsequently assumed its present name ; but the original idea has been preserved throughout. Hereafter, for the sake of brevity and simplicity, it will be called the League.

In the later stages of the Franco-German War, when Napoleon III. had become a prisoner, and France had become a Republic, a strong feeling of sympathy with the French people was expressed by many British democrats, but the Committee continued to make a firm stand in favour of neutrality.

Henry Richard and the committee of the Peace Society naturally desired to encourage any movement in the ranks of labour which tended to assist their work, and for the first few years voted a substantial subsidy. As the income of the Peace Society fell off this subsidy was gradually diminished, till at last the League resolved to become absolutely independent. For some years it was a hard struggle, the balance-sheet almost always showing a deficit. There were times when the League must have collapsed if its secretary, through his past frugality, could not have been content to wait for his small salary for many months.

In 1871 the Committee developed into the Workmen's Peace Association, and offices were taken at 9, Buckingham Street, Strand, a house which for some years was a Radical centre. One floor was occupied by the Land Tenure Reform Association, whose president, John Stuart Mill, first propounded the doctrine of the " unearned increment," to-day best known as the taxation of land values. His chair is now one of the heirlooms of the League.

The first important work of the League was to draw up an " outline of a plan for the establishment of a High Court of Nations," which it will be seen largely anticipated the work of The Hague Congress. It ran as follows :

PREAMBLE.

Whereas, War having signally failed as a means for the settlement of International disputes, and being opposed to the character and spirit of the age, in the belief of this Conference permanent peace and concord between Nations would be promoted by the establishment of a High Court of Nations on the basis set forth in the following articles:

Article I.—CONSTITUTION.

Every separate and independent Government to have the power to appoint an equal number of Representatives to such Court.

Article II.—DUTIES OF THE COURT.

The Court to draw up a Code of International Law, providing for the settlement by the Court, on the basis of such Code, of all disputes that may from time to time arise between the Governments represented.

Article III.—JURISDICTION AND POWER.

The jurisdiction of the Court to extend to all Governments represented, but its power of interference to be limited to the external relations of such Governments, so as under no circumstances to interfere with the internal affairs of any Nation.

Article IV.—Decision of Court.

Any Government represented refusing to be bound by, or neglecting to obey, the decision of the Court within a time specified for that purpose, shall be adjudged, and declared to be Internationally Outlawed, and the other Governments shall thereupon suspend Diplomatic intercourse with such Government and prohibit Commercial intercourse with the Nation it represents until it shall conform to the decision of the Court.

Article V.—Differences for which no Provision is made in International Code.

In case of a dispute arising between Governments for which no provision shall have been made in the International Code, the Court shall have power to arbitrate upon and arrange such dispute, and any Power refusing to accept its award shall become amenable to the Penalties contained in Article IV.

Article VI.—Differences between Governments not represented at the Court.

In case of Differences arising between Governments not represented, the Court to offer its friendly services, as Mediator to adjust such differences.

With this plan was issued a manifesto to the working men, which was drawn up by the present writer at Cremer's request. The following passage will explain the programme of the League :

" We are not fanatic dreamers ; we are not utopian theorists. We share with you that common inheritance of our race, the practical mind, which refuses to attack or destroy until it is ready to reconstruct ; it is not enough for us to denounce the evil of war, and to paint its thousand-fold horrors. You acknowledge the evil—you have been nauseated by the records of its atrocities. But many of you answer, ' The evil is great, but it is inevitable.' It is because we do *not* believe the evil to be inevitable that we appeal to you. We are practical politicians, and have calculated the opposing forces. We have measured the obstacles abroad and at home, and are confident that, sooner or later, a substitute must and will be found for war. It is time that a substitute should be provided. An age that has achieved such marvellous triumphs over all material forces, that has evinced such vast power of organisation in commerce, and that has accomplished such great reforms in government and jurisprudence, is surely able so to reconstruct international relations that, when disputes arise, justice and not force shall be the arbiter."

In the earlier years of the League its most generous supporters were Samuel Morley, John Horniman, and George W. Palmer ; in more recent times Richard and George Cadbury, Andrew Carnegie, and Sir John Brunner.

The first president was Edmond Beales, who retained that office until his death, when he was succeeded by the Rt. Hon. Thomas Burt, M.P., who still survives, and who has more than once crossed the Channel in our service. The first treasurer of the League was Benjamin Britten, a Marylebone shoemaker, who, like most of his craft, was a pronounced Liberal. He had a *penchant* for writing verses, and at one time his lyrics obtained considerable popularity ; indeed, his songs ultimately brought him into the service of a great firm of musical publishers. In the earlier years of the movement Britten served the cause with untiring zeal. Until 1877 various members of the council were elected to the chair ; in that year the present writer was appointed, and has retained the position ever since, mainly because it was necessary that during Cremer's frequent absences abroad on the business of the League some one should have the responsible charge of its office.

CHAPTER IX

PIONEER WORK IN PARIS

THE old International which had so far departed
from its original ideas of fraternity was now practically dead ; the idea of its English secretary,
Cremer, was to create a new International which
should conform more to the original purpose of
the old one. In 1875, Cremer, whose faculty of
initiative was most valuable at all times, proposed
that the Workmen's Peace Association should
commence international operations by holding a
conference in Paris. To the outside world this
seemed a most quixotic enterprise, and the effort
excited no small ridicule both at home and abroad.
Certainly those who laughed had some show of
reason. The Association was a small body of
obscure persons, most of whom had little or no
knowledge of the French language, with an uncertain annual income of perhaps £500 a year. A
Bonapartist or Monarchical restoration in France
seemed highly probable, and necessarily would have
proved a death-blow to our hopes ; while the
most powerful leader on the Republican side was

Gambetta, who constantly urged the people never to talk about the *revanche*, but always to remember the lost provinces. Paris was still legally in a state of siege, so that the right of public meeting was suspended ; many of its public buildings were yet in ruins, and the working classes were thoroughly cowed and disorganised. The last instalment of the war indemnity had only been paid two years before. It was believed, not without reason, that Bismarck was watching for a pretext to invade France a second time. Probably at this period the great majority of Frenchmen regarded it as a patriotic duty to await with eager expectation the hour when a supreme effort should be made to wipe out the disgrace of Sedan, and to extend the frontier to the banks of the Rhine.

Nevertheless the project was not altogether unreasonable. Paris was the only possible basis of continental international operations. Germany was closed to us ; Austria and Italy were alike impossible ; the very instinct of self-preservation would have rallied the smaller States to the movement, but none of them could furnish a hopeful starting-point. For a century France had been the leader in European progress. Moreover, those who projected the effort had a strong faith in the French people and in their democratic institutions. Democracies are essentially pacific unless they are threatened with destruction, or are temporarily beguiled by self-seeking demagogues.

The League was then in its infancy and had not

yet obtained much notoriety either at home or abroad, but Cremer had considerable influence with labour leaders, and a delegation of nearly fifty went across the Channel. We were a hopeful and even a merry party till we arrived in Paris and saw with our own eyes some of the miseries of war. At that time many of the finest buildings in the city were in ruins, and not a few private houses bore traces of the terrible bombardment.

The Conference of September 6 and 7, 1875, was of a comparatively humble character. It was held in a small hall in the Rue d'Arras, the place where Père Hyacinth used afterwards to hold his services. At that period a meeting could only be convened by private invitation, and the police took care that only those who had received personal invitations were allowed to enter. About 170 persons were present, 47 of these composing the British deputation. Among these latter were Joseph Arch, W. R. Cremer, George Procter, myself, and M. Lassasie, all of whom, except Cremer, still survive. The President was Auguste Desmoulins, son-in-law of Pierre Leroux, a Socialist journalist who had been an exile in England during the Second Empire, and who afterwards became a prominent member of the Paris Municipal Council. In his opening speech he mentioned the fact that a conference of jurisconsults had just been held at The Hague and had pronounced strongly in favour of international arbitration.

Cremer was the chief British speaker. He knew

full well that the idea then prevailing among working-class Republicans was that they must have one
more great war, after which would come the social
millennium, and that he was speaking in the
presence of the reporters of half a dozen daily
Paris papers ; but he did not shrink from boldly
expressing his views. He told his audience that
the time for holding the Conference was said to
be badly chosen, because war might break out any
day in Europe, the nations being all armed to the
teeth. But with him this was a reason for continuing the movement in favour of peace with greater
activity and energy. He rejoiced at the reception
they had met with in France and found therein
reasons for encouragement. He hoped that this
progress would continue, and felt sure that but
for the state of siege and the fear of police
espionage their numbers would have been much
greater. Let French Republicans continue that
peaceful, patient, and prudent policy which had
won for them, during the last four years, the
admiration of their English brethren and of the
friends of real progress everywhere. It greatly
depended upon the peaceful attitude of the
Parisians whether Republicanism should exist in
France and extend itself to the various nations of
the Continent, or be crushed out for generations.
If they persisted in the course they were pursuing, allowing nothing to goad them into another
insurrection or war of revenge, the Republic must
be consolidated in France, and the idea of which

they were the guardians would then be extended to other nations.

The course of events has shown that Cremer was right in the main. At that time a popular delusion prevailed in this country that the French people needed a strong despot to hold them down. The despots drenched almost every country in Europe with French blood ; but for nearly forty years past a succession of able Republican statesmen— in spite of such mischief-makers as Boulanger, Deroulède, and Millevoye—have maintained peace and consolidated the liberties of the French people.

The chief French speakers were Limousin, journalist ; de Boutellier, ex-naval officer ; and Henri Bellaire, Secretary of the Paris Peace Society, who died not long after. The chief resolution, which was unanimously adopted, was as follows :

> " That as the commercial and economic advancement of the industrial classes is essential to their intellectual and moral development, and as war between nations diminishes production, increases the cost of food, entails heavy financial burdens, retards national progress, and does not permanently decide disputes between nations, this conference gives its hearty adhesion to the principle of international arbitration as a practical, rational, and economical means of settling international differences."

A second resolution entered a solemn protest against bloated armaments.

This conference was not without results, for a Workmen's Peace Committee was at once formed in Paris, with which the League was in frequent

correspondence. One of its prominent members
was M. Murat, who had taken an active part in the
Paris Commune, and who rendered valuable service
to Cremer at this time. The Paris committee had
grown so vigorous that three years afterwards it
was able to convene a public meeting in the
Chateau d'Eau Theatre. A large British deputation again crossed the Channel in the company of
Cremer. Among the survivors are James Row-
land, M.P., Greedy, Lassasie, Matkin, Stainsby,
Evans, Clarke, and Henry Taylor. Victor Hugo
would have presided, but enfeebled health made it
necessary that he should only be honorary president, and his place was taken by M. Tolain, an
old comrade of Cremer in the International. The
République Française, Gambetta's organ, refused
to announce the meeting or to report it, and
it was only three days before the date that the
police allowed bills to be posted in the streets ;
but so great was the demand for admission that the
tickets were exhausted in twenty-four hours, and no
less than eight thousand persons applied for them.

  Victor Hugo wrote from Guernsey as follows :
" DEAR FELLOW-COUNTRYMEN OF EUROPE,—I
am at this moment, to my great sorrow, unable to
preside over your labours. What you demand I
demand, I desire what you desire. Our union is the
very beginning of unity. Let us be calm. Without
us Governments may attempt something, but nothing
that they may try to do will be successful against
your decision, against your liberty, against your

sovereignty. Look at their attempts without un-
easiness, always with serenity, sometimes with a
smile. The supreme future is with you. All that
is done, even against you, will serve you. Continue
to march, labour, and think. You are a single
people of Europe, and you want a single thing—
peace."

The chief speakers on the British side were
prominent trade unionists, and on the French side
Desmoulins, Edouard Lockroy, editor of the
Rappel, and Dauthier, a Paris workman. The
proceedings lasted over three hours and were
characterised by the most unbounded enthusiasm.
Subsequently another great meeting was held in the
Theatre at Puteaux, an industrial suburb of Paris.

Not long before, Cremer, with indefatigable
energy, endeavoured to break ground in Germany,
and with that object visited Berlin, Hamburg,
Dresden, Leipzig, Cologne, and Frankfort ; but
though he was cordially received by Dr. Max
Hirsch and other Radicals and Social Democrats,
at that time the obstacles to any organised demonstration were too formidable to be overcome. This
is worthy of mention in view of the splendid success
of the recent fraternal gatherings at Berlin when
the address to German workmen was presented—
the framing of which was the last act of Cremer's
life.

In June, 1879, the French Workmen's Peace
Society invited an English deputation to attend a
banquet in a garden at Ménilmontant. Cremer and

half a dozen others of us attended as well as a
deputation from the Italian League of Liberty,
Fraternity, and Peace. M. Wynants, a Paris workman, presided, and an address was presented from
the British Workmen's Peace Association, signed
by 432 officers and representatives of working
men's organisations, in which the French were
strongly urged to lead in the peace crusade.
Speeches were delivered by MM. Naquet and
Laisant, both of them Deputies, while M. Dauthier
sang a peace song which he had written, the last
verse of which ran as follows :—

> " Des nations l'alliance féconde,
> O Béranger, rejouit nos esprits.
> La paix enfin s'empare de ce monde ;
> A leurs foyers sont rendus les proscrits.
> Unissons-nous, nous tous fils de la France,
> Italiens, Germains, Belges, Anglais,
> Pour assurer enfin la délivrance
> Des peuples par la paix !"

Signor Eaudi represented Italy at this banquet,
where the movement had already made great progress, mainly through the exertions of Signor
Moneta, editor of *Il Secolo*, of Milan. A little
while previously a great meeting had been held
in a Milan theatre, attended by four thousand persons, and addressed, among others, by Aurelio
Saffi, formerly a Triumvir of the Roman Republic,
Garibaldi sending his adhesion.

On the morning after the banquet Cremer and
the other English delegates waited on Victor Hugo

at his Paris residence, who in reply to an address, said : " You are men, you are workmen, you love peace, and you struggle against war. I am with you in this combat ; I have been in this battle already a long time, and I intend to continue to serve this beautiful cause during the few years I may yet have to live. I am an old man—I am seventy-seven years of age—but thanks to Him who orders all things, I feel myself still capable of continuing the struggle, and so long as I have breath I will combat war ; I will defend our common cause, the cause of labour and peace."

CHAPTER X

THE EASTERN CRISIS

THE League, while continuing its persistent efforts in France, steadily pursued its propagandist work at home, and held a large number of meetings in all parts of the country. Cremer's close connection with the Trades' Union movement enabled him to largely focus working-class feeling in favour of peace. At the Trades' Union Congresses which were held annually in various towns he caused a resolution to be carried in favour of international arbitration and a reduction of armaments. Advantage was taken of the presence of so many Trades' Union Leaders to hold public meetings in such towns at the time when the Congress met.

When the war between Russia and Turkey broke out, the League assumed an attitude of increased vigilance and activity. It would be foreign to our present purpose to follow in detail the course of events at that time. Suffice it to say that Lord Derby, who was then Foreign Secretary, was a man of eminently pacific mind, who declared that the

7

greatest of British interests is peace. On September 11, 1876, a deputation from the League waited upon Lord Derby at the Foreign Office, and presented to him an address of a pacific character, in which he was asked to use the influence of Great Britain in favour of the independence of the Christain races in Turkey. Lord Derby returned a sympathetic reply, in which he said that the British Government was in consultation with the various European Powers, and he should be heartily glad if the end of it was a satisfactory peace.

In the crisis of the Russo-Turkish War, when a large party in this country were clamouring for British intervention in favour of Turkey, Cremer obtained the signatures of over three hundred officers of Trade Unions to a manifesto which was placarded all over the country. It contained some home truths which may be recalled with advantage at the present time, as will be seen from the following extracts :

" What does war mean? To the landowners it means keeping up high rents which have lately shown a tendency to fall ; to mercenary capitalists it means lending money at high rates for the purchase of murderous weapons, the interest on which the industry of the country will have to pay ; to the sordid section of the Press it means coining gold out of human blood by increasing the largest circulations of the world. To military and naval officers it means employment, promotion, and gain. To the obstructives it means the arrest of reform and the paralysis of progress. But what does it mean to you? War means heavier taxation, which sooner or later comes out of labour, decreases the wages fund, and diminishes the chance of employment. With the exception of the few trades that supply war material, war means bad trade to the nations that engage in it. Yet more—it means dear food, hunger and starvation at home, and misery and disease and wholesale slaughter abroad. Have you forgotten the years of the Crimean War? Many of you at that time could not earn food enough to feed your children. Your sons and brothers were forced by want into the army, while many of you who have grown to manhood since that time knew then by hard, bitter experience that to the workman's child war meant hunger and wretchedness.

" Woe to us at this time if we fail to read the warnings of history ! Eighty years ago we went to war to crush Republicanism in France, and to this hour we pay the interest of £40,000,000 of debt incurred therein. Twenty years ago we went to war to maintain Turkey, and she has grown more fierce, corrupt, and infamous ever since. Who regrets now that we held aloof from the Franco-Austrian War, the Schleswig-Holstein War, the American Civil War, or the Franco-German War? In all these cases the same agencies were at work, and the same vile arts were used, which are so active now. The people then turned a deaf ear to their plausible tempters. Let us do so again, and make them know that, clamour as they will, the British people are resolved on peace."

Somewhat later, when the Turks were utterly defeated and the Russian army was almost within sight of Constantinople, the clamour for war became loud and persistent, and it was necessary that the friends of peace should take prompt and decisive steps to counteract the efforts of the Jingoes.

It was a time of extraordinary excitement. The savage passions of the music-hall mob were inflamed to the utmost pitch of intensity. Mr. Gladstone's windows in Harley Street were smashed ; parcels of human excrement were sent to editors of Liberal newspapers ; an anti-war meeting convened by Charles Bradlaugh in Hyde Park resulted in a desperate free fight ; when a Working Men's Peace Conference was held at the Memorial Hall a blatant Jingo harangued a mob in Farringdon Street in the vain hope of persuading them to take the hall by storm. For such exhibitions of brute force the war press of the period was as directly responsible as when, twenty years after, Mr. Chamberlain's organ at Birmingham instigated a riot outside the Town Hall, which resulted in a lamentable loss of life.

The late Mr. Arthur Albright, of Birmingham, interviewed Cremer and the present writer, and placed £1,000 at our disposal. In four days 470 men from east, west, north, and south were brought together, representing nearly all the industries of the country. On April 10, 1878, the

National Conference met in the Memorial Hall.
The numbers present would have been increased
to a thousand but for the shortness of the notice,
hundreds of trades' union leaders expressing their
regret and inability to attend on that account.
This conference was presided over by Mr. Thomas
Burt, M.P., and subsequently by Mr. Bailey, President of the Amalgamated Tailors. An address was
presented to the conference, in which it was declared that " a war on behalf of Turkey is a year
too late ; a war to obliterate the treaty of San
Stefano must fail in its object ; a war to modify
that treaty would be a monstrous crime, at any rate
till all means of obtaining a peaceful settlement
were exhausted. . . . We believe in the principle
of arbitration. The governing classes of this
country constantly recommend to us a resort to
arbitration in trade disputes. We demand the
application of the same principle to the disputes
of nations in general, and if necessary to this
particular dispute at the present moment."

Resolutions in accord with the spirit of this
address were moved, and speeches in support of
them were made by a number of the most prominent trades' union leaders. Then, to the surprise
and delight of those present, Mr. Gladstone made
his appearance and received a most enthusiastic
reception. At the close of a long speech he said :
" I hope we shall be enabled to avert the calamity
of war, and perhaps also to do some little good
by taking as a nation an honest and cheerful part

in a peaceful congress, and in consolidating the triumph of justice and freedom in the East of Europe. . . . I have never seen a more practical or enthusiastic meeting. I hope that its effect will be to encourage us to persevere in the work that we have taken in hand until that work is complete."

This conference was succeeded by a second, which was held on the 4th of May at the Memorial Hall, when 656 delegates attended from Agricultural Labourers' Unions. Nearly every one present was either a district or branch officer, so that the conference was as thoroughly representative as it was possible to make it. These men came from no less than twenty-nine counties. Joseph Arch presided, and this conference was as unanimous and enthusiastic as the previous one.

These great gatherings struck the right keynote at the right moment. They were followed by large anti-war meetings in nearly all the great towns. There could be no doubt that such popular demonstrations exercised a powerful influence on the Government. The malicious activity of the music-hall patriots and other Jingoes of a more influential kind was effectually thwarted. The Tory Government found it desirable to enter into secret negotiations with Russia, and Lord Beaconsfield and the Marquis of Salisbury went to Berlin with a secret agreement in their pockets. They came back declaring that they had brought " peace with honour," but afterwards it became known that the principal points in dispute had been previously settled by negotiation.

Shortly afterwards Cremer was the recipient of a modest testimonial for his services in the cause of democracy, accompanied by an illuminated address, which is here given *in extenso* because it shows the variety of the movements in which he was engaged :

" The important services which, on various occasions, during a long series of years, you have rendered to the cause of Freedom and Peace at home and abroad, merit hearty and generous recognition. That recognition we, who have been associated with you in one or more public movements, for the social and political well-being of the people, desire to express, by the present testimonial. From the time when you helped to inaugurate the movement for shortening the hours of labour, and when you united with some of us in the reception of Garibaldi, to the present hour you have taken an active part in such movements. In the great struggle between freedom and slavery in America, at a time when an aristocratic attempt to sympathise with the insurgent slave-owners threatened to disgrace and degrade our country, you laboured assiduously and successfully to resist the attempt. In the formation of the Reform League, and in its struggles for a more complete representation of the people, you took an honourable and conspicuous part. More than once you have sought to establish, in your own person, the great principle, that a man should not be disqualified from representing others because he is a workman. The cause of popular education, of land tenure reform, of the emancipation of the agricultural labourers, and other progressive movements, have ever found in you an earnest advocate. But most especially we desire to recognise the services which you have rendered to the sacred cause of Peace as secretary of the Workmen's Peace Association from its formation. Twice, when a powerful party in this country were loudly clamouring for war, you have most effectively marshalled against them the forces of the sons of industry, to whom war would have been the most disastrous of calamities. In the late great crisis, the main burden fell upon your shoulders, and most gallantly and ably was it borne. To you is mainly due the propagation of peace principles among the workmen of the Continent, and of France especially. The undersigned, therefore, on behalf of many friends who have been associated with you at various times, in earnestly striving to advance the cause of Freedom and Peace, feel sincere pleasure in presenting you with this address, together with a purse of £65 as a mark of their respect and admiration."

CHAPTER XI

SOUTH AFRICA AND EGYPT

AT the conclusion of his Midlothian Campaign, Mr. Gladstone was returned to power with a splendid majority of eighty-six at his back. The country was heartily sick of a warlike policy, and the heavy burdens of taxation which it involved. Twenty millions had been spent on the unnecessary war in Afghanistan, and five millions more on the war in Zululand, to say nothing of the cost of calling out the reserves, and other warlike preparations when it seemed probable that Great Britain would intervene on behalf of the " unspeakable Turk." Mr. Gladstone inherited several grave difficulties from his predecessor. Turkey was indisposed to carry out certain provisions of the Berlin Treaty, and the smouldering fires in the Balkan Peninsula threatened to break out once more. Pressure was therefore brought to bear upon the Sultan by the Powers, Great Britain leading the way.

The Zulu War was ended before Mr, Gladstone came into office, but a new trouble had arisen in

South Africa. In 1877 Sir Theophilus Shepstone
had formally annexed the Transvaal, promising
the Boers at the time the full retention of their
self-governing powers. Soon after Sir Bartle
Frere, the High Commissioner, found the dis-
contented Boers collected in a huge fortified camp,
and entered into negotiations with them. A little
later Lord Wolseley declared that henceforth the
Transvaal should be treated as a Crown Colony.
In December, 1879, the Boers made a determined
stand for independence, and in February, 1881,
they gained a great victory at Majuba Hill. A
loud outcry for revenge arose when the news of
our defeat arrived.

To counteract this, Cremer drew up an address
to Mr. Gladstone, which was signed by over six
hundred representative working men, denouncing
the " nefarious practices " by which the annexation
of the Transvaal was attended, and urging Mr.
Gladstone to treat the Boers with justice. In
this address the memorialists said : " We are not
insensible to national honour and greatness, but
our love of justice is not blinded by the glamour
of extended empire ; and we hope that neither
you nor your Government will order or sanction
further wrongs by the shedding of more blood to
satisfy an insane craving for revenge before daring
to do what is right."

Mr. Gladstone did not turn a deaf ear to these
and similar appeals, and when the Boers proposed
an armistice it was granted, and ultimately a con-

vention was signed, under which the Boers secured the rights of self-government, with a British Protectorate. When the second Boer War broke out Mr. Gladstone was fiercely denounced by its authors as though he had committed a crime. He will be amply justified by history. Had this country continued to treat the Boers with justice, it would have saved many thousands of lives and many millions of treasure. The pacification of the Transvaal under General Botha shows what might have been accomplished if the British Government had not become the accomplice of greedy financiers and alien adventurers.

The intervention of Great Britain in the affairs of Egypt, which commenced with the bombardment of Alexandria, and led to John Bright's resignation from the Gladstone Government, caused great dissatisfaction to the friends of peace in this country. The League vainly protested against the bombardment, and a subsequent expedition of a British army to Egypt under the command of Lord Wolseley. In this protest Cremer was especially prominent, and addressed a number of public meetings. There can be no doubt, however, that public opinion generally was in favour of the intervention. When the Government demanded £2,300,000 toward the expenses of the Egyptian War, only 29 Members voted against it, the majority of them being Irish Nationalists. One of the strongest reasons against intervention in Egypt was the knowledge that it would produce ill-feeling in France, as, indeed, it did for some years afterwards. On more than one occasion France vainly protested, and demanded that Great Britain should fulfil the promises made by our Government to withdraw from occupation. Another strong reason was the fact that British intervention was mainly the work of bondholders who were threatened with the loss of the money they had invested in Egyptian securities. It is unnecessary here to discuss the right of British intervention in this case ; but, doubtless, many who at the outset were opposed to active interference have been subsequently convinced that not only were the interests of investors protected, but that the administration of Egyptian affairs by Lord Cromer and other British officials resulted in the establishment of Egyptian finances on a sound basis, and proved of great benefit to·the industrial population.

CHAPTER XII

IN PARIS AGAIN

ONE of the most exciting gatherings that the
League ever held in Paris was that held on
February 22, 1885, which was held in the Tivoli-
Wauxhall, a famous dancing saloon in the centre
of Paris. A thousand seats had been provided, but
the greater number of the audience had to stand.
In all, there must have been nearly four thousand
present. Nine French Deputies appeared on the
platform, one of whom, M. Henri Maret, occupied
the chair, with M. Laisant, Deputy, and Citizen
Joffrin as assessors, or as we should say, vice-
presidents. M. Henri Maret, editor of *Le Radical*,
was physically unable to contend against the
clamour of a group of some fifty Anarchists, who
came to the meeting bent upon disturbance, and
whose object was not to give a hostile reception
to the English deputation, but to show their dislike of the French Deputies on the platform. No
sooner had the chairman taken his seat than a
dozen men were shouting at the top of their
voices : " Down with the Deputies ! " " Down with

the twenty-five francs." French Deputies were at that time paid twenty-five francs a day for their services. The chairman for a while struggled in vain against the noise, and then Citizen Joffrin came to the rescue.

Joffrin, a journeyman engineer who had worked for some years in England, and who subsequently became a Deputy for Paris, was at that time the most popular leader among French workmen. Physically, he was a powerful man with a strident voice, but no single human voice could contend successfully against the clamour. On the chairman's table was a huge bell, which Joffrin grasped with both hands and continued to ring with all his might until the clamour subsided. Joffrin shouted to the Anarchists, " If you do not respect the Deputies, respect at least the strangers who received us in 1871 " (Joffrin alluded to himself and others who had to go into exile after the insurrection of the Paris Commune). " Do not make an organised disturbance ; we beg the Anarchists, whose theories I combat and shall ever combat, to respect the liberty of speech."

M. Maret, the clamour having somewhat diminished, made an eloquent speech, in the course of which he said : " Citizens, there are two sorts of patriotism. There is the patriotism of the past, selfish, cruel, and destructive, whose glory it was to cause the flow of rivers of blood. There is the patriotism of the future, that of peace and labour. Its glory is to excel in industry and in freedom, and its battles are for victories of progress. That patriotism is ours. We love France, the land of our birth, of our adoption, and we shall be the more proud of her flag when it floats over civilisation and fraternity in lieu of gathering in its folds slavery and death. Therefore, in common indignation against those who would revive the days of massacres and mournings, we grasp the hands of our English brothers who come to us to speak of justice and of peace."

The applause of the great majority of the vast assembly showed that they were in full sympathy with the sentiments uttered by the chairman.

Mr. Burt, who received an ovation, made a brief speech in English, which was translated, and presented an address from the British workmen to the working men of France. It is noteworthy that in this address the journalistic mischief-makers on both sides of the Channel were denounced in scathing language, and a strong protest was uttered against the ever-increasing armaments of the Great Powers. The French Chamber had just voted some additional millions for Tonquin, and the British Parliament had voted five and a half additional millions for ironclads, torpedoes, and fortifications.

M. Notelle, a Paris workman who had taken part in all our previous efforts from the first gathering in the Rue d'Arras, moved a resolution cordially responding to the sentiments expressed in the address. Towards the end of his speech another disturbance arose, and one of the Anarchists who rushed on to the platform was ejected therefrom. Subsequently a few others mounted the platform, and one of them was allowed to speak. His words showed that even Anarchists were by no means hostile to our movement, for at the outset he thus spoke : " The English come to fraternise with us ; others will come from other lands ; there will soon be but one people, the people of workers." He concluded with moving an amendment to the resolution, and as in the opinion of the president and others on the platform, it did not conflict with the resolution itself, it was agreed to make it a rider. The resolution as amended was then unanimously adopted.

In explanation of this somewhat disorderly scene, it should be stated that not long before several Anarchists had been prosecuted by the French Government and sentenced to various terms of imprisonment. Their comrades naturally seized every opportunity to manifest their discontent, and they used the Tivoli-Wauxhall meeting to make a collection for the wives and families of those who were in prison.

M. Clemenceau would have been present at this meeting but for an engagement in the country. At that time he was the Deputy for Montmartre, and editor of *La Justice*. He arranged to receive the English deputation at his office at midnight. Of all French newspapers, M. Clemenceau's organ had been the steady friend of the *entente cordiale*, and the constant opponent of a turbulent and aggressive foreign policy, and a brief address was presented to him thanking him for the services which he had rendered. Mr. Burt introduced the deputation, and the address was read by the present writer. M. Clemenceau thanked the deputation for their kind expression of opinion in regard to *La Justice*, and added that when Radical Republicans like himself objected to an aggressive foreign and colonial policy, French Ministers replied by pointing to the annexation policy of the British Government. He, however, earnestly hoped that when the Radical Republicans of France succeeded to power they would be faithful to their principles of peace and progress. It is noteworthy that in reporting this agreeable interview with M. Clemenceau, the *Arbitrator* expressed the belief that at no very distant day he would probably become the Prime Minister of France.

CHAPTER XIII

THE first Reform Act of 1832 gave a very grudg-
ing representation to what was then suburban
London. Under that Act the Tower Hamlets, which
had then a population of 360,000, 10,000 of whom
were electors, returned two Members. The Tower
Hamlets then extended from Tower Hill to Stam-
ford Hill, and from Ball's Pond to the East India
Dock. By the second Reform Act Hackney was
made a separate borough and included the parishes
of Hackney, Bethnal Green, and Shoreditch,
formerly represented by Sir Charles Reed and Mr.
Henry Fawcett. The third Reform Bill of 1885
still further divided the borough of Hackney into
seven constituencies, each returning one member,
the parish of Shoreditch being divided into the
separate constituencies of Hoxton and Haggerston.

About half a century ago Haggerston might be
said to possess a population almost equally divided
between the lower middle and upper working class.
I can remember the time when the carriage of
one of the members for the Tower Hamlets used

to stop at the residence of his mother in one of the principal streets, and when a considerable number of the householders possessed domestic servants. In later years the population has largely changed. Those of the middle class have almost entirely migrated into the outer suburbs, and into regions beyond across the Essex border : and this is mainly true also of the upper working class. By the time that Haggerston was made a separate constituency the larger and older houses were mostly let in apartments to separate families, and save the shopkeepers, the inhabitants were almost entirely of the working class, consisting largely of gas-workers, costermongers, labourers, but more especially of shoemakers. It was this constituency to which Cremer appealed in 1885. At one time the old church of St. Mary, Haggerston, sufficed for the whole district, but three or four new churches of a decidedly ritualistic type had been erected, and these were distinctly a Conservative force, more especially among that part of the population which could be influenced by the distribution of soup and coals and blankets. From the first Cremer had to contend against this pernicious influence, and more than once he had to fight an uphill battle against candidates who were notoriously chosen on account of their wealth rather than on their merits. The only wonder is that he should have been again and again returned, and a tribute of respect is due to many of his impoverished voters who steadily supported him at their own personal loss, and the wives of such men were equally worthy with their husbands.

Cremer had conceived the idea of standing for West St. Pancras, of which borough he had long been a resident, and he actually issued an address to the electors. It was very doubtful, however, whether he could have succeeded in such a constituency, which largely consisted of middle-class electors. Ultimately Mr. Harry Lawson, son of the proprietor of the *Daily Telegraph*, was chosen as the Liberal candidate, much to Cremer's annoyance. It was fortunate in the end for Cremer that he had to seek a more congenial constituency. Even at Haggerston his path was not easy. Sir Sydney Waterlow, Mr. Benjamin Whitworth, and two or three other well-known politicians were also before the Liberal and Radical Association. Ultimately the choice lay between Cremer and Whitworth. Mr. Whitworth, a wealthy Manchester man, and a munificent contributor to the funds of the United Kingdom Alliance, was the favourite of the temperance section of the party ; but Cremer was supported by the clubs and trade unions and was finally selected by a majority of more than two to one.

The Conservative candidate was Mr. Denny Urlin, a barrister, who was better known as a champion of Church defence and as a lay representative of advanced ritualism in the columns of the *Church Times* than as a party politician. He was, however, exactly the kind of candidate to suit the High Church clergy, and their male and female helpers whose charities were calculated to influence the impoverished class of voters. During the election a slanderous report was circulated that Cremer was an avowed enemy of religion, but this falsehood was counteracted by a letter from Samuel Morley expressing hearty good wishes for his success.

Cremer was triumphantly returned at the head of the poll, the figures being :

CREMER	...	...	...	...	...	2,736
URLIN	...	...	...	...	...	1,259
Majority	...	...	...	...	...	1,477

An election fund was raised by the present writer, the chief contributors to which were Samuel Morley, Andrew Carnegie, George Palmer of Reading, Lord Hobhouse, and Arthur Albright of Birmingham. Cremer's election expenses were under £300 and a balance of £120 was carried forward in preparation for the next contest.

At the General Election of 1886, Cremer was opposed by Mr. E. Lawrence, a Liberal Unionist, but was again returned, the figures being :

CREMER	...	...	...	...	...	2,054
LAWRENCE	...	...	...	...	...	1,677
Majority	...	...	...	...	...	377

In 1892 the Conservatives put forward Mr. J. S. Firbank, a wealthy contractor, but again

they failed to capture the seat. The numbers at
the declaration of the poll were :

CREMER	...	...	...	...	...	2,543
FIRBANK	...	...	...	...	...	1,662
Majority	...	...	...	...	...	921

After Cremer's first election in 1885 the success
of four London Labour candidates—Cremer,
Howell, Durant, and Leicester—was so gratifying
that a dinner was arranged in their honour at the
" Criterion " with Lord Hobhouse in the chair. Sir
Charles Russell had to propose the toast of the
evening, and as he knew hardly anything of the
antecedents of the Labour men the present writer
had to coach him beforehand. Unfortunately, a few
stubborn Republicans not only refused to stand up
when the health of the Queen was proposed, but
actually hissed, and this fact was reported in some
of the papers. A Tory member was so shocked that
he asked a question in the House about the matter.
The reply of the Minister was that he would make
inquiries of the noble lord who presided at the
banquet. When the question was repeated the
House was assured that Lord Hobhouse heard no
hissing, which was quite true as his lordship
happened to be deaf. I am afraid that the Minister
who answered the question was well aware of this
physical infirmity.

CHAPTER XIV

DE PROFUNDIS

SOMEWHAT late in middle life Cremer married a second time—his bride being Lucy Coombes, of Oxford, to whom he was devotedly attached. They were both great lovers of natural beauty, and he used to delight to speak to his intimate friends of their week-end rambles on the Surrey hills and elsewhere. Thursley Common, Hindhead, Haslemere, and Blackdown, were their special places of resort. In the company of his wife, who was some years younger than himself, he renewed his youth. Having no children, they were little vexed with household cares, and as often as possible they left the great city behind to sun themselves in the meadows, explore woodland bye-paths, and gather wild flowers. As I look upon an earlier portrait of Cremer's bright, hopeful face I vividly recall those days when he was full of innocent gaiety, and spoke with the freedom of friendship about the happiness of his married life.

Suddenly a great calamity fell upon him. The wife whom he so fondly loved was stricken with a painful, lingering, wasting, internal disease. No woman was ever more carefully tended by her husband ; no man was ever plunged in deeper sorrow for the wreck of his life. I saw him often at this period, but he had so steeled himself to endurance that, though I knew he was deeply troubled I had no idea of the depth of his despair. I know now that he lamented that the cause was suffering from his absorption in his own private grief, although, as a matter of fact, he tore himself away from the bedside of his wife to attend a series of meetings in Scotland shortly before her death. The letters written to his sister, which are before me as I write, are indeed a revelation of the inner man, and almost overcome me as I read them. I hesitate to use these sacred confidences, but have determined to do so in part, because I desire to present a faithful picture of the whole man, and those who only knew the solitary recluse of recent years could have no idea otherwise of the wealth of love within him. There is yet another reason. Because Cremer was opposed to woman suffrage he has been slanderously accused of being a woman-hater ; it is as well to set this accusation at rest once for all.

Anything more pathetic I have seldom read than the letters which he wrote to his sister at this period. Among his friends he appeared to bear up wonderfully, but in writing to his sister the fountains of the great deep were broken up and he poured out all his heart to her. The sister had evidently sought to comfort her brother with the consolations of her own simple Christian faith ; the brother replied that myself and others had vainly tried to do the same thing, but he was still a doubter. Let me lift just the corner of the veil. He wrote to his sister as follows :

" I had doubts and fears against which I struggled and prayed in vain. No doubt it is incomprehensible to you, but it is true, and strange to say, my poor darling with her infantile mind had the same sceptical turn. During her long illness I have tried to comfort her with the hope of immortality ; and although you did not know it, every day after she was removed upstairs into what proved the chamber of death I prayed with her, and on the fatal morning, as soon as I had sent the telegram to the hospital she said to the nurse, ' You need not wait, my husband is going to pray with me.' On previous occasions I had taken her hand in mine while praying with her, notwithstanding that the scalding tears rained down upon her beautiful but wasted hand. That morning I did not at first take her hand until she said, ' Are you not going to take my hand? ' I did so, and in choking utterances, her poor, dear hand bathed with my tears, I prayed for her and my forgiveness, and that she might be received into heaven ! Poor darling ! she evidently knew that the end was near, but, faint and weak as she was, she repeated a great deal after me. You know the rest ; as shortly after you arrived she only just knew you, and then the stupor which precedes death put an end to all consciousness."

I may add that when the body of his wife was taken to the grave the minister had mistaken the hour of the funeral. Cremer vainly looked round for me, but I was far away in the country at the time ; then he took the book and with a faltering voice read the Burial Service over the body of her whom he so dearly loved. Subsequently he designed a beautiful memorial card containing a vignette portrait of his wife, surrounded by forget-me-nots, with an inscription in which he expressed the hope of meeting her hereafter.

In a subsequent letter Cremer wrote to his sister : " I cannot write any more. If you knew what it has cost me to write so much, and the torrents of tears I have shed while doing so, you would comprehend the intensity of my grief. Yet after all, what passed between us that morning at the bedside affords me some ray of hope—infinitesimal, but still a ray."

I refrain from quoting from other despairing letters, written weeks and even months after his wife's death, in which Cremer continually expressed his longing to be speedily laid in the same grave with her. Time, the great healer, had reserved him for further splendid services to humanity at large. He who had his own Gethsemane consecrated the remainder of his life to the deliverance of suffering womanhood from the miseries of war.

CHAPTER XV

FIRST INVASION OF WASHINGTON

In 1886 Andrew Carnegie published " Triumphant Democracy," a work whose militant Republicanism somewhat shocked the upper classes of this country by its bluntness and boldness. Its author showed that the policy of American statesmen had been eminently pacific, embodying the maxim of Jefferson : " Peace, commerce, and honest friendship with all nations, entangling alliances with none." Mr. Carnegie thus wrote :

" How easily within our grasp, fellow-citizens of the world, seems the day when—

> 'The drum shall beat no longer and the battle flags be furled,
> In the Parliament of man, the Federation of the world.'

We may not look, however, for quite so wide and complete a union. Oceans divide the races, and this fact will keep them apart, for permanent political aggregations must ever be coterminous ; but as far as the continents of the world are concerned there is no insuperable obstacle to their union each into one nation upon the federal system.

*   *   *   *   *

" A league of peace to which each continent will send delegates to decide international differences is not quite so far in the future as may at first sight appear. This would remove from the world its greatest stain—war between man and man."

These words seem prophetic ; Mr. Carnegie has lived long enough himself to provide that Palace of Peace at The Hague, which will be the permanent home of such a gathering as he anticipated. Advancing years have only made Mr. Carnegie still more sanguine. It is but a few months ago that, in conversation with Cremer and other representatives of the League, he expressed the belief that some of those with whom he talked would see the final abolition of war between civilised nations.

Early in the summer of 1887 Cremer had an interview with Mr. Carnegie, and invited him to attend a meeting of the Council and friends of the League. To some of us Mr. Carnegie was already no stranger. Mr. Burt, our president, had already visited him at Pittsburg ; the present writer edited the *Echo* when Mr. Carnegie was one of the syndicate who owned that paper ; but this was the first time that Mr. Carnegie actually came in contact with the League. The connection ever since has been close and cordial, in spite of occasional differences as to policy. As will be seen hereafter, Mr. Carnegie has repeatedly assisted the League, both in America and in Europe, sometimes with pecuniary assistance, but more especially by his personal influence.

On the 16th of June Cremer arranged a meeting at Anderton's Hotel to confer with Mr. Carnegie as to the best means of obtaining a treaty of arbitration between Great Britain and the United States. Mr. Thomas Burt, M.P., presided, and several Members of Parliament were present, including Mr. R. B. Haldane, the present Secretary for War. Cremer explained that he was already obtaining signatures of Members of the House of Commons to a memorial to the President and Congress of the United States urging the adoption of a treaty of arbitration. The Chairman of the Council of the League then put a few questions to Mr. Carnegie as to the feeling in the United States, as to the terms of the memorial, and as to the best manner of presenting it. The reply to most of these questions was eminently satisfactory. Mr. Carnegie declared that " for years there had not been a political platform formulated by any party in the United States which did not contain the clause ' We are in favour of submitting to arbitration all questions of international dispute.' " Mr. Carnegie ridiculed the possibility that two great nations like Great Britain and the United States could go to war over a paltry dispute concerning the fisheries. Mr. Carnegie rather favoured the idea of first approaching the American Minister (Mr. Phelps), but he thought that probably Mr. Phelps himself would advise the presentation of the memorial by a deputation, and he strongly urged that any

Members of Parliament who should visit Washington for that purpose should be accompanied by some of the chief Labour leaders of this country. He readily promised his own hearty co-operation, and, as will be seen hereafter, that promise was amply fulfilled.

In the summer of 1887 Cremer drew up the following memorial from Members of the British House of Commons to the President and Congress of the United States of America :

MEMORIAL.—"The undersigned Members of the British Parliament learn with the utmost satisfaction that various proposals have been introduced into Congress, urging the Government of the United States to take the necessary steps for concluding with the Government of Great Britain a Treaty which shall stipulate that any differences or dispute arising between the two Governments, which cannot be adjusted by diplomatic agency, shall be referred to Arbitration. Should such a proposal happily emanate from the Congress of the United States, our best influence shall be used to ensure its acceptance by the Government of Great Britain. The conclusion of such a Treaty would be a splendid example to those nations who are wasting their resources in war-provoking institutions, and might induce other Governments to join the peaceful compact."

This address was signed by 175 Liberals, 44 Liberal Unionists, and 13 Conservatives—232 in all. Among those who signed were Mr. Asquith, Mr. Bright, Mr. Bryce, Sir John Brunner, Mr. Chamberlain, Mr. Courtney, Sir Edward Grey, Mr. Haldane, Sir H. H. Howorth, Sir John Lubbock, Mr. John Morley, Sir Charles Russell, Mr. Philip

Stanhope, Mr. Thomas Shaw, and the present Lord Selborne. Letters of approval were also received from a number of peers, including the Archbishop of Canterbury, the Bishops of London, Durham, Carlisle, and Bath and Wells, the Marquis of Ripon, the Marquis of Bristol, the Earl of Derby, the Earl of Kimberley, the Earl of Aberdeen, the Earl of Iddesleigh, and Lords Hobhouse, Bramwell, Lawrence, Monkswell, Blachford, and other peers.

This address was presented to President Cleveland at the White House, Washington, by ten Members of the House of Commons, one Peer, and three representatives of the Trades Union Congress. These were Sir Lyon Playfair, M.P., Mr. Halley Stewart, M.P., Mr. B. Pickard, M.P., Mr. O. V. Morgan, M.P., Mr. Munro Ferguson, M.P., Sir George Campbell, M.P., Sir J. Swinburne, M.P., Mr. A. Provand, M.P., Mr. Caleb Wright, M.P., Mr. Cremer, M.P., Lord Kinnaird, Mr. John Wilson, Mr. Charles Freak, and Mr. J. Inglis.

The deputation was introduced in an appropriate speech by Mr. Andrew Carnegie. Sir Lyon Playfair, Mr. John Wilson, and Mr. Cremer addressed the President, who returned a sympathetic reply, in the course of which he said : " I am sorry to be obliged to confess that the practical side of this question has received but little of my attention. I am reminded, too, that in the administration of government, difficulty often arises in the attempt to carefully apply ideas which in themselves

challenge unqualified approval. Thus it may be
that the friends of international arbitration will
not be able at once to secure the adoption, in its
whole extent, of their humane and beneficent
scheme. But surely great progress should be made
by a sincere and hearty effort. I promise you a
faithful and careful consideration of the matter ;
and I believe I may speak for the American people
in giving the assurance that they wish to see the
killing of men for the accomplishment of national
ambition abolished, and that they will gladly hail
the advent of peaceful methods in the settlement of
national disputes, so far as this is consistent with the
defence and protection of our country's territory,
and with the maintenance of our national honour,
when it affords a shelter and repose for national
integrity, and personifies the safety and protection
of our citizens."

The reply of President Cleveland was as cordial
as could be expected at this juncture. Among Irish-
American voters the feeling against this country
was very bitter. The presidential election was
approaching, and both the Democratic and the
Republican parties were anxious not to take any
steps which would alienate the Irish vote.

Subsequently at the opening of Congress the
deputation paid a visit to the House of Representatives and the Senate, where they were warmly
received, and in each case were accorded the privi-
lege of " the Floor of the House." Cremer and
others also had an interview with the Foreign

Affairs Committee of the Senate, the Chairman of which, the Hon. J. S. Sherman, showed himself favourable to arbitration.

On June 14th of the following year both Houses of Congress passed a concurrent resolution :

"That the President be, and is hereby, requested to invite, from time to time as fit occasions may arise, negotiations with any Government with which the United States has or may have diplomatic relations, to the end that any differences or disputes arising between the two Governments which cannot be adjusted by diplomatic agency may be referred to arbitration, and be peaceably adjusted by such means."

Immense meetings were held at Philadelphia, Boston, Richmond, New York, and other cities, attended by enthusiastic audiences. On one or two occasions the Irish caused some disturbance, which was only partially allayed when Cremer, Mr. Halley Stewart, and other members of the deputation reminded them that they had voted in favour of Mr. Gladstone's Home Rule Bill.

At Boston the deputation was royally entertained at a banquet, at which the chief speakers were the Governor of Massachusetts and Dr. Oliver Wendell Holmes ; the latter concluded his speech with an extract from one of his own poems :

"Land of our Fathers, ocean makes us two,
    But heart to heart is true !
Proud is your towering daughter in the West,
Yet in her burning life-blood reign content
Her mother's pulses beating in her breast.

9

> This holy fount, whose rills from heaven descend,
>   Its gracious drops shall lend—
> Both foreheads bathed in that baptismal dew,
> And love make one, the old home and the new!"

During his American visit Cremer made a call upon the venerable Quaker poet Whittier, who said : " You are just the man I wanted to see. I was afraid you were all gone without coming to see me." Whittier showed the keenest interest in the mission of the British deputation, and presented Cremer with a volume of his poems, inscribed on the fly-leaf : " With hearty sympathy in the noble mission of my friend Cremer, I am glad to place my name in this volume."

At Pittsburg Mr. Carnegie had arranged a splendid reception for the deputation, and a visit was paid to Grapeville, about thirty miles distant, which is another of Mr. Carnegie's mammoth mines of industry.

Cremer thus describes that which he saw : " The steamer landed us just as it was dark. Ascending a small hill, we saw an iron pipe about 25 feet high and 4 feet in diameter. In a few minutes the gas, which is obtained by simply boring into the earth, was turned on, and so deafening was the noise from the rush of the gas through the pipe that not even by shouting in one another's ear could the slightest sound of the voice be heard. To light the gas a rocket is fired across the top of the pipe, and the sound produced by the ignition is almost equal to that which comes from firing a cannon. Three rockets were discharged before the gas united, two of them being badly aimed ; and then immediately following the report up went a volume of flame quite 70 feet high, and so intense was the heat that those of us who were near the pipe had to run for fear of being cremated ; but apart from the noise, which was deafening, and the heat, which was unendurable,, that almost mountain of fire, rushing up from the earth into the darkness of the night, and the variety of the shadows reflected by surrounding objects, produced a picture the weird grandeur of which I must leave to be imagined. Descending the hill, we were startled by the sudden appearance of a similar spectacle on the opposite side of the river, and I think most of us returned to Pittsburg with the impression that we had witnessed the eighth wonder of the world."

The concurrent resolution of the United States Congress was not fruitless. Early in 1900 the representatives of seventeen American Republics met at Washington and drew up the text of a treaty of arbitration, containing nineteen articles, in the preamble of which those who signed it said, " Considering it their duty to lend their assent to the lofty principles of peace which the most enlightened public sentiment of the world approves (they) solemnly recommend all the Governments by which they are accredited to celebrate a uniform treaty of arbitration in the articles following."

Mr. Andrew Carnegie, who was one of the

representatives of the United States, wrote as
follows to Cremer :

April 28, 1890.

" My Dear Mr. Cremer,—The Conference of
American Republics did more for arbitration, I
believe, that any body of men that were ever convened. No subject interested the delegates so
deeply, and upon none was there such enthusiasm.
I send you documents showing that they unanimously resolved to settle all questions by arbitration, and to avoid future conquests of territory,
Chili alone abstaining from voting. I think the
action of this conference has thrown around the
continent an impregnable shield of peace. It will
be a rash foreign nation that lights the torch of
war upon the continent. Seventeen Republics have
resolved that peace shall reign over this entire
continent. Let us see the nation that will disregard
their wishes. For my part I do not believe this
will ever be done more than once. I hope to have
the pleasure of seeing you next month in London."

At the final meeting of this Pan-American Conference Mr. J. G. Blaine, who presided, delivered
a concluding speech as follows :

" Gentlemen,—I, withhold for the moment the
word of final adjournment of the International
American Conference, in order that I may express
to you the profound satisfaction with which the
Government of the United States regards the work
that has been accomplished by the International
Conference. The importance of the subjects which

have claimed your attention, the comprehensive intelligence and watchful patriotism which you have brought to their discussion must challenge the confidence and secure the admiration of the Government and people whom you represent, while that larger patriotism which constitutes the fraternity of nations has received from you an impulse such as the world has not seen before. The extent and value of all that has been worthily achieved by your conference cannot be measured to-day. We stand too near it ; time will define and heighten the estimate of your work ; experience will confirm our present faith ; final results will be your vindication and your triumph. If, in this closing hour, the conference had but one deed to celebrate, we should dare call the world's attention to the deliberate, confident, solemn dedication of two great continents to peace, and to the prosperity which has peace for its foundation. We hold up this new Magna Charta, which abolishes war and substitutes arbitration between the American Republics, as the first and great fruit of the International American Conference. That noblest of Americans, the aged poet and philanthropist Whittier, is the first to send his salutations and his benediction, declaring : ' If in the spirit of peace the American Conference agrees upon a rule of arbitration which shall make war in this hemisphere well-nigh impossible, its session will prove one of the most important events in the history of the world.' "

CHAPTER XVI

THE idea of an Interparliamentary Peace Party was first mooted as far back as 1875. In the autumn of that year Dr. Albert Fischoff, who was in correspondence with Henry Richard, brought the subject forward at a meeting of the Austrian and Hungarian delegations, his primary object being to secure a gradual disarmament throughout Europe. He proposed that an annual Conference should be held of the Deputies of all nations, whose first task should be to endeavour to reduce the heavy burden of standing armies. This proposal was communicated to a number of French and Italian Deputies, who warmly approved it ; it was also laid before members of the German Reichstag by Baron Ducker and nearly fifty of its members expressed their adhesion. The first Conference was to have been held in 1877, when the quota of reduction was to be discussed and agreed upon. Then arrangements were to have been made for the introduction of the following resolution into each Parliament :

" The House expects with confidence that the Government will shortly declare to all continental Powers, or at least to all the great Powers on the Continent, their readiness to reduce their standing armies by the quota arranged by the Conference in case the respective Powers do the same."

This movement was premature and proved abortive, but the men who conceived the idea deserve recognition.

As a matter of fact the Bulgarian atrocities and the outbreak of the war between Russia and Turkey for the time paralysed the efforts of the friends of peace. It was utterly useless to discuss a reduction of armaments while Russia was invading Turkey, while Austria was pouring its troops into Bosnia and Herzegovina, and the British Fleet was anchored at Besika Bay, and only awaiting instructions for an advance through the Dardanelles to Constantinople. From the same cause a peace demonstration which Cremer had arranged in Berlin, after several disappointments, to his great chagrin had to be indefinitely postponed. For the time being the Peace Party in this country had to concentrate its strength upon a strenuous effort to prevent our Government from plunging into a terrible war. Who would dare to say at the present moment that they were not better patriots than the Jingoes of the music-halls? As it was twelve years had to run their course before the next advance could be made.

The presentation of the memorial of Members of the British House of Commons at Washington excited much interest in France, and in 1888 some fifty French Deputies co-operated with M. Frederic Passy in introducing into the French Chamber a proposition in favour of a permanent Treaty of Arbitration with the United States. M. Goblet, a Radical Republican, was then Minister of Foreign Affairs. He spoke with some reserve, but intimated that no objection would come from his side. On June 11th the Chamber adopted a Report which was distinctly favourable. Shortly afterwards when Cremer was in Paris M. Goblet sent for him to make inquiries and was accompanied by several Deputies. M. Goblet appeared to be thoroughly sympathetic, and the French Deputies arranged that a small number of British Members of Parliament should meet them in the autumn. The British representatives were nine in number, the survivors being Mr. Thomas Burt, Mr. Charles Fenwick, Mr. Agg Gardner, and Sir Charles Schwann. The French Deputies were twenty-four in number and included MM. Passy, Jules Siegfried, Jules Simon (ex-Prime Minister), Yves Guyot, and Camelinat. A series of resolutions was adopted, the most important of which provided that a larger conference should be held in the following year and that a committee should be appointed to convene it. This Conference assembled on June 29th and 30th. Cremer and the present writer went over to Paris two or three days before to make the final arrangements. The conference had been convened at the " Mairie," in the Place St. Sulpice, but when we looked at the room we were filled with dismay. At once we hurried off to the Continental Hotel, and on behalf of the League, engaged the " Salle des Fêtes," one of the most handsome rooms in Paris. There was no time to notify those who were coming of the change of rendezvous, so we had to station men with cards at the doors of the " Mairie " intimating the altered arrangements.

At the Hôtel Continental no less than fifty-six French Senators and Deputies attended, including Jules Simon (ex-Premier), Trarieux (afterwards President of the Senate), Frederic Passy (the veteran leader of the Peace Party), Jules Siegfried (afterwards Minister), J. Bourgeois (who afterwards represented France at The Hague), and Jean Jaurés (the eloquent Socialist leader).

Twenty-eight Members of the British Parliament were present, including two Irish representatives. Among these were Mr. Philip Stanhope (Lord Weardale), Mr. Burt, Mr. Fenwick, Dr. Clark, Sir Francis Channing, Sir Thomas Roe, Sir George Newnes, Sir Charles Schwann, Mr. H. J. Wilson, Mr. Halley Stewart, and Mr. Thomas Shaw.

There were also a few representatives from Italy, Spain, Denmark, Hungary, Belgium, and the United States.

M. Jules Simon, who presided, spoke as follows : " Representing divers nations of the world, we can make the most excellent use of the greatest power which exists, namely, that given to us by the electors. I wish a welcome from the bottom of my heart, in the name of all pacific Frenchmen, to the representatives of all nations. You know, gentlemen, the majority of our countrymen are friends of peace. Allow me, therefore, to acclaim with warmth, in agreement with the French people, the representatives of countries which might not yet be able to send delegates to an official congress. To give proof of the feelings of perfect agreement and of cordiality between the members of the parliamentary conference, it is requisite that many nations should be represented in the bureau."

The conference then proceeded to elect its officers as follows : Presidents : Frederic Passy (French Deputy), the Marquis Alfieri (Vice-President of the Italian Senate), Hon. Philip Stanhope (British Parliament), J. R. Whiting (United States Congress) ; Vice-Presidents : W. R. Cremer, (Great Britain), Marquis De Marcoartu (Spain), M. Bajer (Denmark), and M. Anspach (Belgium). As secretaries, M. Gaillard (France), Burt (Great Britain), M. Mazzoleni (Italy).

At a subsequent meeting of the committee of the conference, which was held in one of the rooms of the Chamber of Deputies, Mr. Philip Stanhope was elected president of the committee and Sir Charles E. Schwann treasurer, Cremer being elected secretary for Great Britain, which meant that the main work of the next conference would devolve upon him, inasmuch as the next meeting was arranged to take place in London during the following summer.

Those who, like the present writer, attended this first Paris conference were delighted with its success, but it was only the earnest of still greater efforts in European capitals and in the United States, as will be seen hereafter.

The Interparliamentary Union, in accordance with the arrangements made in Paris the previous year, met in London on July 22 and 23, 1890. The meeting-place was at the Hôtel Métropole. It was a great advance on the Paris conference, no less than twelve Parliaments being represented, viz., Great Britain, France, Germany, Austria, Italy, Holland, Spain, Denmark, Sweden, Norway, Belgium, and Greece. About two hundred representatives were present. Among the English representatives were Bishop Westcott (Durham), Mr. Bradlaugh, Lord Kinnaird, Lord Eversley, Sir George Newnes, Lord Playfair, Sir C. E. Schwann, Mr. Thomas Shaw, Mr. H. J. Wilson, and Mr. Halley Stewart. Among the French representatives who were present were M. Passy, M. Trarieux (afterwards President of the Senate), Henri Maret, and C. Sabatier. For the first time a number of members of the German Reichstag attended. Some fifty Italian Deputies would have been present but for official duties elsewhere, and through the same cause representatives of the United States were absent. An extraordinary number of adhesions had been forwarded. Amongst the leading French Deputies who thus sent their good wishes were ex-Ministers like Jules Simon, Ribot, and St.

Hilare, and Count de Mun, the head of the Catholic Party. Amongst the Germans were Professor Virchow and Prince Carolath-Schonaich, who presided at the Berlin conference in 1908. Adhesions were also received from Signor Crispi, the Italian Prime Minister, and the Duke of Tetuan, the Spanish Minister for Foreign Affairs. Perhaps the most remarkable adhesion of all was that of Mr. John Sherman, Chairman of the Foreign Affairs Committee of the United States Senate, which is given *in extenso* as showing the progress that had been made.

MY DEAR SIR,—Your note of the 14th inst. is just received. I am much pleased with your kindly approval of the action of Congress on arbitration in international disputes. It does seem to me that the next step in this good cause would be some recognition by Parliament, or at least by your ministry, of a somewhat similar character. The feeling in favour of arbitration in all national disputes that do not involve the autonomy of a country, and especially questions involving merely matters of claim, or of disputed boundaries, or of commercial privileges, is that they should be in every case, which cannot be settled by ordinary negotiation, submitted to arbitration, organised upon some basis which would secure confidence in the judgment to be rendered. No nation is too great and none too small to resort to such a peaceful remedy for disputes that are incident to all human affairs. In the recent American conference the principle of arbitration was approved and has been since ratified by a great majority of the nations represented in the conference, and I believe will be formally agreed to by the Governments represented. If it is possible under your forms of proceeding to have such a resolution assented to by Parliament, it will be by far the most effective step yet taken to promote the peace of nations.

" Very respectfully yours,

" JOHN SHERMAN."

A similar letter was sent by Mr. R. Hitt, Chairman of the Foreign Affairs Committee of the House of Representatives. Mr. Gladstone also wrote excusing his absence on the ground that he made it a rule to avoid extra-parliamentary action in connection with associations out of doors in which, officially or otherwise, he had been called to take a prominent part. He added : " Undoubtedly it is not without regret that I forego any occasion of protest against the devouring mischief of militarism which is consuming the vitals of Europe, and which operates even in this country, although we have so many advantages of resisting it."

As will have been anticipated, the success of this conference surpassed even Cremer's sanguine expectations. The whole burden of organisation had fallen upon him, and the financial responsibility upon the League, and this arrangement continued until the Interparliamentary Union set up its bureau at Berne.

Lord Herschell (ex-Lord Chancellor) presided at the first sitting. At the conclusion of his speech he said : " They did not suppose that the triumph of such a cause as they were met to promote could be immediate or complete, but they did not regard that as a reason for holding their tongues and remaining still. There were difficulties in the matter of arbitration, but notwithstanding those difficulties they believed that the principle was a sound one, and that the more men reflected upon it the more those difficulties would disappear."

In the course of the proceedings the delicate question of Alsace-Lorraine cropped up in a discussion on one of the resolutions, but ultimately the resolution was adopted unanimously in the following amended form : " That as closer relations between the members of various Parliaments would make for peace, the conference recommends the appointment of a parliamentary committee for each country with a view to the interchange of ideas and the consideration of disputes as they may arrive."

At the closing banquet Sir Lyon Playfair (afterwards Lord Playfair) presided, the Marquis of Bristol occupying the vice-chair. The chief British speaker was Mr. Shaw-Lefevre (Lord Eversley), who was the first to propose the settlement of the " Alabama Dispute " by arbitration in the House of Commons. The United States was represented by Mr. David Dudley Field, one of the pioneers of the cause, who had advocated international arbitration many years before at the sittings of the

Social Science Association. Representatives of France, Germany, Austria, Italy, and Spain also took part, and Cremer at the conclusion of the proceedings said : " I am amply rewarded for my labours by the successful conference we have held, and the splendid banquet of this evening, where the remarkably able speeches delivered have formed a fitting sequel to the discussions of the last two days."

At the final sitting of the London conference it was resolved to meet annually in some European capital, and Rome was chosen for the following year.

At the beginning of 1890 a dispute arose between Portugal and Great Britain. That small country was our ancient ally, and may be said to have owed us no small debt of gratitude ; but it owned a considerable portion of the south-east coast of Africa, with undefined claims on the Hinterland. The explorer Livingstone had penetrated inland through a district known as the Shire Highlands, and had found no trace there of Portuguese dominion. In the course of time certain Scotch missionaries followed and established missionary settlements. The quarrel arose over the high-handed proceedings of a certain Major Pinto. This person had enlisted an army of Zulus for a military expedition, and had mowed down with machine guns a large number of natives who were reckoned to be under British protection. Lord Salisbury thereupon took prompt and decisive

action, much to the wrath of the populace at Lisbon,
who hauled down British flags, smashed the
windows of British Consuls, made bonfires of
British goods, and started a public subscription for
one new ironclad. Such childish demonstrations in
reply to Lord Salisbury's ultimatum were, of course,
very absurd ; but on the Continent the action of
Lord Salisbury produced a disagreeable impression, and some of the friends of peace abroad
strongly deprecated the threatened withdrawal of
the British Ambassador and the commencement
of hostilities as the bullying of a weak Power by
a stronger one. On this occasion Cremer, in the
House of Commons, expressed regret that arbitration had not been resorted to, but at the same time
he insisted in the *Arbitrator* that the British view
of the dispute was the right one. This incident is
suggestive, as it furnishes an answer to those who
falsely declare that the British advocates of peace
are the friends of every country but their own. As
in the case of the Fashoda dispute with France,
when Major Marchand suddenly confronted the
victorious British troops at the head waters of the
Nile, we held that our own country was in the
right.

The *Arbitrator*, of which Cremer was editor,
fairly stated the case on both sides and commented
thereon thus : " Here certainly is a dispute in
which arbitration might well be called in for the
settlement of rival claims. It has been sometimes
urged against the Peace Party that, whenever a

dispute arises, they invariably maintain that their own country is in the wrong. The reproach is not justified by the facts. In this instance we are free to confess that the case of the Portuguese appears to be decidedly weaker than our own. The stronger our case, the more ready we should be to submit it to impartial arbitrament. In this Portuguese dispute, however, there have been names freely flung about as possible arbitrators whose owners are distinguished only by their unfitness. It appears that while Lord Salisbury was negotiating with the Portuguese Government hostile proceedings continued. If our information is correct, the Portuguese Government wanted to go to arbitration at home, and at the same time continue its warlike proceedings in the Shire Highlands. This was not the way to secure arbitration, especially from a Minister like Lord Salisbury, who is hostile to the principle." At the time when this last sentence was written it was quite correct, but, as will be seen hereafter, Lord Salisbury became a convert to the principle in his later years.

It is due to Lord Salisbury to add that he foresaw the danger of disputes arising between various European Powers in regard to the interior of Africa, and that consequently he concluded conventions under which these Powers agreed to the limitations of their respective spheres of influence in regard to the Hinterland. Almost invariably Lord Salisbury as a Foreign Minister was as pacific

10

in his policy as any succeeding Liberal statesman, and this is equally true of the Marquis of Lansdowne.

In no continental country had the idea of international arbitration been more warmly welcomed than in Italy. It will be remembered that some fifty Italian Deputies had sent their adhesion to the Interparliamentary Conference in London, but were prevented from attending by stress of circumstances. Italy was the weakest member of the Triple Alliance, and felt much more severely than either Germany or Austria the terrible burden of bloated armaments. Its adhesion to the Triple Alliance had produced somewhat strained feelings on the part of the French, so that the situation was far less favourable than it is at the present moment. The sacred cause of arbitration, however, had devoted friends in such Italian statesmen as the Marquis Pandolfi and Signor Bonghi, and they worked earnestly to make the conference at Rome a splendid success. The distant place of meeting, and the unfavourable time of the year caused the attendance of representatives from Great Britain to be comparatively few—only fifteen being present. The Hon. Philip Stanhope, Burt, and Cremer were the chief British members of the conference. But there was ample compensation in the advance otherwise made. Members from no less than sixteen European Parliaments were present, and the Marquis Pandolfi announced that more than fourteen hundred adhesions had been received.

As compared with the London conference the German representatives had increased from six to eighteen, and the Austrian from one to twelve, while Hungary sent four representatives, and Roumania twenty-one. Portugal and Servia were represented for the first time. The chief German representatives were Dr. Baumbach (Vice-President of the Reichstag), and Dr. Max Hirsch, who always proved a stalwart friend of the cause, and whose successor, Herr Goldschmidt, in the leadership of the " Hirsch-Duncker " trades' unionists has been equally earnest.

The conference at Rome was especially noteworthy because for the first time it obtained something like official recognition. The sitting was opened in the Hall of the Capital, the seat of the municipality, and was presided over by Signor Biancheri (President of the Chamber of Deputies), who was supported by the Duke de Sermoneta, Mayor of Rome. On two evenings the members of the conference were entertained at *soirées* in the Chamber of Deputies itself. More than once during the sittings the conference was disturbed by the persistence of Signor Imbriani, the champion of " Italia Irredenta," but his ill-timed interruptions hardly disturbed the harmony of the proceedings.

The chief subject of discussion was a proposal to set up a permanent bureau, with a secretary, on which there was much difference of opinion, but ultimately it was agreed that such a bureau should be established at Berne. Cremer himself was very doubtful as to whether the establishment of the bureau was not premature, and whether Berne was really the best place for meeting.

This conference, noting the advance of public opinion in favour of arbitration treaties in the United States, recommended that the subject should be discussed in the various Parliaments of Europe. To some extent this course was followed, more especially in the British Parliament and in the German Reichstag, but the honour of leading the way belongs to Denmark, where such a motion was carried by a majority of fifteen, mainly through the exertions of M. Bajer, who attended the first conference in Paris, and has ever since been a loyal and earnest friend.

In Rome the assembly of the conference was hailed with the greatest enthusiasm, not only by the people, but also by the press. The only discordant note was struck by the priestly organs of the Vatican, which declared that the conference might as well pass resolutions against the action of the winds and the waves, the priestly idea of arbitration being that the Pope should be the arbitrator-in-chief.

The conference was followed by a large gathering of representatives of Workmen's Associations in Rome, at which Cremer was the chief speaker. The warmth of Italian hospitality was almost boundless. Not only were the palaces of some of the chief Italian nobles at Rome thrown open, but an excursion was arranged to Naples, and some other of the chief towns in the South of Italy, where the members of the conference received a popular ovation. Simultaneously with the gathering in Rome great peace demonstrations were held in Milan and other Italian cities. Italian readers of this biography will learn with no little satisfaction that Cremer returned to this country full of joy. Not only he but his successor, Mr. Maddison, from their youth upward had been largely inspired by the writings of Joseph Mazzini, the purest and noblest of international patriots.

Cremer had preserved quite a collection of *jeux d'esprits* of his friend Sir Wilfrid Lawson, mostly written on the backs of envelopes and other odd scraps of paper. Here is Sir Wilfrid's apology for not going to Rome, with a cheque enclosed :

> "My dear Mr. Cremer,
> You excellent schemer,
> Your note says you are shortish of tin ;
> As I don't go to Rome,
> But am staying at home,
> It's but right I should pay for my sin.
>
> Next year if we live
> Should an impetus give
> To the cause of true peace with each nation ;
> So good luck to your motion,
> In spite of old Goschen,
> In favour of sound arbitration."

CHAPTER XVII

OPPORTUNITY AT LAST

IN these modern days the opportunities of private
Members are few and far between. At the close
of the session of 1891 Cremer gave notice of a
motion expressing the hope that the British
Government would open negotiations with the
Government of the United States for the conclusion of a treaty of arbitration. This resolution
was put upon the notice paper again and again, but
from various causes it was impossible to bring it
forward, the main reason being that the Government found it necessary to appropriate so much of
the time of private members. At length, on June
16, 1893, the opportunity was reached. It was a
Friday evening, at which time it was no easy
matter to secure a house ; but by means of a whip
and a personal canvass of Members a quorum was
obtained, almost exclusively of Liberals and Irish
Members. Among the distinguished visitors who
listened to the debate were the United States Ambassador, Mr. and Mrs. Carnegie, and the Presi-

dent of the New York Chamber of Commerce, who afterwards congratulated Cremer upon his speech, and upon the victory which he secured.

Mr. Cremer at the outset recalled the fact that an address to the President and Congress of the United States was signed by 234 Members of the House of Commons. He stated that this address had been favourably received by the President and Congress, and that both Houses had passed a concurrent resolution inviting international arbitration as to differences between nations. He added that shortly afterwards a Pan-American conference was held at Washington, and a treaty of arbitration, between the various Governments there represented was discussed and adopted. The American Government forwarded copies of the resolution of the Pan-American conference to other Governments. No European Government accepted the invitation given ; apparently each Government was waiting to see what the others would do, and had not the courage to take the initiative. He recalled the words of Mr. Gladstone in speaking of the negotiations concerning the Alabama difficulty, when he said : " Both sides of this House are animated by one sentiment, that we should make progress in gradually establishing in Europe a state of opinion which would favour a common action of the Powers to avert the terrible calamity of war." He assured the House that the workers of both countries were in full sympathy with his object, and he concluded with this appeal to Mr. Gladstone : " From the experience which I have gathered amongst the masses of the people in various countries, I am satisfied that if the Prime Minister is bold enough to make this step and lead the way, he will not only earn the gratitude of the toiling millions, but make for himself a name in history which the whole world will look upon with admiration."

The resolution read as follows :

"That this House has learnt with satisfaction that both Houses of the United States Congress have authorised the President to conclude a Treaty of Arbitration with any other country ; and this House expresses the hope that her Majesty's Government will, at the first convenient opportunity, open up negotiations with the Government of the United States with a view to the conclusion of such a treaty between the two nations, so that any differences or disputes arising between the two nations, which cannot be adjusted by diplomacy, shall be referred to arbitration."

Sir John Lubbock (Liberal Unionist) seconded the motion and dwelt specially on the enormous burden entailed by ever increasing armaments. The unnecessary expenditure on the Army and Navy compelled every man and woman in Europe to work an hour more a day than they otherwise need.

Mr. Gladstone, who had been occupied in the House all the week with exacting Home Rule debates, returned a most sympathetic reply. He declared that he was heartily glad, even after an exhausting week, that Mr. Cremer and Sir John

Lubbock had found an opportunity of striking a stroke on behalf of humanity. He said : " In those speeches, while they were hearty from the first word to the last, I do not think the most zealous critic could detect a single unhealthy or exaggerated sentence. They were the speeches of men of humanity, the speeches of men of enlightenment, and the speeches also of sober-minded men of business. The more they are read and pondered the better it will be for the great interests that are at stake." Mr. Gladstone proceeded to discuss at length the actual situation, and pointed out some of the difficulties which occurred to him. In conclusion he added :

" There is another method of proceeding, which, I think, in our limited sphere we upon this bench have endeavoured to promote, and to which I have attached very considerable value, and that is the promotion of what I may call a central Tribunal in Europe, a council of the Great Powers, in which it may be anticipated, or at all events may be favourably conjectured, that the rival selfishness, if I may use so barbarous an expression, may neutralise, and something like impartial authority may be attained for settlement of disputes. I am quite convinced that if selfishness were to be sunk, and each State were to attain to some tolerable capacity of forming a moderate estimate of its own claim, in such a case the action of a Central Authority in Europe would be of inestimable value." Mr. Gladstone concluded by suggesting that a resolution should be adopted in the following modified form :

" That this House has learnt with satisfaction that both Houses of the United States Congress have, by resolution, requested the President to invite, from time to time, as fit occasion may arise, negotiations with any Government with which the United States have, or may have, diplomatic relations, to the end that any differences or disputes arising between the two Governments which cannot be adjusted by diplomatic agency may be referred to arbitration, and peaceably adjusted by such means ; and that this House, cordially sympathising with the purpose in view, expresses the hope that her Majesty's Government will lend their ready co-operation to the Government of the United States upon the basis of the foregoing resolution."

Mr. J. W. Lowther, late Under Secretary for Foreign Affairs in the Conservative Government, followed with a speech which was on the whole sympathetic, and Mr. Stansfeld on the Liberal side, and Sir George Baden-Powell, Conservative, also took the same line, as also did Captain Cecil Norton. Cremer expressed his willingness to accept the resolution in the form proposed by Mr. Gladstone, whereupon Sir William Harcourt said :

" I only rise for the purpose of asking the House to pass this resolution. The resolution, which is of immense importance, was supported by the authority of the Prime Minister, and it affords me the greatest satisfaction to know that the House is about to pass it unanimously. I trust that the House will now take such steps as are necessary to place upon the Journals one of the most im-

portant resolutions ever submitted to it." The
resolution, having been again read by the Speaker,
was unanimously agreed to amid general cheering.

It is worthy of note that the number of those
who had petitioned in favour of the motion, either
through their organisations or by personal signature, exceeded one and a half millions ; and if to
the number of petitioners are added the persons
represented by the Chambers of Commerce and
the religious bodies who expressed their opinion
by the resolution, upwards of two millions expressed their desire for the conclusion of a treaty of
arbitration with the United States.

I think it must be in reference to this speech
that Cremer wrote to his sister as follows : " You
probably heard little or nothing of the speech
which I made in the House about three weeks ago,
but everybody who heard it—and the House was
full—said it was the best I ever made in the House.
I don't think so, but I received such a shoal of
congratulations that if I was inclined to be vain
it would turn my head. Even Mr. Gladstone, who
was an attentive listener throughout, sent me a
message of congratulation by one of his trusty
friends. I presume that I owe my invitation to
dine with him to that speech. At dinner I sat
next to his son Henry, who was most effusive in
his congratulations on what he termed my admirable speech. You will see in *Punch's* ' Essence
of Parliament ' what a flattering term is applied

to me, but not on account of the speech. Well, it is pleasant to be described in *Punch* as ' honest Bill Cremer.' "

That year the cause was further advanced by the conclusion of the Behring Sea Arbitration. A few months previously Lord Salisbury and the Government of the United States had agreed that the dispute in regard to the seal fisheries in that sea should be referred to an Arbitration Court sitting in Paris, consisting of two representatives of Great Britain, two of the United States, and one each of France, Italy, and Sweden.

Sir Charles Russell, who was the chief counsel on the British side, at the conclusion of his speech said : " These nations are here before you, friendly litigants, peaceful suitors in your court, asking by pacific means the adjustment and determination of their rights in times of peace. This is indeed a fact of great moral significance. This arbitration is a victory for peace. It will be, it must be a victory for peace if, as I cannot permit myself to doubt, it conform to and leave untouched and undoubted the principles of the law which have been consecrated by long usage, stamped with the approval of generations of men—that law which has grown up in response to that cry of humanity heard through all time, a cry sometimes inarticu- late, sometimes drowned by the discordant voices of passion, pride, ambition, but still a cry that has gone up through all ages for peace on earth and goodwill amongst men."

It is unnecessary to dwell in detail on the points in dispute. Suffice it to say that the judgment of all the arbitrators except those of the United States was favourable to Great Britain, though, as will hereafter be seen, there was considerable dissatisfaction in America. The decision of the arbitrators was not seriously called in question, but the amount of damages to be paid was disputed.

CHAPTER XVIII

SECOND VISIT TO WASHINGTON

MEANWHILE progress was being made in the United States, as the following letters of the American Secretary of State and the British Ambassador will show :

MR. GRESHAM TO SIR JULIAN PAUNCEFOTE.

WASHINGTON, *December* 5, 1893.

" EXCELLENCY,—With regard to your note of the 9th August, 1893, of which acknowledgment has been hitherto unavoidably deferred, I have now the pleasure to inform you that the President will feel great satisfaction in bringing to the knowledge of the Congress, in his forthcoming Annual Message, the resolution of the House of Commons on the 16th of July last, whereby that high body expressed its cordial sympathy with the action taken by the Senate and the House of Representatives in the concurrent resolution of the 14th February and 3rd April, 1890, requesting the President ' to invite from time to time as fit occasions may arise, negotiations with any Government with which the United States has or may have diplomatic relations, to the end that any differences or disputes arising between the two Governments which cannot be adjusted by diplomatic agency may be referred to arbitration and be peacefully adjusted by such means.'

" In manifesting the hope that her Majesty's Government will lend their cordial co-operation to the Government of the United States upon the basis of this concurrent resolution of Congress, the House of Commons has afforded a most gratifying proof of the sentiment of the two nations in favour of the settlement of international disagreements by honourable resort to impartial arbitration, a mode of adjustment of which the United States and Great Britain have, by mutual accord, given to the world conspicuous illustration on several recent occasions.

" I have, &c.,

" W. Q. GRESHAM."

SIR J. PAUNCEFOTE TO THE EARL OF ROSEBERY.

WASHINGTON, December 7, 1893.

" MY LORD,— In accordance with the instructions contained in your lordship's dispatch of the 28th July last, I transmitted to the United States Secretary of State the copy of the resolution passed by the House of Commons expressing sympathy with the action taken by Congress in favour of the settlement of international disputes by arbitration, and I informed Mr. Gresham that her Majesty's Government would be glad if the President should see fit to lay it before both Houses of Congress.

"I have now the honour to enclose copy of Mr. Gresham's reply, in which, after stating that it had been unavoidably deferred, he informs me that the President will feel great satisfaction in bringing the resolution in question to the knowledge of Congress in his forthcoming Annual Message.

"I transmitted to your lordship a copy of this message, which was communicated to Congress on the 4th inst., in my dispatch of the 5th inst., and your lordship will observe that, in alluding to the receipt of the resolution, President Cleveland remarks : "It affords me signal pleasure to lay this Parliamentary resolution before the Congress, and to express my sincere gratification that the sentiment of two great and kindred nations is thus authoritatively manifested in favour of the rational and peaceable settlement of international quarrels by honourable resort to arbitration.'

"I have, &c.,
"JULIAN PAUNCEFOTE."

During the session of 1894 Cremer drew up a second memorial to the President and the Congress of the United States, and obtained the signatures of no less than 354 Members of the

House of Commons. The majority of these were Liberals, but a number of Conservatives, Liberal-Unionists, and Irish Nationalists signed the memorial, which ran as follows :

"In response to the resolution adopted by Congress on April 4, 1890, the British House of Commons, supported in its decision by Mr. Gladstone, on June 16, 1893, unanimously affirmed its willingness to co-operate with the Government of the United States in settling disputes between the two countries by means of Arbitration. The undersigned members of the British Parliament, while cordially thanking Congress for having, by its resolution, given such an impetus to the movement and called forth such a response from our Government, earnestly hope that Congress will follow up its resolution, and crown its desire by inviting our Government to join in framing a Treaty which shall bind the two nations to refer to Arbitration disputes which diplomacy fails to adjust. Should such a proposal be made, our heartiest efforts would be used in its support, and we shall rejoice that the United States of America and the United Kingdom of Great Britain and Ireland have resolved to set such a splendid example to the other nations of the world."

Cremer presented this memorial to President Cleveland at the White House on January 18, 1895, and a copy was at once sent to each member of the Congress.

An interview with the President had been arranged by Mr. Gresham, the Secretary of State, who was an earnest supporter of the cause. Cremer's interview with President Cleveland, upon whom he had waited seven years before, lasted for an hour. He explained the reasons which

11

prompted the memorialists, and pointed to the number of influential names appended to the document. He further explained the reasons which induced Mr. Gladstone to suggest a modi- fication of the arbitration resolution, and he came away well satisfied with the interview.

His reception by members of both Houses of Congress was equally cordial. The floor of the Senate and of the House of Representatives was graciously accorded to him. The Committee on Foreign Relations in both Houses favoured him with an interview, and discussed the object of his mission.

Cremer wrote home at the time : " The task is by no means so easy as some sanguine friends imagine. My visit has made me better acquainted with the delicate and difficult character of the undertaking ; but we are fortunate in having as our Ambassador Sir Julian Pauncefote, as I know from interviews with him that the conclusion of a treaty is a subject dear to his heart. The Secretary of State is equally in earnest upon the matter, and if they undertake the task I feel sure they will succeed. At the present moment there are two resolutions and a Bill upon the subject before Congress. The resolutions are by Senator Allison and Mr. Coombs ; the Bill has been intro- duced by Senator Sherman, but as Congress adjourns at the end of February, and will not reassemble until December next, the prospect of either resolutions or Bill being discussed this year is very remote, especially as they have been referred to the Committee on Foreign Relations. But the adoption by Congress of either resolutions or Bill is not absolutely necessary. Of course, if Congress requested the President to open up negotiations with our Government his hands would be strengthened, but he had the power to prepare a Treaty without any authorisation by Congress, and it would not surprise me to learn that the Secretary of State is already engaged with our Ambassador at Washington in drafting such a treaty."

Probably Cremer would have remained longer at Washington had he not been suddenly summoned home to attend to his parliamentary duties.

Before leaving Washington, Cremer had a long interview with Mr. Gresham, than whom the cause of arbitration had no warmer friend. His last words were : " Do you know if Sir Julian has received instructions to begin? When you see him, tell him I am ready whenever he is." In the following May Mr. Gresham died. Cremer felt his loss as a terrible blow. He wrote : " To our cause his decease is a severe, almost irreparable, loss. None in the United States better understood the far-reaching results which the conclusion of a treaty of arbitration between the two nations must have —not only upon the future relations of the two countries, but upon the civilisation of the world. He had thought out the subject to the end, and his mind was made up in regard to it."

Two somewhat untoward events occurred in 1895 which were calculated to retard the cause. The first was the refusal of the House of Representatives at Washington to vote 425,000 dollars in payment of the damages for which the United States were held to be liable by the Behring Sea Arbitration Tribunal. As a matter of fact, the arbitrators did not fix the amount of damages, which were to be ascertained afterwards; but the Canadian Government, acting on behalf of claimants, offered to accept a lump sum of 425,000 dollars as payment in full. President Cleveland accepted the offer, but the House of Representatives refused to vote the money on the ground that many of the claims were fraudulent, having been made by men who palmed themselves off as British subjects, and were flying the British flag, but who were really United States citizens. The difficulty was finally overcome by the appointment of a Joint Commission to investigate the *bonâ fide* character of the claims, and the actual amount of the damages which were eventually paid.

The other event was the somewhat menacing message of President Cleveland to the American Congress in December, wherein he claimed that the long-standing dispute between Great Britain and Venezuela should be settled by arbitration. This dispute had remained unsettled for the greater part of a century. British Guiana, which had been taken over from the Dutch, adjoins Venezuelan territory. The difference was as to the proper boundary-line, and it had been rendered more acute by the discovery of gold in the disputed territory. The message of President Cleveland, who, it should be remembered, was a warm friend of arbitration, caused some excitement in this country. It was a disagreeable surprise, for very few of the British people knew anything at all about the dispute in question. The League at once took the alarm, and a great public meeting was held at the Memorial Hall, presided over by Sir John Lubbock, and addressed by Canon Scott-Holland and several leading Free Churchmen and Labour representatives, urging a peaceful settlement of the Venezuelan question, and the conclusion of a permanent arbitration treaty.

The following letter, addressed to Cremer, was read at the meeting from Dr. Guinness Rogers ; it is given *in extenso* as showing how warmly that veteran Free Church leader appreciated Cremer's efforts :

" As I feared would be the case, I am quite unable to be with you to-night. It is very difficult to interpolate an engagement into a week already too full. In this case it is impossible.

" I very much regret that it is so, not that you will need my advocacy, but because I feel it a pleasure as well as a duty to associate my name with your endeavour to avert what would be an unmeasurable calamity as well as a gigantic crime. Happily we may hope that the danger has passed, or at all events is passing away. For myself, I can

never think of the Americans as a different nation,
and even the painful events of the last three weeks
have been bringing out new proofs of our unity.
The men who would break the ties which bind us
together are enemies of both.

" You yourself have been the constant advocate of arbitration through evil report and good
report. If out of this unfortunate controversy
there shall arise a strong conviction that this is
the only way of settling international differences
which could approve itself, not only to Christians
but to all rational beings, this trouble will not
have been endured in vain."

At the opening of the parliamentary session in
London, Lord Rosebery said that he viewed with
delight the movement which had set in on both
sides of the Atlantic for some form of permanent
machinery of arbitration, and Lord Salisbury returned a sympathetic reply. In the House of
Commons Sir William Harcourt expressed the
opinion that there could be no objection to referring
the dispute to the arbitration of a third Power, and
Mr. Balfour declared that he should rejoice if out
of this evil there should spring the good fruit of
some carefully guarded system of arbitration.

About the same time a similar dispute in regard
to boundaries was settled between the Republics
of Chili and Argentina, the Pope being invited
to act as arbitrator. He appointed two South
American archbishops to draw up a report, and
his award was accepted by both republics, which

afterwards erected a statue of " Christ the Pacificator " to celebrate the happy event. They subsequently sold some of their ironclads, for which they had no further use.

Before the year had run out an Arbitration Tribunal was appointed for the settlement of the Venezuelan difficulty. Two members were to be appointed by the Supreme Court of the United States, two by the Supreme Court of this country, the four so appointed to choose a fifth.

Not only was the Venezuelan dispute amicably settled, but a general treaty of arbitration between Great Britain and the United States was signed on January 11, 1897. This treaty was drawn up by Mr. Olney, the American Secretary of State, and Sir Julian Pauncefote, the British Ambassador, to both of whom a high meed of praise is due. When Cremer paid his second visit to Washington, he was frequently in communication with Sir Julian, who said to him :

" I have set my heart upon getting a treaty concluded during the time I am here as British Ambassador, and when it is concluded we shall all be very greatly indebted to you. What you have done has not only given a powerful impetus to the movement, but rendered my task much easier."

The treaty consisted of fifteen Articles, the first of which ran thus : " The high contracting parties agree to submit to arbitration, in accordance with the provisions and subject to the limitations of the treaty, all questions in difference between them which may fail to adjust themselves by diplomatic negotiations." Under the treaty each of the high contracting parties was to nominate as an arbitrator a jurist of repute, and these two were to select an umpire. In the case of a controversy involving territorial claims, three judges were to be appointed on each side, whose award by a majority of not less than five to one should be final. If the majority was smaller, or the tribunal was equally divided, the mediation of one or more friendly powers was to be sought. The remaining clauses further defined the machinery of arbitration.

The conclusion of this treaty was hailed with unbounded delight by Cremer and other active supporters of the arbitration movement in both countries. Unfortunately, their rejoicing was premature. There is many a slip betwixt cup and lip, as will be seen in the events subsequently recorded.

CHAPTER XIX

THE INTERPARLIAMENTARY AT THE HAGUE AND
BRUSSELS—A DEFEAT AND A PETITION

THE 1894 conference met in the first chamber of
the Dutch Parliament, where it was welcomed by
M. Van Houten, the Minister of the Interior. The
main business of this conference was to receive
and discuss the Report of Mr. Philip Stanhope
(Lord Weardale) on the organisation of a Permanent International Court of Arbitration. Mr.
Stanhope recalled the desire expressed by Mr.
Gladstone for the establishment of a central
tribunal in Europe, or Council of the Great Powers,
and declared that in his judgment it belonged to
the interparliamentary conferences to take the
initiative for the realisation of this grand and
generous idea, and to study it thoroughly, though
it was evident that a serious project for a central
European tribunal was not the work of a day and
could not be submitted at once to such a conference
as theirs. He sketched the outline of such a Permanent Court, and said that the project would
have to respect the following principles :

1. National sovereignty to remain inalienable and inviolate.

2. The adhesion of every Government to the constitution of the International Court to be absolutely optional.

3. All the adhering States must be on a footing of perfect equality with respect to the International Court.

4. The judgments of the Court must have the force of an executive sentence.

After prolonged discussion the proposals of Mr. Stanhope were accepted by a large majority, and the commission of six members was appointed to prepare a plan for the establishment of a tribunal. M. Trarieux, a French Senator, and subsequently Minister of Justice, read an appeal to the Press which he had drawn up at the request of the bureau, and which was unanimously adopted. The conference agreed to meet at Brussels the following year.

In the summer of 1895 the cause of arbitration made a great stride forward in France. As far back as 1888 M. Passy, the veteran leader of the French peace party, had given notice in the Chamber of Deputies of a resolution in favour of a treaty of arbitration with the United States, but at that time Frenchmen were fully occupied with their own domestic troubles, and the project had to be relinquished. In 1895 the motion was revived by M. Barodet, a Radical Deputy of Paris ; and urgency having been obtained for it, it was unanimously resolved that " the Chamber invites the Government to negotiate, as soon as possible, the conclusion of a permanent treaty of arbitration between the French Republic and the Republic of the United States of America."

The Interparliamentary Conference of 1895 met in August that year at Brussels in the Senate Chamber of Belgium. One of its interesting features was the announcement of the Norwegian delegates that their Parliament had voted 2,850 francs to further its objects. Other Parliaments have since voted considerable sums of money for the entertainment of the conference, and recently the British Government has promised to vote an annual contribution ; but to Norway belongs the honour of having set the example. M. Trarieux, who had taken a prominent part in the conference at The Hague, was now unable to attend, having been appointed French Minister of Justice. The chief business at this conference was the reception of the Report of the Commission appointed to draft a scheme for the formation of a permanent international tribunal. This scheme was embodied in twelve Articles, which, after full discussion, with some amendments, were adopted. The conference agreed to meet at Buda-Pesth, the Hungarian capital, in the following year.

It was a great disappointment to some of those who attended that the bureau, which arranged the order of business, recommended that a resolution on disarmament, which two British members were prepared to move, should not be proposed in the conference. The bureau feared that considerable differences of opinion would arise on this delicate question.

Cremer proposed and carried a supplementary resolution of a practical character as follows :

"The conference empowers its President to inquire into and, if possible, ascertain whether any two or more Governments are willing to take the initiative in establishing a Court for the settlement of their differences by pacific means."

The idea was that if two or three of the smaller States would make a beginning other States would gradually fall in. Little did the author of this modest proposal anticipate that before the close of the century a Permanent High Court of Nations would be set up with the concurrence of the Great Powers.

At the election in July, 1895, Cremer was opposed by Mr. John Lowles, a prominent local Conservative leader in Hackney. The election was keenly fought on both sides, and the Conservatives relied very much upon the material advantages which the electors were supposed to be about to derive from Mr. Lowles's return. Their candidate was connected with two or three limited liability companies in the City who were spoken of as large employers of labour, and the prospect was held out that if Lowles was successful there would be practically work for everybody in Haggerston. The result of the election was the defeat of Cremer by a narrow majority, the figures being :

Lowles	...	...	...	...	...	2,276
Cremer	...	...	...	...	...	2,245
Majority	...	...	...	...	...	31

The way in which this election was conducted may be gathered from the following letter written by Cremer to his sister after his defeat :

July 20, 1895.

" MY DEAR SISTER,—The ten days' strain of the election was terrible. Canvassing all day and addressing three open-air meetings each night for thirty-five or forty minutes each was enough to exhaust the most robust. If we had had a couple of days more I should have won with a good majority. Our opponents admitted that. The onslaught I made upon them in the few days astonished my opponents and called forth the admiration of my friends. The most abominable means were employed to defeat me. Voters were personated, somebody voted for numbers of voters who were dead, the beer-tap ran all day, money was freely expended—and yet with all these influences their majority was only 31. When the poll was declared there must have been 12,000 people outside the Town Hall, wild with excitement and indignation at my defeat. I never knew until that night the amount of affection entertained toward me. It took a number of police to get me through the multitude to the railway-station.

" The Tories will have a big majority, and will probably be in office for five or six years, and then, even if I live, I shall be too old to work as I have done. Alas that when I have piloted our cause so near to port it should be shipwrecked thus ! But for the undying faith I have in the ulti-mate success of our principles I should despair. I am still hard at work in gathering evidence as to the illegal practices of my opponent."

A petition was lodged against the return, the judges being Mr. Justice Bruce and Mr. Justice Wright. The former was the senior, and in the event of a difference of opinion between the judges he would have the predominant voice. I deeply regretted that Cremer did not at once withdraw from the struggle. His counsel, then Mr. and now Judge Willis, K.C., fought the battle resolutely, and the late Mr. Richard Cadbury, who was deeply interested in Cremer's life-work, proved a loyal and devoted friend. The following letter from the judges who tried the election petition was read to the House of Commons by the Speaker :

" We hereby certify that we differ as to whether John Lowles, the Member whose election is com-plained of, was duly elected.

" We differ on the question as to whether any corrupt or illegal practice was proved to have been committed by or with the knowledge or consent of the said John Lowles, and also on the question whether the said John Lowles has been guilty by his agent of any corrupt or illegal practice ; but we agree that no corrupt or illegal practice was proved to have been committed by or with the knowledge or consent of the said William Randal Cremer, and also that the said William Randal Cremer has not been guilty by his agents of any corrupt or illegal practice."

CHAPTER XX

THE Interparliamentary Congress assembled at Buda-Pesth on September 23, 1896. Over 250 members were present, including 19 English representatives. The proceedings of this conference were especially memorable on account of its far-reaching effects upon European politics, as will be seen hereafter. The sittings were held in the Senate Chamber, and every Parliament in Europe was represented, with one exception. The President of the Hungarian Lower House, M. Szilagyi, presided, and warmly welcomed those present, as did also the Minister of the Interior, M. Perzel, in the name of the Hungarian Government. Count Apponyi, in an eloquent speech, declared that it was the glory of Great Britain to make every ideal progress practical. It was only in the previous year that the Hungarian group had been formed, but already it numbered 200 members. M. Franz Kossuth was one of the distinguished Hungarians who took part in the proceedings.

On the second day Count Apponyi proposed that

delegates should be admitted to the conferences who might be appointed by the heads of States or of Governments for the purpose, and further, the members of the Russian Council of State or of any analogous institution in States without a Constitution, two delegates to be appointed for each nation. This resolution, whose importance will be subsequently seen, was adopted with a few dissentients.

Senator Descamps (Belgium) brought up the Report of the Committee appointed at Brussels the previous year on " The Permanent International Court of Arbitration and the Ways and Means which may be used for bringing the Conclusions of the Conference into Practice." The following resolution was subsequently adopted :

" The conference invites the parliamentary groups to examine if it will not be possible to fix a time during which each of the groups shall demand from the competent officials of its country to conclude special or general treaties of arbitration, and particularly to promote the convocation of a diplomatic conference charged with preparing on the basis of the plan voted by the Sixth Inter-Parliamentary Conference the constitution of a permanent Court of Arbitration."

The issue of the proceedings at Buda-Pesth will best be seen from the following statement of the St. Petersburg correspondent of the *Times,* which appeared on December 16, 1898 :

" Soon after the appearance of Count Muravieff's famous circular I pointed out in the *Times* one or more of the influences under which it was believed that the Czar had decided to invite the

12

Governments of the world to the approaching conference to consider the possibility of arresting the ruinous progress of military armaments. I have just received an interesting statement giving some further particulars, and in part confirming what I have previously reported on the subject. My informant says :

" ' You will remember that about a couple of years ago an Interparliamentary Peace Conference on Disarmament was held at Buda-Pesth, and was attended by Members of the different Parliaments of Europe. At that time the Russian Consul-General in the Hungarian capital was M. Basili, who has since been appointed, under Count Muravieff, Chief of the Asiatic Department of the Russian Foreign Office. The promoters of the conference, and especially Count Apponyi, wished to have a Russian delegate, but, unfortunately—or perhaps fortunately, as some persons prefer to think—Russia was the only country not blessed with parliamentary institutions. The Imperial autocratic Government naturally found it quite impossible, and contrary to its professed principles, to send an official delegate to sit together with the chosen representatives of self-governing peoples. Therefore Russia was not officially represented. When, however, the conference came to an end, M. Basili sent a copy of its resolutions to the Ministry in St. Petersburg, where they were duly relegated to the archives and, for the time, forgotten.

" ' Meanwhile Count Muravieff came into power, and M. Basili was recalled and placed at the head of the Asiatic section of the Ministry. His Report on the Peace Conference at Buda-Pesth would probably never have been heard of again had it not been for the discussion in very high places over the heavy call to be made upon the Russian exchequer for military improvements and the increase of the Navy. . . .

" ' In consequence of the discussion that took place in these circumstances as to the expense of armaments, it is said that the Report of the conference at Buda-Pesth, which was calculated to suggest a remedy, was taken out of the pigeonholes and sent to the Emperor.' ".

Mr. W. T. Stead, in his " United States of Europe," as well as in a private letter to Cremer, has confirmed the above statement. He said : " In 1896 the Interparliamentary Conference met at Buda-Pesth. M. Basili, who is now the Chief of the Asiatic Department in the Russian Foreign Office, attended some of its meetings, took a deep interest in the proceedings, and reported to his Government strongly in favour of action in the stay of armaments. His suggestion was not received with approval by his official superiors, and it remained for a long time in abeyance ; then came the notable utterance of Lord Salisbury at the Guildhall on November 9, 1897, deprecating the ever increasing competition of the nations in armaments. After this M. Basili again renewed his representations in favour of an attempt to arrive at an international agreement on the subject.

" He was now established in the Foreign Office, and the suggestion commended itself to Count Lamsdorff, He submitted the proposal to the Emperor, who adopted it with enthusiasm, and after a short time we had the Rescript."

Subsequently a semi-official denial of this statement appeared in the *Journal de St. Petersburg*, but the Special Commissioner of the *Daily News* declared that the story was quite true. He added : " M. Basili is so much in earnest about securing a successful issue for the conference that he is willing even to deny he ever existed, if he could thereby gain a point for peace. But facts are not affected by such excess of zeal, and Mr. Cremer will be glad to know that the only result of the official correction has been to establish more firmly the truth of the original statement."

It was reported to the conference that, in accordance with the resolution moved by Cremer at Brussels, the Governments of Switzerland, Holland, and Belgium had been approached ; but though their replies were sympathetic, for various reasons they did not consider it expedient for smaller Powers to take the initiative. Undeterred by this rebuff, Cremer proposed :

"That the conference should appoint a special Commission to interview European Governments with the view of inducing two or more of them to adopt the proposals agreed to by the Brussels Conference for constituting a Permanent Court of Arbitration.

This motion was not carried.

It is worthy of note that before the close of the year 1896 Baron Pirquet obtained a unanimous vote in the Austrian Chamber of Deputies in favour of the principle of arbitration.

CHAPTER XXI

THIRD VISIT TO WASHINGTON

AT the beginning of 1896 Cremer conceived the idea of presenting a memorial to the President and Congress of the United States in favour of a treaty of arbitration from officers of trade unions and other organisations of working men. This project he carried out with his wonted energy, although the labour of collecting these adhesions was enormous. No fewer than 5,359 signatures were appended. This document ran as follows :

"The undersigned, while holding divers political opinions, are happily all agreed in their desire to see arbitration substituted for war. Unhappily very few of the European Powers have reached that advanced stage ; but we rejoice to know that between the United States of America and our own country a strong desire exists for the conclusion of a treaty which shall bind the two nations to refer to arbitration disputes which diplomacy fails to adjust. The feeling in favour of such a treaty has been manifested in various ways, notably by the resolutions which have been unanimously adopted by the United States Congress and our House of Commons, while 354 members of the latter have further accentuated their wishes by signing a memorial to the President and Congress of the United States. To these expressions of opinion we venture to add our own, and believe that in doing so we are voicing the feelings of the working classes, especially of those who belong to industrial organisations. The enormous advantages which the conclusion of such a treaty would confer upon the commercial and industrial interests of the two nations and the splendid example which would be set to other countries are too apparent to need any argument ; and as Congress and the House of Commons have by resolution affirmed the desirability of settling disputes by arbitration, we earnestly hope that her Majesty's Government will at once take the necessary steps for the conclusion of such a treaty, and thus forge the first link in a chain which shall ultimately bind the English-speaking nations in a peaceful federation."

In June, 1896, Cremer and several members of the council of the League waited on Lord Salisbury at the Foreign Office with a copy of this memorial, and explained to him what had been done. Lord Salisbury's reply, which was very sympathetic in its tone, was not altogether unexpected, for we were well aware that in his Attorney-General, Sir Richard Webster (now Lord Alverstone), we had a warm friend, who had inherited from his father a keen interest in the arbitration movement.

Lord Salisbury said : " I am very glad to see this memorial from you, and I hardly need to assure you that in the minds of the members of her Majesty's Government, as in the minds of all sensible Christian men, there is a most earnest desire that where it is possible arbitration should be substituted for any arbitrament of a warlike character. We have that feeling strongly before us. As you have justly said, this opinion has hardly advanced among the nations of the Continent of Europe to a point at which any definite result can be obtained, but matters are more hopeful in the United States. We have not been neglectful on the subject. We have been in negotiation with America for several months. Sir John Mowbray, in his remarks, made one reservation, which is the reservation which all men who wish to deal with this subject practically and fruitfully should bear in mind, namely, that it must be done, so far as is practicable. These words contain a reservation of unknown extent. Our desire is that the principle should be extended as far as is consistent with the just rights of those whose interests are committed to our charge."

The early utterances of Lord Salisbury in regard to international arbitration were frigid and almost contemptuous. When speaking on the Alabama arbitration on March 3, 1873, he said : " I am afraid that, like competitive examinations and sewage irrigation, arbitration is one of the famous nostrums of the age. Like them it will have its day and will pass away, and future ages will look with pity and contempt on those who could have believed in such an expedient for bridling the ferocity of human passions." Ripened experience in later years had taught him much, and in the summer of 1892, in a speech at St. Leonards, he said : " After all, the great triumph of civilisation in the past has been in the substitution of judicial termination for the cold, cruel, crude arbitrament

of war. We have got rid of private war between
small magnate and small magnate. In this country
we have got rid of the duel between man and man ;
we are slowly, as far as we can, substituting
arbitrament for struggles in international disputes."

A new congress assembled at Washington at the
end of 1896. The treaty of arbitration, which
had been already drawn up and signed, was submitted to the Senate, where a two-thirds vote was
requisite in order to secure ratification.   On
May 5, 1897, the decisive division took place, when
43 senators voted in favour of ratification and 26
against it, so that three votes were wanting to make
the necessary two-thirds. The man who led the
opposition to the treaty was Senator Morgan, of
Alabama. He had previously expressed his approval of arbitration in the abstract, so that his
objections were directed rather to the manner in
which arbitration was to be carried out by the
treaty. According to Cremer, Senator Morgan,
who appeared on the American side in the Behring
Sea Arbitration, was greatly annoyed that the decision was given in favour of Great Britain. Michael
Davitt, who was in the United States at the time,
also used all the influence he possessed against
the treaty, and he certainly carried with him large
numbers of Irish-American voters. It is due, however, to the Catholic hierarchy in the United States,
and to the best men in the Nationalist Party in
the British House of Commons to say that they
took a nobler course.

Cremer's former visits to America had enabled him to understand the various adverse influences that were at work. He was confident that the vast majority of the people of the United States were in favour of an arbitration treaty ; indeed, if the Senators had been able to vote by population the treaty would have certainly been ratified. But from the very position of the United States most of the people could have little more than a benevolent interest in the matter. Since the absurd expedition of the French army sent by Napoleon III. to Mexico, no Power in Continental Europe had dreamed of interference on the American continent ; a war with Great Britain seemed absolutely unthinkable ; the Central and South American Republics were certain to constantly follow the lead of their big sister. To Cremer and his colleagues in the League it therefore appeared necessary to start on a new campaign, mainly with the object of influencing public opinion in the United States in favour of a treaty. This resolution was promptly taken.

The League was especially anxious to enlist the active support of Christian sentiment in the United States. As the vast majority of Protestants across the Atlantic are closely connected with what are known as the Free Churches in England, it was considered desirable to secure the assistance of two or three well-known Free Church leaders, more especially Dr. Charles Berry, of Wolverhampton, and the Rev. Hugh Price Hughes. The

latter was unable to go to America in consequence
of pressing engagements, but Cremer went down
to Wolverhampton to secure the help of Dr. Berry,
who was about to visit the States in the autumn.
Dr. Berry was in full sympathy with the movement,
but he objected that he had already trespassed so
much on the forbearance of his own people that he
could not prolong his visit.   Of all the Free Church
leaders no one was so widely known or commanded
equal influence in the United States as the man
who a few years before had been invited to fill the
vacant pulpit of Henry Ward Beecher, at Brooklyn,
and still further pressure was brought to bear on
him. A request to the members of Dr. Berry's own
church, signed by Mr. George Cadbury, Dr. Guinness Rogers, and other leading Free Churchmen,
surmounted the difficulty, and accordingly Dr.
Berry proceeded to America, fortified with a cordial
message from the National Free Church Council
of which he had been the first president.   Cremer
and Dr. Berry were cordially received at great
public meetings in Washington and other American
cities.

Cremer learned, in conversation with a number
of Congressmen, that the main reason why the
treaty failed to secure a two-thirds majority in
the Senate was that, rightly or wrongly, it was
regarded as interfering with the powers of the
Senate itself.   Under the constitution of the United
States, every treaty with a foreign power must,
before it becomes operative, be sanctioned by two-

thirds of the Senate ; and if the treaty had been ratified, the Senate would, in cases of dispute between the two countries, have been deprived of its right to discuss and pronounce judgment upon the points at issue, as the treaty stipulated that whenever differences arose between the two countries which were found to be incapable of adjustment by the respective Governments, that the matter in dispute should be forthwith referred to the tribunal for which the treaty provided. This many senators regarded as an infringement upon and a curtailment of their constitutional prerogatives ; and while professing to be in favour of arbitration, they claimed their right to consider every dispute upon its merits, also to determine whether it is of a fitting nature to be settled by arbitration.

Cremer had an interview with President McKinley, who declared that he was still strongly in favour of settling disputes by arbitration and had said so in his message to Congress, but he did not regard the moment as opportune for legislative action.

CHAPTER XXII

THE TZAR'S RESCRIPT AND THE FIRST HAGUE CONFERENCE

ALL Europe was amazed when in August, 1898, the Tzar of Russia issued a rescript, a copy of which was handed to every ambassador accredited to the Court of St. Petersburg. This document ran as follows :

" The maintenance of general peace, and a possible reduction of the excessive armaments which weigh upon all nations, present themselves in the existing condition of the whole world as the ideal towards which the endeavours of all Governments should be directed. The humanitarian and magnanimous ideas of his Majesty the Emperor, my august master, have been won over to this view. In the conviction that this lofty aim is in conformity with the most essential interests and the legitimate views of all Powers, the Imperial Government thinks that the present moment would be very favourable for seeking, by means of international discussion, the most effectual means of ensuring to all peoples the benefit of a real and durable peace, and above all, of putting an end to the progressive development of the present armaments.

" In the course of the last twenty years the longings for a general appeasement have grown especially pronounced in the consciences of civilised nations. The preservation of peace has been put forward as the object of international policy. It is in its name that great States have concluded between themselves powerful alliances ; it is the better to guarantee peace that they have developed in proportions hitherto unprecedented their military forces, and still continue to increase them without shrinking from any sacrifice. All these efforts nevertheless have not yet been able to bring about the beneficent results of the desired pacification.

" The financial charges following an upward march strike at public prosperity at its very source. The intellectual and physical strength of the nation's labour and capital are for the major part diverted from their natural application, and unproductively consumed. Hundreds of millions are devoted to acquiring terrible engines of destruction, which, though to-day regarded as the last word of science, are destined to-morrow to lose all value in consequence of some fresh discovery in the same field. National culture, economic progress, and the production of wealth are either paralysed or checked in their development.

" Moreover, in proportion as the armaments of each power increase, so do they less and less fulfil the objects which the Governments have set before themselves. The economic crisis, due in great part to the systems of armaments *à outrance*, and the continual danger which lies in this massing of war material, are transforming the armed peace of our days into a crushing burden, which the peoples have more and more difficulty in bearing.

"It appears evident, then, that if this state of things were prolonged it would inevitably lead to the very cataclysm which it is desired to avert, and the horrors of which make every thinking being shudder in advance.

"To put an end to these incessant armaments, and to seek the means of warding off the calamities which are threatening the whole world—such is the supreme duty which is to-day imposed on all States.

"Filled with this idea, his Majesty has been pleased to order me to propose to all the Governments whose representatives are accredited to the Imperial Court the meeting of a conference which would have to occupy itself with this grave problem. This conference would be, by the help of God, a happy presage for the century which is about to open. It would converge in one powerful focus the efforts of all the States which are sincerely seeking to make the great conception of universal peace triumph over the elements of trouble and discord. It would at the same time cement their agreement by a corporate consecration of the principles of equity and right, on which rest the security of States and the welfare of peoples."

At the end of 1898 Count Muravieff, the Russian Foreign Minister, addressed a circular to the representatives of the Powers in which the Tzar expressed his gratification that nearly all the Powers had received his proposal cordially, and that it had been hailed with approval by public opinion throughout the civilised world. The circular suggested a preliminary exchange of views with the object :

" (a) Of seeking without delay means for putting a stop to the progressive increase of military and naval armaments, a question the solution of which becomes evidently more and more urgent in view of the fresh extension given to these arguments ; and,

" (b) Of preparing the way for a discussion of the questions relating to the possibility of preventing armed conflicts by the pacific means at the disposal of international diplomacy."

For once men were to gather grapes of thorns and figs of thistles. If the invitation had come from the Queen of England, or the President of the French Republic, or the President of the United States, no one would have been much astonished ; but the Tzar of Russia seemed the very incarnation of militarism. He was the man who was supposed to be the absolute master of unnumbered legions of armed men, who was regarded as a menace to peace and progress wherever Russia had a frontier

—in China, India, Persia, Asia Minor, and the
Balkan Peninsula ; even in free Scandinavia men
did not reckon themselves safe from the colossal
Power which had absorbed Poland and Finland.
Who could have dreamed that so soon afterwards
time would number the Tsardom itself among

> "Those pagod things of sabre sway,
>   With fronts of brass and feet of clay"?

There were undercurrents at work, however, at
the Court of St. Petersburg, as will be seen hereafter. A tribute of praise is especially due to
the late Jean de Bloch, a member of the Russian
Council of State, who had been unwearied in his
efforts for the cause. De Bloch held that the
conditions of warfare had so altered of late years
that conscription had become a ruinous absurdity.
In the Tsar's Rescript it will be observed that
there is no direct mention of the High Court of
Nations, and that the one dominant idea in the
mind of its author was a reduction of armaments.
As all the world knows, the first Hague Conference
did not fulfil the hopes of its convener, although
its work in other directions was eminently
successful.

Immediately after the issue of the rescript
Cremer obtained the signatures of over a hundred
members of the British Legislature, including nine
bishops, thanking the Tzar for the action he had
taken. The number would have been much greater
had it not been the holiday season. Lord Tweed-

mouth in his reply declared that the very proposals of the Tzar were in the first instance made by Lord Rosebery.

An address of congratulation to the Tzar was also signed by the members of the Bureau of the Interparliamentary Union, representing fifteen European Parliaments. Mr. Stead also organised in this country a vigorous Campaign of Peace, in which he was assisted by Earl Grey, Sir John Macdonell, Sir Percy Bunting, and Mr. F. W. Fox. The Trades' Union Congress, at the suggestion of Mr. F. Maddison, adopted a resolution of approval, and a similar resolution of the League drew a sympathetic reply from Mr. Balfour.

The conference assembled on May 18, 1899, and was attended by the representatives of twenty-six Powers. The number of representatives was not limited, but each Power, large or small, had only one vote. Baron de Staal, the chief representative of Russia, presided. The chief British representative was Sir Julian Pauncefote, with whom Cremer had a long interview on the eve of his departure. He well knew from previous intercourse with Sir Julian that this country could not be represented by a warmer friend of the arbitration principle. It was especially auspicious for the cause that France was represented by M. Bourgeois, who was one of the founders of the Interparliamentary Union, and Baron d'Estournelles de Constant, a later recruit to whom the cause in France owes a large debt of gratitude. To the honour of M. Bourgeois it should be remembered that he declined the task of forming a French administration because of the importance of the work in which he was engaged at The Hague.

The conference sat about two months and deliberated upon Armaments, Regulations of War, and Arbitration. With regard to armaments the conference passed the following resolutions :

" The conference is of opinion that the restriction of military budgets, which are at present a heavy burden on the world, is extremely desirable for the increase of the material and moral welfare of mankind."

Yet further :

" The conference expresses the wish that the Governments taking into consideration the proposals made at the conference, may examine the possibility of an agreement as to the limitation of armed forces by land and sea, and of war budgets."

Although these resolutions were unanimously adopted they have hitherto had no practical results.

The conference agreed upon a number of Articles tending to the humanisation of war. For example, the employment of arms, projectiles, or material of a nature to cause superfluous injury, and the attack or bombardment of towns, villages, habitations, or buildings which are not defended, was prohibited. It is unnecessary to discuss these provisions at length, though they ought to allay the fears of those timid people who are afraid that some fine morning an enemy will destroy their homes by means of explosives dropped from balloons. We are more immediately concerned with the vital matter of arbitration.

Russia proposed that, while making reservations as to national honour and vital interests, arbitration should be made compulsory where these reservations do not apply. Germany alone opposed the proposal, and the abandonment of the Russian scheme was the price of Germany consenting to the creation of the permanent tribunal at The Hague. Since then Germany has inserted in her last Treaties of Commerce the very clause to which she formerly objected. Thus it was that a chief result of the first conference at The Hague was the creation of a permanent tribunal. The scheme was drawn up in a convention containing fifty-six Articles, which were mainly the work of Sir Julian Pauncefote, who said to Mr. Stead : " We are setting up a tribunal for the benefit of mankind. Any and every State which has a dispute which may involve mankind in the disaster of war is welcome to make use of our Court. There is no limitation, and there are no exclusions." Adhesion to the convention gives to each Power that signs it a right to nominate members of the Permanent Court, but any Power may resort to it.

The *Times* thus summarised the labours of the conference : " The most conspicuous feature about the conference is, as our Special Correspondent remarks, the successful establishment of a permanent Court of Arbitration. This result, Englishmen may recognise with pride, has been attained chiefly by the sound practical instinct of their representative. The arbitration scheme bids fair to be a real success within certain limits, and it does so because Sir Julian Pauncefote realised from the first the only conditions which could give it a chance of succeeding. The principle on which he insisted, and which, with the steady support of the Americans, he had persuaded the conference to adopt, is the principle of permanency in the new tribunal. The creation of a court always ready to adjudicate on such subjects as the parties to international controversies may choose to submit to it is in itself a great gain."

It will be remembered that the first effort of the Workmen's Peace Association was to draw up the outline of a plan for the formation of a permanent Arbitration Court. Here is the preamble :

"Whereas war having signally failed as a means for the settlement of international disputes, and being opposed to the character and spirit of the age, in the belief of this conference permanent peace and concord between nations would be promoted by the establishment of a High Court of Nations on the basis set forth in the following Articles."

Now let us turn to the scheme which was formulated at The Hague. Article XX. runs thus :

"With the object of facilitating immediate recourse to the arbitration of international differences not settled by diplomatic means, the signatory Powers pledge themselves to organise in the following manner a Permanent Court of Arbitration, accessible at all times and operating, unless otherwise stipulated by the parties, in accordance with the Rules of Procedure inserted in the present convention."

The boldest and bravest of the men who founded the Workmen's Peace Association could never have dreamed that within the lifetime of some of them their aspirations would be realised. This result was very largely due to the patient perseverance and indomitable energy of Sir Randal Cremer. It was a proud day for him when he had to move that the establishment of a High Court of Nations should be struck out of the programme of the League because by the action of the Powers it had actually come into existence.

Time alone will show whether the Hague Court which is to be located in the " Palace of Peace " now being erected at The Hague by Mr. Andrew Carnegie will fulfil the high hopes and expectations of Lord Pauncefote, Baron de Staal, M. Bourgeois, and others who formulated the arbitration convention ; but it has not only educated public opinion, it is already in operation ; and the very meeting of a second conference and the promise of a third shows that in the judgment of monarchs and statesmen such official gatherings have the promise and potency of *bon accord*.

In 1897 the Interparliamentary Union met at Brussels, M. Beernaert, the President of the Chamber of Deputies, occupying the chair, but there was no feature of special interest in the proceedings. By this time the British group had grown to over one hundred members, including the present Lord Chancellor, the present Chancellor of the Exchequer, Mr. Haldane, and Sir Samuel Evans, the present Solicitor-General. In 1898 a conference was to have been held at Lisbon, but owing to the great distance of the Portuguese capital the design had to be abandoned. In 1899 the conference met at Christiania.

Norway from the outset had occupied an honourable place in the history of the movement. It was the first country to pay the expenses of its representatives to conferences. Alfred Nobel had made a special arrangement in his will that the peace prize should be awarded by a committee appointed by the Norwegian Chamber. John Lund, the President of the Lagthing, had been one of the most active members of previous conferences. Norway gave to the conference a right royal reception. The Legislature devoted £2,000 for its entertainment ; the hall of the Storthing was placed at its disposal ; the Norwegian fleet went out to meet the members as they arrived from Copenhagen by sea, and greeted them with salvoes of cannon ; twelve thousand people assembled on the wharves to greet them ; and when the sittings commenced the Prime Minister welcomed them in a sympathetic speech. All the Scandinavian railways granted free passes, and the municipality of Christiania provided over a hundred carriages to take the members to a banquet in a mountain suburb.

All who were present were naturally exultant at the success of the first official conference at The Hague. Mr. W. T. Stead, who had been present at The Hague, presented a Report of the proceedings there, which was read by Mr. Philip Stanhope. It commenced thus : " I bring you glad tidings of great joy. If you did but realise the magnitude of the success which has been achieved, you would be singing the *Te Deum Laudamus* in the cathedral rather than discussing abstract propositions in the Storthing. For the great charter of the general peace has been signed, and that which twelve months ago seemed to be beyond the hopes of all the peace societies has now been accepted by all the Powers in the world.

" It is as if a miracle had been wrought before our eyes, but we are too dull to recognise its significance. There may be some, even in the Interparliamentary Conference, who imagine that the Hague conference has failed. I tell you with all earnestness that in the opinion of your members who took part in the work it has achieved a success so brilliant that the triumph crowns the closing century with glory.

" The Reglement Pacifique of the Hague Conference is the first great International Law of Peace. It is more ; it lays the foundation, not only of peace based upon justice : it is the first direct definite step towards the federation of mankind.

" The starting-point of this new, great international charter is the formal declaration by all the Powers that henceforth they will use their efforts to prevent war and to maintain peace."

The Report then proceeded to describe the machinery which the Hague conference had created, and concluded as follows : " What our friends at The Hague bid me say to you is this, that without your help in popularising the work which we have done in educating the peoples as to the new opportunities afforded for avoiding war all our work will be in vain. The battle has been won. It is for you to secure the spoils."

Resolutions were adopted by the conference congratulating the Tzar of Russia on the results of The Hague conference and exhorting the various national groups of members to employ their influence for the following purposes :

(a) To obtain the adhesion of their Governments to the pacific and humanitarian resolutions of the Hague conference —if this adhesion be not already given.

(b) To encourage their Governments to conclude arbitration treaties with as many States as possible.

(c) To facilitate the accession of countries not represented in the convention concluded by the Hague conference.

(d) To bring to the knowledge of their fellow-countrymen the results of the Hague conference with the necessary explanations and appreciations."

Much curiosity was excited in regard to Nobel's famous legacy. He had directed that a sum of 150,000 kroner, together with a diploma and a gold medal bearing his portrait, should be awarded

annually to the person who had laboured the most
or in the best manner to create a fraternal feeling
among the peoples, who had laboured to abolish or
to decrease standing armies, and to form or spread
peace congresses. The first distribution was not
to take place until the end of 1901. At Christiania
the names of Passy, Cremer, and the Baroness von
Suttner appeared to be the most likely favourites,
and each of them has subsequently proved a prize-
winner. It may be here mentioned that a statement
of Cremer's services to the cause, which I drew
up at the request of the Council of the League, was
signed by over a hundred Members of the British
House of Commons.

CHAPTER XXIII

INTERPARLIAMENTARY UNION AT PARIS

IN 1900 was held the magnificent exhibition in Paris which extended along both sides of the Seine from the Place de la Concorde to the Trocadero, and filled the vast expanse of the Champs de Mars. Public feeling towards France in this country was very different from what it is now. Rightly or wrongly French statesmen were charged with adopting a " policy of pin-pricks," and the Fashoda incident, of which Major Marchand was the hero, had caused much angry comment. As a matter of fact the Paris Exhibition was largely boycotted by Great Britain, whose leading manufacturers were conspicuous by their absence. The French people undoubtedly took an unfavourable view of the conduct of the British Government in South Africa. The outbreak of the South African War was a terrible blow to the friends of peace both in this country and abroad. In England the League and most of the members of the Interparliamentary Union uttered strenuous protests against the war, the consequence being that not a few who had worked with us hitherto for the time left our ranks.

Throughout Europe the British people were regarded as a nation of sanctimonious hypocrites. At that time a Briton travelling abroad found it desirable to hide his origin as far as he could, which was not always easy. With the solitary exception of Yves Guyot, no man in all France whose opinion was worth having had a word to say in our favour. One of my most bitter recollections is that in Geneva, that ancient fastness of freedom, I sat in the English Garden, on an Easter holiday, watching a grand procession of the trades, and was suddenly confronted with the collection-box in aid of the Boer women and children. I gave my contribution with tears of shame. For the men whose pride and obstinacy brought us to such humiliation there can be no forgiveness, for they trailed the fair fame of our own dear land in the dust before all Europe at the instigation of polyglot devotees of Mammon, who had degraded and debauched the Press alike in England and South Africa. The British nation which went mafficking in the crisis of the war fever has since learned by bitter experience that it cannot make war on the cheap, and to this day it is suffering from the consequences of its folly.

Great things had been hoped from the second meeting of the Interparliamentary Conference in

Paris, but it assembled under a heavy cloud of disappointment and disaster. It was with sad hearts that Cremer, Stanhope, and about twenty other British members went across the Channel.

The war was not the only drawback. In the time of Bismarck and Crispi, when Italy was a member of the Triple Alliance, the relations of France and Italy had been sorely strained ; in more recent years they had greatly improved. About two hundred Italian Deputies had promised to attend the Paris conference, but almost on the eve of meeting they were suddenly summoned by the news of the cruel assassination of King Humbert. This event not only cast a deep shadow over the conference itself, but impelled the French Committee of Reception to countermand the fêtes and banquets of welcome which had been arranged.

Nevertheless there was much reason for encouragement. The first conference at Paris was attended by barely a hundred members ; at the second three hundred and fifty assembled. At the first conference only seven nations were represented, at the second the number had grown to eighteen. At the first conference Germany was not represented at all, at the second over sixty Germans were present, one of whom announced that the German group already numbered a hundred. At the first conference the League had to hire the dining-room of a hotel as a place of meeting, at the second the gathering was held in the Luxembourg Palace, the Chamber of the Senate, whose president, M. Fallières (now President of the Republic), took the chair at the first sitting. Under the circumstances nothing could have been more cordial than the reception accorded. The Keeper of the Seals welcomed the conference in the name of the Government ; the Paris municipality threw open the Hôtel de Ville for a reception, and the President of the Republic, M. Loubet, also received the members at the Élysée.

Mr. Barrows, a United States Congressman, reported that during the year his own Government had agreed to refer certain disputes with Russia and Chili to arbitration, and that the United States Senate had ratified the Hague arbitration scheme. Baron d'Estournelles de Constant proposed a resolution, which was adopted with unanimity, expressing the hope that the just punishment administered by the Powers for the sanguinary massacres in China would not develop into a campaign of conquest. Count Apponyi and M. Beernaert called attention to ways in which the Hague scheme might be improved and extended.

It was almost inevitable that the South African War should excite strong feelings of disappointment and even anger on the part of some of the speakers, who were more than once called to order by the President. The fact that the British Government had refused arbitration could not be denied, and the necessary absence from The Hague of the African Republics as mere protected States was not regarded as a valid reason for refusal. In the end Mr.

Stanhope appealed to the generosity of the conference and expressed the hope that nothing would be said which would oblige the British members to withdraw. The conference yielded to this appeal, recognising that their friends from this country had done their utmost to allay the war fever.

Cremer, after recounting the efforts which had been made by the British members to obtain the ratification by their Government of the decisions of the Hague conference, proposed the following resolution, which, after discussion, was adopted :

"The conference regrets that the arbitration Convention concluded by the Hague Conference has not yet been formally ratified by all the Governments represented there, and the conference instructs the Council of the Interparliamentary Union to communicate to the Governments who have not yet signed the convention its earnest desire to see this great International Act completed at the earliest possible moment."

Only a few short years ago the mischief-makers who at the present moment are sowing the seeds of distrust and hatred against Germany were engaged in a similar nefarious task in regard to France, and the Nationalist Press of France was not a whit behind the Jingo Press of Great Britain. The Dreyfus affair, which excited great interest in this country, led too many of our newspapers to involve the whole French people in one sweeping condemnation. As subsequent events proved, the splendid efforts of Labori, Zola, Trarieux, and other French champions of justice were ultimately crowned with success. The unfortunate Fashoda incident further fanned the flame of ill-feeling, and the language of some of our leading newspapers gave the Nationalist Press of France an undue advantage. The outbreak of the unhappy war in South Africa and the partial boycott of the Paris Exhibition still further increased bitterness. Both nations were increasing their armaments, and on both sides of the Channel certain journals were cynically discussing the probable results of a war between France and Great Britain as the same papers at the present time are discussing the probable results of a war between Great Britain and Germany. Provocative language was used by Mr. Chamberlain and other prominent English politicians, and on the French side men like Deroulède, Rochefort, and Millevoie were equally indiscreet. The League, therefore, determined to prepare an address from the workers of Great Britain to the workers of France, which was speedily signed by 214 Labour leaders, including nearly every prominent trade unionist in the country.

This address, like subsequent manifestoes, began by denouncing the pernicious influence of those newspapers which inflamed international hatred. It commenced thus : " A new force has been born into the world, a force before which even monarchs bow down, and by which peoples are incited to distrust and hate each other. The force we refer to, and against which we raise a warning voice, is that portion of the press controlled by unprincipled capitalists, and used to inflame popular passion in our respective countries." The address went on to show that the interests of the workers in both countries are practically identical, and that a war between France and Great Britain would mean the ruin of industry. The address concluded thus : " We appeal to you to unite with us in thwarting the base designs of those who are constantly defaming and caricaturing their neighbours in order to excite suspicion and malice. Such men are the worst enemies of their own country and of humanity at large. Your Chauvinists and our Jingoes are the exploiters of honest, simple-minded patriotism, and use it constantly for their own selfish ends. They have had their way too long. We must confront them henceforth with the most resolute opposition, and whatever differences exist or may arise between the two countries which our Governments are unable to adjust, we must persistently demand that before resorting to violent means they shall have recourse to the peaceful tribunal which was created by the great International Conference which assembled last year at The Hague. Unless we do this there is a danger that they may begin the new century with a gigantic crime against humanity and civilisation. We have no cause of quarrel against you ; you have no cause of quarrel against us : we have alike cause to closely watch and combat those who would kindle strife between us. Workers ! the time

14

has come when, in the interests of humanity, we should march shoulder to shoulder, proclaiming that the greatest interest of labour is peace."

No sooner had Cremer regained his seat for Haggerston than he hurried across the Channel to prepare for the great demonstration of fraternity which was held in the Bourse du Travail on October 28, 1900. The Bourse du Travail is the home of 240 Labour organisations, and contains a central hall in which nearly three thousand people can assemble. Long before the time of the meeting the hall was crowded, and as soon as the English delegation appeared on the platform the song of the International was enthusiastically sung by the whole audience. M. Baumé, a prominent Paris trade unionist, was appointed French president, and Mr. Pickles, chairman of the Trades Union Congress, was appointed English president. A considerable number of German and Italian delegates also attended. M. Baumé, in his opening address, said : " By this imposing demonstration, we, both English and French, desire to affirm our unfailing will to maintain universal peace, being perfectly aware that the workers have no interest in making war between one country and another. We know that not only should we have to pay the cost by means of accumulated taxation, but it is we and our children who will have to do the fighting, and how many among us would lose our lives in the battlefields or come home mutilated? We must, therefore, make every effort to protest against such slaughter of one people by another people, and as Pierre Dupont so well said in his song of the soldier, ' the peoples are our brothers and the tyrants are our enemies.' " Mr. Pickles explained to the audience that the British address had been recently endorsed unanimously at the recent Trades Union Congress, where a million and a quarter of organised workmen were represented.

The address was then read in French by M. Adolphe Smith, and was received with the utmost enthusiasm. In M. Adolphe Smith, who is equally at home in the French and English languages, the audience had not only a translator, but an orator, who drove home each sentence of each speaker with telling effect. British and French speakers followed alternately. The British representatives were Mr. George Barnes, secretary of the Amalgamated Engineers ; Mr. Richard Bell, secretary of the Amalgamated Railway Servants ; Mr. T. G. Gray, secretary of the Co-operative Union ; Mr. John Wilson, secretary of the Durham Miners ; Mr. Herbert Burrows, and Mr. Cremer. The French speakers were nearly all members of the Paris Labour Exchange, and of the Labour Exchange of France, and included MM. Briat, Lacour, Bourderon, Griffuelhem, and Levy. Two leading French Socialists, M. Vaillant, formerly Minister of Public Instruction, and M. Jaurès, also addressed the assembly. The speech of the latter excited unbounded enthusiasm.

The French president then submitted the following resolution, which was enthusiastically voted :

"This meeting of French workers is happy to welcome the delegation of the workers of Great Britain.

"It is pleased to receive the manifesto which the British deputation has presented. It unanimously approves the desire expressed in this manifesto to maintain and consolidate the fraternal union of the workers of both countries.

"This meeting affirms that, in spite of all the difficulties that may have existed in the past, or that may arise in the future, all differences between the two nations must be settled by arbitration."

When the great meeting had terminated, the British delegation and all Germans who were present were invited to a separate room, where they were entertained to a " wine of honour " by the administrative commission of the labour exchange, the German delegates profiting by this opportunity to say a few words of general approval. Our French comrades were full of generous hospitality. They had arranged to take the English delegates for an excursion to Versailles on the following day, and on the evening of the demonstration they were entertained at a banquet in the Hôtel Modern. This was a truly remarkable gathering. Among those who took part were Longuet, who was condemned to death after the Commune ; Camelinat, Master of the Mint at the time of the Commune; Vaillant, formerly Communard and subsequently a Socialist Deputy, and Allemane, who had been condemned to penal servitude, and had lived for eight years in New Caledonia with a cannon-shot chained to his leg. It was interesting to find these men who in their youth had been men of war, in after-years becoming veteran champions of peace. One of the chief speakers at this banquet was M. Briand, who pointed out that " the governing classes having failed to prevent war by their conference at The Hague, it was logical that the working classes should now try what they could do. The resolution carried at the meeting seemed very platonic, but the working men would not rest satisfied with mere words. If the capitalists were fatally pushed towards war, the working men felt no such impulse ; they would, therefore, not only protest, but act. When the hour came the British trade unionists would be called upon to use their great strength and wealth to prevent war. The French labour organisations had neither the same wealth nor as many members, but they were animated with the sacred fire that would lead them to sacrifice life itself. Thus peace might be imposed on recalcitrant Governments."

At the Bourse du Travail demonstration a cordial invitation was given to the representatives of the French workers to pay a return visit to London. This took place on June 15 and 16, 1901. In the afternoon of June 15th a crowded and enthusiastic meeting in Shoreditch Town Hall was presided over by Mr. Gregory, chairman of the London Trades Council, and by Citizen Pouget,

as representing the French delegates. As at the
Paris meeting the speeches were alternately in
English and French, and were forcibly translated
by M. Adolphe Smith. The English speakers were
Mr. Hawkins, chairman of the London branch of
the Co-operative Wholesale Society ; Mr. Maddison,
Mr. Will Crooks, and Mr. Cremer, who at the time
was suffering from severe illness. The French
delegates presented an address to the workers of
Great Britain in which they strongly advocated
disarmament, as the following passage will show :
" The general disarmament will only be possible
when we are in a position to impose our will on the
Governments, make them understand that we will
no longer be the accomplices of their homicidal
passions, and when, in the name of human fraternity, we refuse to kill each other, then will peace
become an effective and definite reality. It is
towards this harmonious future that we should
direct all our efforts. It is to realise this glorious
end that, in the name of the workers of France,
we convoke you, our comrades of Great Britain,
to unite with us and to work with us. War against
war ! Hurrah for peace ! Long live international
fraternity ! "

On the following evening the French delegates
were entertained at a dinner at the Crystal Palace,
when Mr. D. Holmes, secretary of the Leicester
Hosiery Trades, presided, the English speakers
being Mr. W. C. Steadman, Mr. J. Macdonald,
secretary of the London Trade Council ; Mr. Isaac

Mitchell, secretary of the Federation of Trades Unions ; and Mr. Howard Evans. Citizen Baumé and other French delegates expressed their gratification at the enthusiastic reception which they had received, not only at the banquet, but at a luncheon at the Co-operative Wholesale Society in the morning. The proceedings were wound up with the song of the International and with " Auld Lang Syne," the latter with hands interlaced, forming a chain of solidarity.

Cremer, to his great regret, was detained from this festive gathering by a serious attack of illness.

CHAPTER XXIV

THE BOER WAR

THE authors of the Boer War will be judged at the bar of history, and there can be no doubt what the verdict will be. From its commencement to its close the public opinion of Europe condemned the conduct of Great Britain, more especially as our Government refused to submit the dispute to arbitration. It is unnecessary in this place to discuss the question at length. Our immediate purpose is to deal with the attitude of Cremer and the League in regard to it. On June 29, 1899, the council of the League adopted the following resolution :

"This Council expresses its regret and alarm at the provocative language used by some of our journals and public men towards the Government of the Transvaal, which is calculated to aggravate differences and lead to an open rupture. Apart from the frightful consequences of a war between the British and the Boers, the conflicting testimony as to the grievances of the Uitlanders and their legitimate demands should impose upon our Government a policy of patience and forbearance."

It will be remembered that the war came upon this country as a surprise. In fact, Sir Edward Clarke subsequently said, amid the cheers of the

Liberals : " I am convinced that if this House had been sitting during the month of August and the first week of September, there would have been no war with the Transvaal."

Many of those who were opposed to the war believed that President Kruger made a fatal blunder when he took the initiative ; but it may be pleaded on his behalf that the circumstances attending the Jameson Raid, and the events which followed, had caused him to lose all faith in the justice and fair dealing of the British Government. From the outbreak of the war the League and the members of the British group of the Inter-parliamentary Union denounced the war in the strongest language. Sir Henry Campbell-Bannerman and other leaders of the Liberal Party manfully protested, but in vain. Mr. Asquith, in particular, denounced the journalists who had done their utmost to provoke a rupture as " irresponsible fire-eaters, professional breeders of mischief between nation and nation, bravadoes and bullies, who at times like this always make themselves heard in the back slums of British journalism." All protests, however, were useless. The Rand magnates had obtained the control of nearly all the newspapers in South Africa, and many of the most widely-circulated journals in this country. The most infamous lies in regard to the Boers were widely circulated and greedily swallowed by the British public, and those who protested against the unrighteousness of the war were hounded down, and in not a few cases were savagely maltreated. The most conspicuous case was that of Mr. Lloyd George when he appeared at Birmingham. Certain papers deliberately provoked a riot beforehand, and a conflict took place between the mob and the police, who were vainly trying to keep order. Mr. Lloyd George barely escaped with his life by departing from the hall in disguise.

One of the saddest features of the whole business was the defection from the peace party of a number of conspicuous ministers of the Free Churches, such as the Rev. Hugh Price Hughes, Rev. W. J. Dawson, and Dr. John Watson, while the pulpits of the Established Church resounded with justifications of the war. To such an extent did the war fever prevail that Mr. Chamberlain was invited to occupy the most prominent position at a luncheon at Wesley's Chapel, in City Road, but the friends of peace in the Wesleyan body were strong enough by their protests to prevent such a scandal. Amongst the advocates of the war the Protestant Archbishop of Armagh occupied a position of bad pre-eminence.

The mob at Scarborough savagely attacked the premises of Messrs. Rowntree, who generously forbore to make any claim against the borough fund for the property which had been destroyed. In doing so they said : " The loss of property, though not light to some of us, is as nothing compared to the peril to which some of those dearer to us than life were that night exposed, all with the loss of free speech, won for us by brave men and women of old. We respectfully submit to our fellow-townsmen of all creeds and parties that the wrecking of buildings, and especially midnight assaults on the homes of women, children, and aged persons, are acts of cruel lawlessness which nothing can justify." This is only a sample of what occurred in various parts of England. In nearly fifty places meetings were broken up and the friends of peace were savagely assaulted by Jingo mobs.

Mr. Chamberlain himself admitted that President Kruger offered to make large concessions, and he added, " We did not accept · everything, but we accepted nine-tenths of the whole " ; and on account of that one-tenth the Tory Government insisted on spending many millions of treasure and of causing the slaughter of many thousands of lives.

The faithfulness of Cremer to the cause of peace and arbitration occasioned the temporary withdrawal from the League of Lord Avebury and other former friends ; but the League remained steadfast to the position it had taken up from the first.

In the midst of the war the Tory Government dissolved Parliament with the object of securing a Tory majority while the country was in the throes of the war-fever. Cremer once more stood for Haggerston. Sir Henry Campbell-Bannerman bluntly declared that the election was a false election, and that the best men among the Unionist Party were ashamed of it. He repudiated with indignation the charge that two-thirds of the Liberals were traitors to their country. His scathing words well deserve to be remembered. "These allegations," he said, "made on the word of a minister and repeated by that minister again and again, marked a depth of infamy and party malice to which no previous Government had ever sunk. What its effect on the voters might be he could not tell, and it would be difficult indeed to estimate it ; but he would say this for himself—that he would sooner see the party with which he was associated suffer the direst defeat at the polls than win a vote by such dishonourable means."

One of the most sensational episodes in this election was the correspondence between Mr. Chamberlain and Mr. Philip Stanhope (Lord Weardale). The latter declared in a speech to his constituents at Burnley that Mr. Chamberlain had whitewashed Mr. Cecil Rhodes because of a threat that if he did not do so a certain correspondence would be read in the House of Commons. Mr. Chamberlain bluntly denied this statement in a telegram ; whereupon Mr. Stanhope declared that he was ready to justify it in a court of law. He subsequently wrote to Mr. Chamberlain as follows :

" SIR,—I am at present without any answer to my letter of the 28th ult., and I observe that in a published letter to a Burnley correspondent you state that I carefully evade any statement which would render me liable to an action for libel. This assertion is the reverse of the truth. What I have said with respect to your attitude in the House of Commons, in regard to the Jameson Raid and your whitewashing of Mr. Rhodes, was said with the utmost deliberation, with a full sense of responsibility, and under the assurance from competent legal authority that I had thereby afforded you substantial ground for action. I took this course as the only one left me after your repeated refusals in the House of Commons to publish the suppressed Hawkesley correspondence and telegrams, which would have settled the matter beyond dispute, and I did so with the avowed intention of provoking you to take the only means to refute the grave charges affecting you. You have, no doubt discreetly, from your point of view, declined to meet me in a court of justice, and everybody can now draw their own conclusions.

" Your obedient servant,
" PHILIP STANHOPE."

Throughout the Haggerston election Cremer strenuously denounced the war as a crime against freedom and humanity. In spite of the war fever, which was still raging, he recovered his seat, the voting being :

CREMER	...	...	...	...	...	2,290
LOWLES	...	...	...	...	...	2,266
Majority	...	...	...	...		24

Among the many congratulations which Cremer received was the following from Sir William Harcourt :

" My dear Cremer,—I do not think any election has given me so much pleasure as your return to Parliament. Your simple, downright, effectual earnestness has been to me always an example of what a real representative of the people ought to be, and I have always regarded you as one of my most trusted comrades in arms. That London should have returned the foremost advocate of the sacred cause of peace is a patch of blue in a black sky."

The trick of the Tory Government in snatching an election before the war was over was highly successful, though their parliamentary majority was out of all proportion to the electoral poll. The total Tory vote was 2,578,492 ; the total Opposition vote was 2,455,518.

During the autumn session of 1900 Cremer managed, notwithstanding repeated calls to order and adverse rulings of the Chairman of Committee, to deliver a strong protest against the vote of several millions for the war. At the conclusion of his speech he ventured on a forecast of the ultimate judgment of the nation as follows :

" I remember what took place during the war in the Crimea. There was then the same difficulty in expressing one's earnest convictions against that war as there has been in reference to the present struggle. But I console myself with the reflection that the verdict of history is always with the friends of peace. There is not a man in this House who will now declare that the Crimean War was a just one, or one that could not have been easily avoided. I am perfectly certain that a rude awakening will come with regard to the South African War, and that before many years have passed we shall have the same kind of feeling expressed by the mass of the people, who have been purposely deluded in regard to the objects of the war, and that it will be difficult to find a man who will stand up and justify the course which has been pursued in South Africa."

That prophecy is already half fulfilled.

CHAPTER XXV

A FRENCH INVASION OF ENGLAND

THROUGHOUT his Parliamentary career Cremer constantly spoke and voted against increased war expenditure. It is unnecessary to speak of these occasions in detail ; suffice it to say that, except when this country was engaged in Indian or Colonial wars the usual plea for an increase of armaments was our strained relations with France, the causes of which need not here be discussed in detail. No doubt there were faults on both sides. French politicians regarded with jealousy our continued occupation of Egypt and our campaigns in the Soudan ; English politicians looked with equal distrust on the French occupation of Madagascar, and the advance of France in Siam and Tonquin. But Cremer's intimate knowledge of the French democracy, and his intercourse with the best men in the Republican party, made him confident that an open rupture with France was inconceivable. His view has been amply justified in recent years. No sane man in this country has any dread of France now. Everybody joins in the *entente cordiale;* it was Cremer's glory that he organised an *entente cordiale* with the French democracy while a large part of the English Press was using the Fashoda incident to clamour for more battleships.

The turning-point was in 1903. Early in that year King Edward paid a visit to President Loubet, which was returned in the summer. Shortly after the King's visit, Cremer expressed his belief that the popularity of our King in France was largely due to the impression that he had used his influence to bring the South African War to a conclusion. Cremer had gone over to Paris just before the King's visit, wishing to ascertain whether members of the French Chamber and Senate would think it desirable to address a meeting of Members of the British Parliament, within the precincts of the House, upon the promotion of an Anglo-French Treaty of Arbitration, and the arrest or diminution of armaments. It would be free from party, and several members on the Unionist side were interesting themselves in the matter.

Cremer had opened up communications with a group of Deputies and Senators in the French Parliament, who had enrolled themselves under the banner of arbitration and disarmament. His object was to get Baron d'Estournelles, who had been instrumental in forming the group, to attend with some of his colleagues and explain to a meeting of British M.P.'s, in one of the grand committee-rooms, the object contemplated by the

French members. The Baron saw at once the advantages of such a meeting.

That success would largely depend upon the nature and character of the invitation may be easily understood. The British group of the Interparliamentary Union or the Liberal Party in Parliament would, if invited, have undertaken to convene the meeting ; but Cremer and his friends felt that it would be a great advantage if the meeting was held under neutral auspices, or even convened by those who had hitherto looked askance at the arbitration movement. So he approached a Committee consisting of M.P.'s belonging to all political parties, whose object was simply to watch over commercial interests. The scruples of the Chairman of this Committee were ultimately overcome, and upwards of a hundred of its members invited eighty members of the French Parliament to a friendly gathering, which ultimately took the form of a banquet. Throughout the negotiations Cremer kept himself as much as possible in the background, and from the moment when the Commercial Committee entered upon the scene he retired, and took no further part in the matter except when privately consulted. This was by no means the first time that the League had initiated a great movement and then effaced itself, leaving the honour and rewards to others. The League, the British group of the Interparliamentary Union, and Mr. Philip Stanhope cordially supported Cremer's efforts, and the friends of arbitration in both countries had cause for rejoicing that the carefully prepared scheme so far succeeded that many politicians who had not previously supported the principle of arbitration by this remarkable demonstration now committed themselves to our cause, and that the Prime Minister, Mr. Balfour, in his frank and manly speech at the banquet, almost expressed his approval of a treaty of arbitration between France and Great Britain.

Baron d'Estournelles, who was the chief speaker, paid a tribute to Cremer and other lifelong workers in the arbitration movement. The Baron's speech was an impassioned appeal for commercial, industrial, and international peace. The Prime Minister, Mr. Balfour, was in capital form ; his reference to a treaty of arbitration between France and England was received with great enthusiasm. Sir H. Campbell-Bannerman's utterance was most felicitous, and that part of his sympathetic speech which was delivered in French was greatly appreciated by the Frenchmen. The only speech which contained a jarring note was that of Mr. Chamberlain.

As soon as Baron d'Estournelles de Constant returned to Paris he wrote the following letter to Cremer :

" My dear Colleague,—I have come back here, and my first duty has been to write to the committee to let them know what an inestimable service you have rendered once more to the cause of arbitration and peace, in preparing, as you did, the reception of my group at the House of Commons. I consider it is my part now to explain what you have done. You have remained willingly behind, but active and devoted. I must acknowledge now your disinterestedness and precious help. I am only sorry not to have seen you ; I think that you ought to have shown yourself afterwards. When I looked for you, you had disappeared like a good fairy."

The Anglo-French Arbitration Treaty was signed on October 14th of the same year by the Marquis of Lansdowne, British Minister for Foreign Affairs, and M. Paul Cambon, French Ambassador to Great Britain. The text of it was as follows :

" The Government of the French Republic and the Government of his Britannic Majesty, signatories of the Convention, concluded at The Hague on July 29th, 1899, for the peaceful settlement of international disputes,

" Considering that by Article 19 of that Treaty, the high contracting parties reserve to themselves the right of concluding agreements with a view to recourse to arbitration in all cases which they shall consider it possible to submit thereto,

" Have authorised the undersigned to agree to the following provisions :

" Article I.—Differences of a juridical order, or such as relate to the interpretation of the Treaties existing between the two contracting parties which may arise between them, and which it may not be possible to settle by means of diplomacy, shall be submitted to the Permanent Court of Arbitration established at The Hague by the Convention of July 29th, 1899, on condition however, that they do not involve either the vital interests or the independence or honour of the two contracting States, and that they do not affect the interests of a third Power.

"Article II.—In each particular case the high contracting parties, before addressing themselves to the Permanent Court of Arbitration, shall sign a Special Arbitration Bond, setting forth clearly the subject under dispute, the extent of the powers of the arbitrators, and the details to be observed as regards the constitution of the Arbitral Tribunal and the procedure.

"Article III.—The present arrangement is concluded for a term of five years from the date of signature."

The following Memorandum was issued from the Foreign Office on the same day that the treaty was signed :

"Lord Lansdowne signed to-day with the French Ambassador an agreement providing that questions of a juridical character or relating to the interpretation of existing Treaties which might arise between Great Britain and France should, if found incapable of settlement by diplomatic means, be referred to the Permanent Court of Arbitration at The Hague.

"It is, however, further stipulated that this

arrangement shall apply only to such questions as do not involve the vital interests, the independence, or the honour of the two contracting parties, and do not affect the interests of a third Power.

" The agreement is the outcome of a movement which, it will be remembered, has recently received a considerable amount of support in both countries, in favour of affirming the general principle of recourse to arbitration whenever that method can be safely and conveniently adopted."

It is a curious fact that the present Prime Minister of France, M. Clemenceau, publicly expressed his disappointment at the limited character of the treaty ; he considered that it contained too many reservations.

It may be added that this treaty has since been renewed for another five years.

The Interparliamentary Conference was held at Vienna in September, 1903. The Austrian Government had placed the Palace of the Reichsrath at the disposal of the Union for its sittings. It was reported that the number of adherents was 2,022, belonging to nineteen different parliamentary groups. Those actually attending were—Austro-Hungary, 62 ; Germany, 29 ; France, 33 ; Great Britain, 14 ; Belgium, 18 ; Denmark, 11 ; Holland, 8 ; Italy, 53 ; Roumania, 34 ; Switzerland, 8 ; Sweden, 5 ; Norway, 4 ; Portugal, 2 ; Spain, 1 ; Bulgaria, 1 ; United States, 1 ; Monaco, 2—in all, 286.

The president was M. Ernest von Plener, ex-minister, president of the Cour des Comptes. At the opening of the first sitting M. de Koerber, President of the Austrian Ministerial Council, said :

Gentlemen,—I have the honour to salute you in the name of the Austrian Government ; and allow me to express our true satisfaction at the high aim which you have pursued during some years. The obligatory introduction of arbitration in case of international disputes between any of the States of the civilised world will be, we trust, the crown of your efforts."

M. von Plener, who presided, said :

" Both States and peoples are penetrated with the great necessity for peace, and the desire to avoid war. This is the clear lesson of the political development of the last twenty years. Treaties of arbitration are more and more multiplying, and public opinion is constantly working in this direction, like the latest approach of the English and French Parliaments, which will strengthen and further the movement for arbitration ; and if this conference did its share to facilitate and hasten this development, it would do a good work, and render a great service to the general progress of humanity."

Count Nigra, the Italian Ambassador, having stated in an address to the conference that Italy was the only Power that always introduced arbitration clauses in all international treaties, a resolution was adopted that in all treaties an arbitration clause should be inserted.

Dr. Gobat (Switzerland) recalled the attitude of Great Britain towards the expressed wish of the President of the United States to bring about a peaceful settlement of the conflict between the South African Republics and Great Britain by offering his good offices, and declared that the proffered intervention was not persevered in because Great Britain made it known that she would be compelled to regard such an offer as an unfriendly act. Dr. Gobat therefore proposed a resolution, which was adopted, providing that an offer of good offices was never to be looked upon by any State as an unfriendly act, and that in the same way no State was to decline the good offices of another.

Sir John Brunner moved a resolution recalling the fact that the first Hague conference was convened, among other things, to consider the burden of armaments. The resolution went on to say :

"Whereas since the Hague Conference the burden of armaments has continually increased, this conference is of opinion that the time has arrived when the project submitted by Russia in 1898 should be again submitted to and considered by another conference."

Some of the German representatives, though expressing a desire for reduction, intimated that they could not vote for the resolution in its present form, but it was carried by a good majority.

Cremer then proposed a resolution which suggested the formation of a Court of First Instance in case of a dispute, consisting of representatives of the Powers concerned, who should appoint a president or request the Hague tribunal to appoint him.

Cremer urged strong reasons on behalf of his proposal. He said :

That the Hague tribunal had for some reason or other not more frequently been resorted to was a matter of regret. Various reasons had been assigned for it ; one distinguished Frenchman who had been a member of the Hague Convention declared that some of the European Powers were attempting to " boycott " the tribunal. Whether they agreed or differed with Baron d'Estournelles, it was clear that from some cause or other many Governments did not look with a friendly eye upon the new authority. It was possible that some nations still entertained a lingering prejudice against submitting their differences to " outsiders," or " foreigners," upon the ground that their verdicts would be influenced by racial, religious, or commercial considerations. If that were so, the nations entertaining these prejudices would be sure to do their very best to settle their differences in a Court of First Instance. The heavy expense incurred by putting the international machine in motion was also assigned as a reason why the small Powers hesitated to appeal to the Hague tribunal. That objection would disappear if Courts of First Instance were established. His resolution, which was only recommendatory, aimed at doing something to fill up the gap between the negotiations of Governments and an appeal to the Hague tribunal. That gap was now too great, and he believed that if it was filled up by a Court of First Instance, the machinery for settling disputes by peaceful means would be vastly improved, if not perfected.

Considerable differences of opinion were expressed in regard to this proposal, and in the end it was withdrawn. The meeting of the conference was attended with a round of hospitalities, the Austrians appearing desirous to surpass anything that had been previously done in that direction.

CHAPTER XXVI

BRITISH INVASION OF FRANCE

In November, 1903, a large number of Members of the House of Commons and several peers paid a return visit and were welcomed, not only in Paris, but throughout France. It was by no means a party demonstration, for a considerable number of the Parliamentarians were Conservatives. The British invaders were received in France from end to end with an unbounded enthusiasm which only an eye-witness could properly describe. I have therefore thought it desirable that in this chapter Cremer should speak for himself ; the account of the progress will serve to show how well this man, who left school at twelve years of age, could express himself in the Press as well as on the platform :

The invading host left Victoria Station on November 25th, by a special train, and crossed the Channel by special steamer ; indeed, the whole journey through France was made by special trains of first-class carriages at very nominal fares, and,

where long distances necessitated, sleeping cars
were provided, and meals in the restaurant cars
were supplied at half the usual charges.   The
hotels through France were equally liberal in their
charges for sleeping apartments.

On arriving at Calais the Prefect of the Department, the Mayor, Municipal Councillors, and
crowds of people welcomed the little army with
enthusiasm.   Instead of being received as past
invaders were, with bullets, bayonets, and the roar
of cannon, refreshments galore were provided in
the buffet, which was charmingly decorated, the
French and British flags being gracefully entwined,
toasts were proposed, fraternal speeches delivered,
the band playing alternately " God Save the King "
and the " Marseillaise."   It was interesting to see
every Britisher, Liberal or Tory, uncover when this
soul-stirring air was being played, and to remember that for generations it was regarded as
the symbol of revolution.   The cordial welcome
and hospitality of Calais was, however, only the
beginning of the triumphal progress which awaited
the invaders in Paris and provincial France.
Amidst vociferous cheering from invaders and invaded the train left Calais and on reaching Paris
the invaders were warmly welcomed in the large
waiting-room at the railway terminus, the room
being decorated for the occasion.   Baron d'Estournelles and the Committee of Reception, which
consisted of fifty Deputies and Senators, had a
kind word for everybody. The Customs authorities,

to the delight of the ladies, who had brought with them piles of trunks, politely declined to examine any luggage ; no prying official was allowed to ruffle the gorgeous costumes and millinery ; these costly adornments were reserved for display at subsequent banquets, receptions, and operas. The following telegram had already been despatched to President Loubet :

"The English Members of Parliament, on setting foot on French soil, send their homage to the Chief of State, and express their joy at the *entente cordiale,* an irrefutable proof of the sincere and lasting friendship existing between the two countries."

Although the travel and the events of the day had been somewhat fatiguing, it was rest itself compared to what was undergone during the next fortnight. The whirl, the rush, the excitement, the receptions, *déjeuners,* banquets, operas, suppers, sight-seeing, excursions, speech-making, hand-shaking, late hours, and early rising, were such as to make it difficult to understand how any one survived to tell the story.

On the following morning the party was divided into groups of about twelve, each group being conveyed to the residences of Senators or Deputies, and entertained at a charming *déjeuner.* The proprietors of the *Siècle* entertained a good number at the Café Durand, and at three o'clock the entire company visited the Chamber of Deputies and the Senate. The Buffet at the Senate had been decorated with flowers, refreshments were proffered, and each lady was presented with a bouquet provided by the President of the Senate.

At five o'clock President Loubet and Madame Loubet gave a reception at the Élysée.

Addressing the company in the great dining-hall, where refreshments had been provided, the President said :

" I thank you who have come here and returned the visit paid by our countrymen to you in London some months ago. I have had from them an account of the sympathetic and cordial reception with which they met in your country. I have by no means forgotten with what courtesy I myself was received in London. The reception accorded to me by his Majesty the king, by her Majesty the Queen, and by all the Royal Family, by all the public authorities, and by the people of Great Britain went to my heart. I desire that your journey, at the same time as it establishes bonds between the Parliaments and societies of the two nations, should help us to draw nearer to the aim which we are together pursuing, in the interests of peace, of civilisation, and of humanity. I cannot allow these few charming moments, which you procure me, to pass without raising my glass to propose the toast of his Majesty the King of England, her Majesty the Queen, the Royal Family, and the whole British nation. In proposing this toast I cannot refrain from recalling the work of peace to which you are so sincerely attached. I have, perhaps, some right to associate myself with it within the limits allowed me by the Constitution, since I have had the honour of receiving the first instigators of this great idea since his Majesty the Tzar of Russia had been kind enough to confide in me on that subject from its inception. The work inaugurated at the Hague Conference is still in its infancy. The two great nations of Western Europe should rejoice at having been the first, by signing a treaty of arbitration, to give an example which will, I hope, be followed by many others. This movement, I am convinced, will not stop, and I am sure of responding to your sentiments, as I respond to those of my fellow-countrymen, in expressing the hope that the work in which we are together engaged may receive its crown."

M. Combes, Prime Minister of France, regretted that as there was no universal language for orators he was forced to speak in French. He was happy to confirm by his presence his adhesion to the splendid work of the International Arbitration Group. No work since the abolition of slavery better deserved the help of generous minds. It was not too much to say that the recent treaty, which consecrated it, did honour to the diplomacy of the two countries. It certainly represented the inner feelings of the two countries. They, the members of the two Parliaments, were representative of the two countries, and it was the two nations, without distinction of parties, who were seated round the tables that night to celebrate the final burial of all their old difficulties. Objections were made to the reservations in the treaty, but they were necessary. M. Combes recalled the ancient dictum that time alone consecrated works in which it had participated. Time had certainly consecrated the diplomatic work which they fêted that night ; imperfect it was, but destined to grow in the future. It was open to every one to consider it as a fruitful germ. The feeble tree would grow into a sturdy oak, beneath which the two peoples would be able to settle such outstanding questions as remained. M. Combes predicted that as time sanctioned arbitration, the reservations which had been made in the treaty would collapse.

The Banquet.

The banquet in the evening at the Grand Hotel, in the magnificent hall, was a sight to be remembered. About six hundred were present. Not only were the members of the French Arbitration Group present, but Deputies and Senators of all shades of opinion. The hall was brilliantly illuminated and decorated with flowers. Over the top table was a trophy of English and French flags, beneath which, in the centre, sat Baron d'Estournelles, supported by Lord Brassey and Sir W. Houldsworth, M. Combes (the Prime Minister), M. Trouillot (Minister of Commerce), General André (Minister of War), M. Pelletan (Minister of Marine), M. Fallières (President of the Senate), M. Jaurès (Vice-President of the Chamber), and

M. Deschanel (ex-President of the Chamber). As
the guests arrived they were received by the bureau
of the Arbitration Group, and as they proceeded
to their places in the banqueting-hall " God Save
the King " and the " Marseillaise " were played.

Everything had been done to charm the eye and
gratify the taste—flowers, music, banners, and a
sumptuous feast, with eloquent speeches to follow.
The menu-card presented to each guest formed a
most interesting souvenir of the occasion. The
front page was devoted to a symbolical picture by
Eugène Carrière, and bore Michelet's prophecy,
" In the Twentieth Century France shall declare
peace to the world." Baron d'Estournelles presided with his usual charm and ability. Appetites
having been appeased, the Baron rose amidst great
applause to address the audience, but before doing
so he read numerous letters of sympathy and regret
at their ability to be present from Members of our
Parliament and Government. Mr. Balfour sent
the following telegram :

"I waited till the very last moment to reply to your invitation
in the hope that circumstances would permit me to come. I am
really grieved to find that official and public engagements
prevent me from accepting your hospitable invitation. It would
have given me great pleasure to return the visit of the members
of the French Parliament, and I beg you to express to them the
great disappointment I feel at being obliged to abandon that
idea."

The Chairman then addressed words of cordial
welcome to the Members of the British Parliament.

He regretted that in the Palais Bourbon there was no hall, as there was at the Palace of Westminster, where a great banquet could be given. The Members of the French Parliament, who, without distinction of party, had associated themselves with the present demonstration of sympathy, were very numerous. The Prime Minister had not waited till now to affirm his attachment to the principle of arbitration. He had enrolled himself in the Arbitration Group when he pronounced last summer in favour of international conciliation. That speech had just been confirmed by the conclusion of the Arbitration Treaty of October 14th. M. d'Estournelles then paid a tribute to M. Frédèric Passy, who had spent his life in the service of peace. He also thanked his guests and all the eminent men who on both sides of the Channel had laboured in the cause of arbitration. Before resuming his seat, he recalled the fact that, as in London, all shades of opinion were represented at the gathering. It was a great achievement to have united all the parties in France. It was the realisation of the speaker's dreams.

Senator Berthelot, Sir W. Houldsworth, M.P., M. Combes (Prime Minister), Lord Brassey, M. Deschanel (Deputy), Sir H. Vincent, M.P., M. Denis Cochin (Deputy), and M. Jaurès followed.

While Lord Brassey was speaking I remembered that the last speech I heard him make was at Stafford House some five years ago, when he ridiculed arbitration treaties, especially an Anglo-

American Treaty of Arbitration. If one had been in a reminiscent mood, it would have been easy to recall the time, not very long ago, when a number of the British M.P.'s then present had pooh-poohed arbitration, and in the House of Commons had sneered at me as an advocate of peace at any price. When Lord Brassey changed his opinions is not known to me, but his speech on this occasion appeared so hearty and sincere that I seized the first private opportunity to thank and congratulate him.

To me, however, the most interesting and remarkable feature of the proceedings was the reception of M. Jaurès, and the effect of his oration. When he rose to address the great gathering very few and very faint cheers greeted him ; but every moment the interest in his utterances visibly increased, bodies were bent forward and necks craned to catch every word, the climax being reached on the conclusion of his beautiful peroration, when the cheering was loud and long. The great Socialist orator and courageous supporter of the disarmament movement in France had extorted admiration from an unwilling audience.

During the evening the following telegram was despatched to King Edward in the name of the French Senators and Deputies :

"The members of the French Parliamentary Group of International Arbitration, assembled this evening with a great number of their colleagues of the English and French Parliaments, address to your Majesty the expression of their hope that these exchanges of visits, of which you set the beneficial example, may continue to strengthen the friendship between France and England, and ensure the maintenance of the peace of the world."

Early on the following day the invaders, by no means exhausted with the previous day's proceedings, gathered together, prepared for another crusade. One wing of the army invaded the studio of M. Toche, the artist who has painted a very large picture commemorative of the great gathering which assembled at The Hague in response to the Tzar's rescript. The picture, which is to be executed in tapestry and placed in the Palace of Peace, contains the portraits of all the delegates to the Hague Convention.

At a reception and *déjeuner* by the Chamber of Commerce several fraternal speeches were delivered. From the Chamber of Commerce to the Hôtel de Ville went the invaders, where they were received by the President of the Municipal Council, the Prefect of the Seine, and a host of other functionaries. Of course, more cordial speeches were delivered, and everybody was shown over the splendid building, which is probably the most beautiful and artistic municipal palace in the world. We then wended our way to the Bank of France, where we were received by the Governor and his wife, Baron Alphonse Rothschild, &c.

The reception and *soirée* at the Palais Bourbon in the evening was sadly marred by the rain,

which descended in torrents, and the absence of
M. Bourgeois, President of his Chamber of
Deputies, who was prevented from receiving the
guests by the serious illness of his wife. To
explain his absence, M. Bourgeois sent the following letter to the Senior Vice-President :

" MY DEAR VICE-PRESIDENT AND FRIEND,—
You know the sad reason which prevents me from
being with you to-night to receive our guests at
the Palais Bourbon. I am extremely sorry for
more reasons than one. The President of the
Chamber would have been most happy to welcome
our colleagues from that British Parliament whose
glorious traditions have so often served as an
example to free assemblies. And the former
French delegate at The Hague would have greeted
with joy the representatives of the great nation
with which we have just concluded a preliminary
arbitration convention. I should have liked to
have fêted with them that treaty, which confirms
the principles symbolised by the Congress at The
Hague. As time goes on, enlightened men of the
world will know how to extend and develop them,
and to secure the triumph of those two great
causes."

M. Bourgeois was represented by MM. Jaurès,
Etienne, and Lockroy, Vice-Presidents of the
Chamber. During the evening I had a long chat
with M. Jaurès and other working-class leaders
upon the remarkable progress and ultimate triumph
of our cause. With M. Jaurès it is a settled con-

viction that the practical stage of the present movement dates from our great demonstration three
years ago at the Bourse du Travail.

The visit to the historic Palace of Versailles on
the day following was delightful. The special
train which had been provided reached Versailles
at noon, and the visitors were heartily welcomed
by M. de Nolhac, Curator of the Museum, representatives of the Municipality, M. Berteaux, and
several other local Deputies and Members of the
General Council of the Department. Leaning over
the upper balustrade of the marble staircase,
M. Berteaux, speaking in excellent English,
reminded his visitors of the many notable
embassies which, in bygone times, had come to
that palace. But, he added, the embassy which
had gathered there that day was the most magnificent of all. The outcome of the visits of some of
those former embassies had not always been happy,
nor had they been peaceful. The outcome of the
visit of the Members of Parliament would, he felt
sure, be not only peaceful, but also beneficial to
the great cause of humanity at large, and that
was why he and his colleagues had so much
pleasure in welcoming their English friends
there.

The Curator then escorted the party through
the various galleries, and returned to the Galerie
des Glaces. Here a halt was called, seats were
provided for the ladies, and in a few minutes
there appeared through the old glass doors a trio

of dancers in delightful eighteenth-century costumes. To the accompaniment of a grand piano and violin, the three ladies, who were the Mlles. Minck, of the Opéra, executed, in a most fascinating manner, a series of eighteenth-century dances.

At five o'clock most of the party returned to Paris, and many of them assembled in the Salle des Fêtes at the Hôtel Continental to receive a medal which the *Siècle* had struck as a souvenir of the occasion. The editor, M. de Lanesan, delivered an eloquent speech, in which he said that the *Siècle* had always contended for a close friendship between Great Britain and France. Three or four English M.P.'s having briefly orated, the party hastened to the Élysée Palace Hotel, where they were received by the British Chamber of Commerce. Municipal Guards, in full uniform, acted as a guard of honour. M. Boddington, President of the British Chamber of Commerce in Paris, welcomed the company, and Lord Brassey replied. The final part of the day's programme was an entertainment, supper, &c., by the Automobile Club in their palatial premises and theatre, which was said by those who attended it to have been delightful. The next day being Sunday proved a veritable day of rest, the only break being a reception at the British Embassy, where there was a great crowd of French and English, the guests being received by Lady Monson, wife of the British Ambassador.

RECEPTION IN THE PROVINCES.

Except the enthusiastic cheers of the crowd at Calais, there had not been, up till now, any proof that the Senators, Deputies, municipal bodies, &c., which had entertained us really reflected the opinions of the people. There was no doubt in my mind upon the subject, and those who were a little apprehensive upon the point had their fears dissipated before we had been many hours *en route* from Paris to Bordeaux, &c.

At Angoulême, although the train was timed to stop only forty minutes, elaborate arrangements had been made for our welcome. A band played the British National Anthem. A large number of the local authorities and notabilities, including the Prefect and Deputy Prefect of the Department, General de Miéry (the Commander of the Garrison), the Presidents of the Chambers of Commerce of Angoulême and Cognac, delegates from Charente, and many others were on the platform. The visitors were escorted to a handsomely decorated saloon, where cordial speeches were exchanged, and the *entente cordiale* toasted in the wines of the country. The ladies were loaded with flowers, baskets of fruit, and other souvenirs. Hearty cheers were given on either side as the train steamed away, the band again playing the national hymns of the two countries. As far as the outskirts of the town crowds had gathered, who cheered as the train went past on its run to Bordeaux.

At Bordeaux the railway terminus had been lavishly decorated. All sorts of functionaries and a crowd of people numbering several thousands were waiting to receive us. There was no longer any doubt concerning the feeling of the people. The banquet given by the Chamber of Commerce was a most brilliant function. About two hundred leading people of the city and department had been invited to meet us. Naturally a great feature of the dinner was the wonderful selection of Bordeaux wines.

The next day the whole party, accompanied by a little host of local notabilities, were taken in a special train to Pauillac, in the Medoc district, so well known to every claret-drinker, and from thence in brakes to the famous Château Lafitte, where, in one of the extraordinary wine-vaults, a *déjeuner* was partaken of by some two hundred guests, Baron Eduard Rothschild presiding. The healths of his guests was proposed by the Baron. Toasts of King Edward and President Loubet were drunk in the costly wines for which the Château is famous all over the world, and in the afternoon the party were taken for a drive through the wine-growing district, back to Pauillac, which was beflagged, and where, at the Hôtel de Ville, the Mayor and Councillors invited us to attend for a few minutes a special meeting of the Town Council. The request was readily granted, and the Mayor, on behalf of the Council, expressed their delight with the object of our visit to France. The cordial welcome extended to us having been acknowledged, the company drove to St. Julien, and then returned to Bordeaux, where the proceedings of the day ended with a special performance at the theatre, and a reception in the concert-hall of the theatre after the performance.

At Marseilles, the second city in France, our reception was equally enthusiastic : delightful drives all through the beautiful city, to every place of interest, along the miles and miles of quays and lovely coast ; by steamer through the wonderful series of docks, a short trip on the Mediterranean ; a *déjeuner* by the " Syndicat d'Initiative de Provence " ; an official reception at the " Bourse du Commerce " ; a banquet by the " Council of the Department " at the Prefecture ; and a reception by the Mayor and the Municipal Councillors at the ancient and historic Hôtel de Ville, or Town Hall.

A Dramatic Incident.

After receiving the guests at the Hôtel de Ville, the Mayor, in very complimentary terms, referred to my long-continued efforts to cultivate and cement friendly relations between France and England, especially between the workers of the two countries. Up till this time I had not spoken at any of the various functions. I knew, however, that several Liberal M.P.'s had insisted that the newly-converted arbitrationists who were bossing the tour should accord me a place in the programme, but how the Mayor could have become so well acquainted with my labours was a surprise, unless he had been coached either by a deputation of workmen members of the Departmental Council General, who had come from the Department to see me and shake hands again, or had gained his information from some of my colleagues. As, however, the Mayor had spoken of me in such eulogistic terms, I could not refuse his request to address the audience. In my ten minutes' speech I referred to the cordial feeling between the two countries, and the Arbitration Treaty which had been concluded as the outcome of efforts, some of which I mentioned, which were begun by the workmen of England and France thirty years ago, and which had been continued ever since ; between the French and British workmen there had never been any feeling of jealousy or animosity. In England and France they worked together harmoniously, and the victory which had recently been gained by the signing of the Arbitration Treaty was really a people's victory. On the conclusion of my speech the Mayor left his place, came out and embraced me, and kissed me on both cheeks.

This unexpected and dramatic incident, which startled everybody present—no one more than myself—ended with a hearty cheer from the audience. Several Frenchmen, the British Consul, and the British chaplain thanked me for what I had said. Indeed, one enthusiast went so far as to say that the speech ought to be fully reported

and circulated all over France. A charming concert followed, and on the following morning, amidst
hearty cheers from a great crowd assembled at
the railway-station, we left for Nice.

From Marseilles to Nice, through the beautiful
Riviera, is an ideal journey. It was a glorious day
of sunshine, the blue water of the Mediterranean
rippled and sparkled, the olive-trees were in leaf,
the orange and lemon trees were loaded with fruit,
and in the distance towered the snow-clad Alps.

At Cannes there was a brief halt while the Mayor
came on board the train to welcome the party and
express the pleasure it would afford him to receive
them on their return journey.

Welcomed at Nice by the Municipal Authorities,
on the evening of our arrival, a gala performance
of *Pagliacci* was given at the Municipal Casino,
followed by supper in the magnificent reception-
rooms. Several speeches were made, all couched
in the most cordial tone of friendship and goodwill. Next day the whole party were taken in
motor-cars to Monte Carlo.

No language could adequately describe the
matchless scenery on the thirty miles' route from
Nice to Monte Carlo; but the terrific speed of the
cars, up and down hills and round sharp curves,
kept our nerves in a state of tension, and rendered
it impossible for any one to fully appreciate the
wonderful panorama.

An excellent *déjeuner* had been provided, at the
Grand Hotel, by the Automobile Club, and all of

us visited the Casino, famous (or infamous) for the gambling that goes on there. To visit table after table, and watch the continually varying moods of the gamblers, is an object-lesson.

In the evening, at Nice, a splendid banquet was given by the municipality, followed by a gala performance at the opera, and a midnight lunch. On the following day a number went to Cannes, lunched with the Mayor, and made more fraternal speeches. Before leaving Nice, all the ladies of the party were presented with a magnificent bouquet of Riviera flowers—indeed, splendid bouquets were presented to them at every place where the train stopped, and at all the banquets, receptions, *déjeuners*, &c.

Three stoppages were made on the journey from Nice to Lyons, the first at Agan, where the Mayor and Councillors came to greet us and present us with boxes of dried fruits, a speciality of the district. At Toulouse Station the party were received by the Mayor, Councillors, a great crowd of people, and a band of music. Toasts were proposed, healths were drunk, speeches made, the crowd cheered, the band played the National Anthems of both countries, more floral tributes were offered to the ladies, and everybody was delighted at the heartiness of our reception.

At Carcassonne two hours were occupied in visiting the ancient castle and seeing the quaint old town. I have seen a great many castles, but none so remarkable as this. So extensive is it

that in former times the whole population lived
within its walls. Proud of their historic building,
the local authorities had provided us with vehicles
from the station to the castle and back.

On arriving at Lyons it poured with rain, and
had, as we were informed, done so for several
hours. What our reception would have been had
the weather been fine can only be imagined ; as it
was, the big railway-station was filled with all the
functionaries of the city, anxiously awaiting the
arrival of our train, which was two hours behind
time. Outside the station the scene was still more
remarkable, an enormous crowd, numbering at least
three thousand people, were standing, and, as we
were told, had been standing there in the rain for
two hours. The right hearty welcome accorded
us by the crowds inside and outside the station
was indicative of what followed.

Commenting upon what occurred at Lyons, the
Special Correspondent of the *Standard*, who was
with us during the whole tour, said, on December
8th, in his telegraphic message to that journal :
" One of the most notable features of the
reception at Lyons was the part played in it by
the working-class population. The crowd which
greeted the delegates at the railway-station was
many thousands strong, whilst for nearly three
hours a mass of at least five thousand people stood
patiently in the rain outside the brilliantly illumin-
ated Hôtel de Ville in order to cheer the Englishmen as they drove to the banquet. So anxious

have all the co-operative bodies of the city been
to entertain the British visitors, that the greater
part of the day has been occupied with two banquets
and the reception which the Prefect of the Rhône
Department is giving in their honour this evening.
At noon to-day the delegates were the guests, at
the Hôtel de l'Europe, of the Republican Committee of Commerce and Industry—that powerful
organisation which quite recently entertained in
Paris the members of the London Commercial
Association. M. Mascuraud, the president of the
association, was in the chair, and he was supported
by the Prefect and the Mayor of Lyons, and about
a hundred and fifty of the commercial and industrial notabilities of the city. M. Mascuraud,
in an interesting speech, pointed out that it was
the commercial representatives of the two countries
who had been specially responsible for the
rapprochement. He was sure the Parliaments of
the two countries would help them in their efforts."

The banquet at the Hôtel de Ville was a brilliant
affair, and it was past midnight before the toast
list and fraternal speeches were concluded. In
his opening speech the Mayor, who is a Socialist
doctor, said in a much applauded speech that if
they desired peace with anybody, it was with Great
Britain, whose markets were so widely opened to
the products of the industry of Lyons.

On the occasion of the Mayor's opening
address, he called upon me to speak. In response
to the invitation, I thanked the workmen of Lyons

for their past co-operation in the efforts we had made, congratulated them upon the success which had been achieved, and hoped they would continue their efforts until the end had been reached. Referring to the Treaty of Arbitration just concluded, I said that I did not regard it as the end, but as a means to the end, that end being a mutual and simultaneous reduction of armaments, the burden of which had become intolerable. President Loubet and our King had carefully noted the signs of the times and seized the proper moment to unite France and England by a treaty of peace. It was true that the treaty was limited in its scope, but it will go on gathering strength ; every example it sets will become a precedent, precedents will multiply, crystallise, and harden into rule, rules will become law, and, ultimately, law will triumph over brute force. It was very gratifying to receive from so many of my colleagues and others congratulations upon the remarks I had made.

What struck me as the most remarkable feature at this great gathering was, not that Lyons should have a Socialist Mayor, and that he should be advocating arbitration and peace, but that he should be supported upon the occasion by the Prefect of the Department, by the military Governor of Lyons, the Commander of the local Army Corps, a Divisional General, and many others occupying responsible positions. It was a good omen, full of significance.

At every banquet, &c., which we had attended the menu cards were so artistic that many brought them away as souvenirs, but Lyons eclipsed all that had been done in the way of menus. Instead of cards, satin, which is largely manufactured in the city, had been used. For beauty of design and exquisite workmanship it would be difficult to surpass the Lyonnaise menus ; they were quite works of art, which will be long treasured as mementos of the historic visit. In addition to the list of dishes, wines, &c., upon the menus, one of them had inscribed upon it, in beautiful letters, the following :

" BANQUET OFFERT À L'HOTEL DE VILLE DE LYON AUX PARLEMENTAIRES ANGLAIS."

The inscription on the other was :

" BANQUET OFFERT À MESSIEURS LES MEMBRES DU PARLEMENT BRITANNIQUE PAR LE COMITÉ REPUBLICAIN DU COMMERCE ET DE L'INDUSTRIE, SECTION LYONNAISE, HOTEL DE L'EUROPE, LYON, LE 8 DECEMBRE, 1903."

Our second day at Lyons was occupied in partaking of an excellent *déjeuner* given by the " Republican Committee of Commerce and Industry," visiting silk factories and the wonderful waterworks which supply the whole city with electricity, finishing up with a magnificent banquet and concert in the " Palais du Commerce." Again it rained and yet again a great crowd had gathered outside the imposing edifice in which the banqueting-hall was situate. The building, the banquet, the speeches, and the music, were alike unique. It happened to be a fête day. The whole city was illuminated, partly on account of the fête and partly in honour of our visit.

On the following morning we left for Paris, the Prefect, councillors, and others being at the station to bid us adieu. A two hours' stay was, however, made at Dijon, where a deputation from the Chamber of Commerce was waiting upon the platform. A large cheering crowd had gathered outside the station in the pouring rain. The streets through which we were driven to the historic palace of the former Dukes of Burgundy were lined with people, and nearly every house displayed French and English flags. Having inspected the palace (which is now the Town Hall) and museum, we were escorted to the Chamber of Commerce, which had been converted into a tastefully decorated dining-hall, and, having partaken of an excellent *déjeuner*, made fraternal speeches and drank toasts in the wine of the country.

Our tour was now at an end ; the events which had been crowded into the seventeen days since we had left London were epoch-making events. We had been making history, the first page of which was begun in July with the banquet at the House of Commons, the last page concluded with the extraordinary reception at Dijon. With my rôle in initiating the first " Great Invasion," which led up to the Second Invasion, I am delighted.

About 8 o'clock we arrived at Paris, where I found a telegram which ten days before had been forwarded by the Nobel Committee, announcing that they had awarded me the Nobel Prize.

CHAPTER XXVII

WHEN the Interparliamentary Union met at Vienna, Mr. Richard Bartholdt suggested that the next conference should be held at St. Louis, where a great international exhibition was to be held. The enormous distance to be travelled seemed at first a formidable obstacle, but ultimately the invitation was accepted and, as will be seen, with the happiest results. The United States Congress voted £10,000 to provide hospitality for the guests, who visited New York, Philadelphia, Pittsburg, Chicago, Kansas, Denver, and other American cities. Out and home, the British members of the conference, twenty-four in number, travelled over ten thousand miles and everywhere were received with enthusiasm. At St. Louis representatives attended from fifteen Parliaments—some hundred and fifty in number.

Mr. Richard Bartholdt presided over the conference, and it was reported that ten additional arbitration treaties had been signed since the last gathering at Vienna. Naturally the disastrous war between Russia and Japan was a prominent topic of discussion, and the conference adopted the following resolution :

"The Interparliamentary Conference, shocked by the horrors of the war that is being waged in the Far East between two civilised States, and regretting that the Powers signatory of the Hague Conventions have been unable to have recourse to the clauses thereof which invite them to tender their mediation at any time after the outbreak of hostilities, entreats the Powers signatory of the Hague Conventions to intervene with the belligerents, either collectively or individually, in order to facilitate the restoration of peace, and instructs the Interparliamentary Bureau to bring the present resolution to the knowledge of said Powers."

It will be recollected that President Roosevelt took the initiative in bringing this struggle to a conclusion, and thus rendered a great service, not only to the Powers concerned, but to humanity at large.

Mr. T. E. Burton, a United States Congressman, moved an important resolution, which had been drawn up by Mr. Bartholdt, requesting the President of the United States to convene a second Hague Conference, which after full discussion was adopted in the following form :

"Whereas, enlightened public opinion and the spirit of modern civilisation demand that differences between nations shall be settled in the same manner as controversies between individuals—that is, through courts of justice and in conformity with well-recognised principles of law—therefore,

"The Conference asks that the different Powers of the entire world delegate representatives to an international conference,

which shall meet at a time and place to be designated by them,
to deliberate upon the following questions :

" (a) The subjects postponed by the Hague Conference ;

" (b) The negotiation of arbitration treaties between the
nations which shall be represented in this conference ;

" (c) The establishment of an International Congress which
shall meet at stated periods to discuss international questions ;

" And decides to request, respectfully and urgently, the President of the United States to invite all the nations to send
representatives to such a conference."

Originally it had been intended that the members
of the conference should proceed first to Washington, but as the visit was deferred they had the
opportunity of presenting the resolution in person
on September 24th, when President Roosevelt made
a memorable speech. After expressing his hearty
sympathy with the objects of the Interparliamentary
Union he went on to say :

" In response to your resolutions, I shall at an
early date ask the other nations to join in a second
congress at The Hague. I feel, as I am sure
you do, that our efforts should take the shape
of pushing forward toward completion the work
already begun at The Hague, and that whatever is now done should appear, not as something
divergent therefrom, but as a continuance thereof.
At the first conference at The Hague several questions were left unsettled, and it was expressly provided that there should be a second conference. A
reasonable time has elapsed, and I feel that your
body has shown sound judgment in concluding that
a second conference should now be called to carry

some steps farther toward completion the work of the first. It would be visionary to expect too immediate success for the great cause you are championing, but very substantial progress can be made if we strive with resolution and good sense toward the goal of securing among the nations of the earth, as among the individuals of each nation, a just sense of responsibility in each toward others. The right and the responsibility must go hand in hand. Our efforts must be unceasing, both to secure in each nation full acknowledgment of the rights of others and to bring about in each nation an ever-growing sense of its own responsibilities. At an early date I shall issue the call for the conference you request."

This announcement was received with the utmost gratification, most of all by Cremer. It was seventeen years since he first visited the White House to advance the cause of arbitration, and after many difficulties and almost heart-breaking delays, at seventy-six years of age he stood there triumphant.

At the end of October President Roosevelt redeemed his promise by the issue of a circular note, signed by Mr. Hay, the Secretary of State, which the United States Ambassadors were directed to present to the Foreign Minister of the country to which they were accredited.

During this visit Cremer addressed large gatherings at New York, Boston, Cambridge, Worcester, and Niagara Falls, and a final banquet was held at the Arlington Hotel, Washington. The thanks

of the Interparliamentary Union having been
tendered to Mr. Bartholdt, he called upon Mr.
Slayden, a Member of Congress, to "propose a
toast to the man most worthy to be toasted that
night." The whole assembly rose and drank to
Cremer, who was then called on to speak. He
recalled the fact that he and a few others, one of
whom was present (Mr. John Wilson, M.P., of
Durham), had presented to the then President of
the United States a memorial for the promotion of
an arbitration treaty. He believed the President
alone might succeed in accomplishing the aims of
the resolution by inviting the nations to assemble,
as suggested therein. But Edward VII. of England
was devoted to the cause of peace, was justly called
Edward the Peacemaker, and if the President of
the United States, in issuing the invitation, would
associate himself with Edward VII., the cause was
won, without doubt and without delay.

Cremer, who was almost overcome with emotion,
added : "This day is the crowning event of my
life." He did not anticipate that there were greater
triumphs yet to come.

Early in 1908 Mr. Elihu Root, the United States
Secretary of State, and Mr. Bryce, the British
Ambassador, drafted and signed a treaty of arbitra-
tion which was subsequently ratified by the Senate.
In this treaty it was declared that, with certain
reservations, differences between the two Powers
should be referred to the Permanent Court at
The Hague for a period of five years. The second
Article, however, ran as follows :

" In each individual case the high contracting parties, before appealing to the Permanent Court of Arbitration, shall conclude a special agreement defining clearly the matter in dispute, the scope of the powers of the arbitrators, and the periods to be fixed for the formation of the arbitral tribunal and the several stages of the procedure. It is understood that such special agreements on the part of the United States will be made by the President of the United States by and with the advice and consent of the Senate thereof, his Majesty's Government reserving the right before concluding a special agreement in any matter affecting the interests of a self-governing Dominion of the British Empire to obtain the concurrence therein of the Government of that Dominion. Such agreements shall be binding only when confirmed by the two Governments by the exchange of notes."

This provision was adopted in order to satisfy the United States Senate, which has always been jealous of its powers in regard to the making of treaties. Cremer expressed a strong opinion that this treaty was very inferior to those which had previously been drafted, and he was probably right ; but considering the cause of the failure of former efforts, Mr. Root and Mr. Bryce went as far as they could go with any hope of success. When Cremer first visited Washington, in 1887, he doubtless would have been content with the conditions laid down in the second Article, but the cause had greatly advanced since then, and the delays involved with reference to the Senate appeared to him very disappointing and even dangerous, inasmuch as the success of arbitration depends largely upon the fact that the machinery is quite ready for use. In my own judgment Cremer's view was too pessimistic ; the treaty was not all that could have been desired, but it was well worth twenty years of patient and persistent effort. On this occasion, in consequence of the poverty of the League, Cremer for a second time crossed the Atlantic at his own charges.

CHAPTER XXVIII

THE NOBEL DINNER

In December, 1903, it was announced that the Norwegian committee had awarded the Peace Prize to Cremer, who happened to be travelling in France at the time. Alfred Nobel, a Swedish chemist, who was the inventor of dynamite, devoted his fortune to the annual distribution of five great prizes to the men who had done the most in literature, medicine, physics, chemistry, and the promotion of the peace of the world. The first four prizes under his will are awarded by the Swedish Academy ; but the fifth is awarded by a committee of five Norwegians, of whom Björnson is the most distinguished member.

From the first a few of Cremer's comrades knew of his intentions as to the disposal of the money, more especially the five persons whom he invited to become trustees ; but the Annual Report of the League, which was presented in March, 1904, was altogether silent on the subject. Probably many of those who assembled at the Holborn Restaurant on May 4th of that year to do honour to Cremer had

no idea whatever of the surprise that was in store.
It was quite enough for them that the splendid
services that Cremer had rendered to the cause
had been so fully recognised. So many had been
the applications for tickets that the issue had to be
stopped. Some two hundred guests assembled in
the Venetian Chamber, including Lord Kinnaird,
Lord Monkswell, Lord Weardale, the Bishop of
Hereford, Mr. Andrew Carnegie, Mr. Thomas
Burt, M.P., who presided, and about twenty other
Members of Parliament. Nearly all the members
of the council of the League were present, and a
goodly contingent of Cremer's constituents from
Haggerston. Karl Blind represented the older
generation of Continental democrats ; M. Brœk-
stad represented Norway ; M. Danielson, the
Swedish Consul, represented Sweden ; Mr. Naoroji
and Sir Henry Cotton, India ; the Mayors of
Shoreditch and several Aldermen and Councillors
represented municipal London, while Fareham,
Cremer's birthplace, sent the chairman of its Urban
District Council ; journalism was represented by
Sir F. Carruthers Gould, the great cartoonist, Mr.
Wm. Hill, Mr. A. E. Fletcher, Mr. Passmore
Edwards, and Mr. Chiozza Money ; literature by
Mr. Silas Hocking ; law by Sir John Macdonell,
Mr. Thomas Shaw, M.P. (now Lord Shaw), Mr.
Corrie Grant, and Mr. B. F. Hawkesley, the legal
adviser of Mr. Cecil Rhodes, who must have felt
himself in strange company ; Mr. Isaac Mitchell,
Mr. Charles Freak, Mr. Washington Chapman,

Mr. W. Coffey, and Mr. W. Matkin stood for trades unionism ; Mr. Vivian, Mr. Gray, jun., and Mr. Maddison for the co-operators."

The greetings of absent friends were numerous and hearty. Lord Hobhouse wrote of Cremer : " He has worked for peace, the greatest of blessings, with a single eye and heart and in a most practical manner by promoting the construction of living machinery for its preservation." Sir William Harcourt wrote : " It has been to me a sincere satisfaction to know that Cremer had received in the Nobel prize a recognition which he has so worthily earned, and in which his friends are assembled to rejoice. He has happily lived to see some happy developments of the cause to which he has been so long devoted and in which he knows how heartily I sympathise with him." Earl Carrington wrote : " May I be permitted to express the deep feeling of gratitude so many of us feel towards a great Englishman who has devoted his life to so great a cause? He strives for an ideal, not for fancy." Lord Avebury wrote : " Please express to Mr. Cremer my warm congratulations. He will remember I seconded his resolution in the House of Commons." The Baron d'Estournelles de Constant wrote : " Nobody admires Mr. Cremer's work more than I do, and it would give me deep satisfaction to express my congratulations on behalf of my French colleagues for the well-deserved reward he has received from the Nobel committee." Dr. Clifford wrote : " I heartily congratulate Mr. Cremer, and rejoice in this recognition of his long and eminent services, not only to England, but to the larger life of the world.   As much as, yea, more than most, he has proved that he holds that God is not the God of the Anglo-Saxon only, but of all men and of all peoples."   Similar congratulations were sent by the Norwegian committee, the Marquis of Ripon, the Marquis of Bristol, Sir George Newnes, Sir Wilfrid Lawson, Mr. Hodgson Pratt, and many others.

The chairman, Mr. Burt, in proposing the toast of " The King as Pacificator," suggested that a telegram should be sent to his Majesty expressing the thanks of those present for the noble efforts he had made on behalf of peace and goodwill between the nations.   This was agreed to by acclamation.

Mr. Burt, in proposing the toast of the evening, said :

" LADIES AND GENTLEMEN,—We have met tonight to do honour to my good and esteemed friend Mr. Cremer.   Mr. Cremer has for many years—for nearly forty years to my own knowledge —been associated with great and good movements for the improvement of man.   He has devoted his talents, his energies, devoted all that he has, with rare courage, persistency, and disinterestedness to the promotion of the great cause of peace between nation and nation.   Well, we all rejoice that his services in that respect have been recognised in a very tangible way. It is, indeed, an instance of a deserving man getting the right thing, and we know that whatever the future may have in store of life, time, and strength will, as in the past, be devoted to the improvement of humanity. We hope that he will long live, and I should like him to be happy too. I feel perfectly sure that he will live a noble, useful, and honourable life as in the past, and I ask you now to drink to the health of Mr. Cremer."

Cremer, on rising to respond, was enthusiastically received. After describing the provisions of the Nobel trust and the circumstances under which he had received the Nobel prize he went on to say :

" It is thirty-three years since a handful of working men started the organisation which is now known as the International Arbitration League. What we have succeeded in doing during that long period is a tempting theme upon which I should like to discourse ; but I leave that pleasurable task to others.

" One instance, however, of ' something attempted, something done,' I cannot refrain from recording.

" When we started, the first of the three objects embodied in our programme was *to advocate the settlement of all international disputes by arbitration, and the establishment of a High Court of Nations for that purpose.*

" Of course, we were scoffed at, and ridiculed as dreamers, or idiots ; but to-day Governments and nations appear to be vieing with each other in concluding treaties of arbitration, and a High Court of Nations HAS been established.

" A great tribunal has not only been set up, but it has come to stay ; and, thanks to the munificence of our friend Mr. Carnegie, it will have its permanent home in a Palace of Peace.

" It would be interesting to trace the modern development of the arbitration movement ; how the question was lifted on to a higher plane, and first took a practical form by the joint efforts of the British Parliament and the United States Congress to conclude an Anglo-American Treaty of Arbitration ; what a great impetus was thereby given to the movement ; how the Interparliamentary Conferences grew out of that effort ; how the Tzar was influenced by the Interparliamentary Conference at Buda-Pesth to issue his Rescript, which led to the Hague Convention, from which sprang the Hague Tribunal. All these things, however, are matters of history.

" I confess, Mr. Chairman, to having been an idealist and a dreamer, but many of my dreams have been fulfilled, and to-day I think I can see the near realisation of another long-cherished dream and hope which I scarcely dared believe would ever be realised.

" Only those of us who during the long, long years worked, watched, and waited for the advent of a new era, and who opposed any Government which left the path of peace and embarked in warlike enterprises, can understand the tremendous odds against which we had to contend, or the number of times the League has been penalised for daring to practise the precepts of Christianity.

" The penalty which the League several times had to pay for this fidelity to principle was an empty treasury, and for months the secretary had to live without the receipt of his scanty wages.

" These repeated attempts to intimidate the League, however, failed, and it was the experience gained during those trial times that made me long for an opportunity of doing something to place the League in a position of independence.

" Well, thanks to the Nobel committee, I am now in a position to make an effort to do so, and I trust I am not too sanguine in the hope that my feeble efforts may be supplemented and completed by others.

" What I want to do is to permanently establish a great organisation to promote the cause of arbitration and peace.

" There is still a mighty work to be done. All the vested interests will be marshalled to oppose disarmament, which is, of course, the great object at which we aim—arbitration as the means, disarmament as the end, has always been our motto.

" So far, therefore, as I am able, I am going to endow the International Arbitration League, taking care that in the trust deed which has been prepared a condition of receiving and continuing

18

to receive the interest upon the endowment shall
be that the sum so received shall be supplemented
by a specified amount derived from subscriptions
and donations, that the council of the League shall
never number less than twenty-four, and that two-
thirds of that number shall be working men.   I
have purposely specified working men, because the
industrial classes are, for weal or woe, going to be
the future rulers of the world.

" Before I conclude I wish to thank my dear old
friend for presiding upon this, to me, momentous
occasion.   It is nearly forty years since we
joined hands and began to toddle on the path
of progress.

" To Mr. Carnegie, both for his presence and
the inestimable services he has rendered to the
cause of peace and progress, I tender my sincere
thanks.   What he has done for the cause no one
present is so well acquainted with as I am.

" I also heartily thank my brother Members of
Parliament for their presence.   To the electors of
Haggerston, who by four times returning me to
Parliament greatly increased my power and influ-
ence, I wish, through those that are present, to
express my gratitude.

" Finally, sir, I tender to the council of the
League my heartiest thanks for their unselfish devotion and zeal.   Some members of the council have
been my kind friends and co-workers ever since the
League was formed ; and during those long years
there has never been (except on very few occasions,

when questions of policy were being considered) any difference between us.

"To the perfect harmony which has prevailed I largely attribute whatever success has attended our efforts.

"The best proof I can give of my confidence in them, and my sincere belief that when I am gone they will continue the great work, is to hand over to them the trust deed, which has been carefully prepared, a deed which conveys to them the sum of £7,000.

"No act of my life has afforded me greater delight, and I earnestly hope that the amount will, either by gift or bequest, be increased to £25,000 —a sum which, if properly invested, would provide the League with a permanent annual income of £1,000."

Amid a scene of great enthusiasm Cremer then handed over the Nobel prize to the trustees whom he had previously selected. These were—Howard Evans (journalist), George Procter (engineer), Charles Greedy (carpenter), John Morgan (cabinetmaker), and Isaac Mitchell (secretary of the Trades Union Federation). The deed of gift imposes upon the trustees certain conditions, the most important of which is that they shall only pay to the League the interest on investments provided the subscriptions and donations do not fall below a certain amount.

A pleasing incident of a personal character may here be placed on record. Cremer had lost some

part of his savings in the " Liberator " smash.
Quite unknown to him, a friend whose name I
have forgotten, happened to mention this fact to
Mr. Carnegie, who thereupon wrote to Cremer
saying that he had long desired to show his appreciation of Cremer's services to the great cause,
but did not know how to do so. He thought that
the time had now arrived, and intimated that he
had placed to Cremer's credit in the Pittsburg
Company an amount covering his loss.   This
amount, with interest, remained untouched till the
Nobel prize was awarded, when it was added to the
Cremer trust.

Here it may be stated that Cremer was so
anxious to secure a permanent home for the International Arbitration League that he subsequently
handed to the trustees an additional £1,000 to
serve as a nucleus of a building fund. This sum
has now been merged in the Cremer trust, inasmuch as by the deed of gift the trustees have
power to devote any of the funds of which they
have charge to the purchase or erection of a
building.

This was not the last of Cremer's benefactions
to the League. Very shortly before his death he
intimated his intention to make a further gift of
some hundreds of pounds. Death prevented the
direct accomplishment of his purpose, but under
his will the League is the residuary legatee. Probably, from first to last, Cremer returned to the
League the whole of his small salary and some

£4,000 besides—a splendid record for a man who in his earlier days was sometimes reproached as a professional agitator.

Mr. John Wilson, M.P., who had accompanied Cremer on his mission to America and had attended most of the Interparliamentary Conferences, proposed the toast of "Our Friends Across the Sea," coupling with it the name of Mr. Carnegie. Mr. Thomas Shaw, K.C., M.P., in an eloquent speech, supported the toast.

Mr. Andrew Carnegie declared that he had never witnessed a nobler act of self-abnegation than that of Mr. Cremer. He added : " I wish, on behalf of your friends across the sea, to say that they participate with their friends here in placing upon your head, sir, the laurel, not as the hero of barbarism, the man who has won victory over his fellows, but as one who has gained the glorious victory over his lower self and consecrated his highest powers to the cause of humanity. Among the greatest of those who have worked in this noble cause will be the name of William Randal Cremer." Mr. Carnegie subsequently added £1,000 to Cremer's gift.

The Bishop of Hereford, who followed, said : " I feel, and you feel with me, that the real men to whom we owe the chief debt of gratitude for all the progress which has been made, and which we are hoping to see, some of us, before we die, are not the great ones as they are called, but, if I may use the phrase, the men who have been doing the spade work, the pioneers who have been living their lives and doing their work in this great cause : to such men as Mr. Cremer, and many others who might be mentioned, we owe the chief debt of gratitude ; and I think our greatest gratitude of all is owing to them, not for the work which they do, but for the spirit which they infuse into the common life, and our hope is that there may rise up an army of younger men who may be worthy to carry on this warfare of peace in which Mr. Cremer has been our great leader, and whom we are proud to follow.''

Mr. Henry Cust, M.P. (Conservative), Lord Weardale, Mr. H. L. Brœkstad (Norway), and Mr. F. Maddison also spoke. The latter said : '' Our friend Mr. Cremer for over forty years has been in the forefront of the battle for human betterment. Beginning as a trade unionist, he remains one. Starting his public life with a passion for liberty, he is still an ardent fighter for freedom. In his early manhood he dreamed of a world without war ; in his old age he has seen international arbitration enter the domain of practical politics, and even into the sphere of high world statesmanship. Our cause can never be lost, for it is as undying as the Eternal Light. When Mr. Cremer is called to pass to the higher life, in that supreme moment it will be a source of enduring satisfaction that he has tried to do good.''

A little while previously a number of Cremer's

constituents presented him with a handsomely illuminated address, which ran as follows :

THIS TESTIMONIAL PRESENTED

AT THE SHOREDITCH TOWN HALL ON
WEDNESDAY, FEBRUARY 17TH, 1904,

TO W. RANDAL CREMER, M.P.,

By his Friends and Admirers to Commemorate the
awarding to him of the

NOBEL PRIZE

For his indefatigable Labours in the CAUSE OF PEACE,
extending over a Period of 30 Years, culminating in the
signing of a Treaty of Arbitration between
England and France. With the sincere Hope that he
may be spared for many Years to continue his Labours in so
sacred a Cause.
Signed, on behalf of the Committee,

J. J. FREEMAN, Chairman.

CHAPTER XXIX

THE INTERPARLIAMENTARY UNION AT WEST-
MINSTER

CREMER'S crowning triumph was the assembly of
the Interparliamentary Union in the Royal Gallery
of the House of Lords in 1906. The British
Group had grown to 350 members, Lord Weardale being president and Cremer hon. secretary.
Upon these two, more especially upon the latter,
fell the main burden of organising the gathering,
which was itself a formidable task ; and they
had efficient co-workers in the treasurers, Sir John
Brunner and the late Colonel Sir Howard Vincent.
It may be observed here that the League had never
been an exclusively Liberal organisation, but has
numbered among its supporters men like the late
Marquis of Bristol, Lord Avebury, and Mr. Agg-
Gardner, who do not belong to that party. It
was at first contemplated to hold the meetings
in the Foreign Office ; but the accommodation
proving insufficient, by the gracious permission
of the King, and with the cordial co-operation of
Mr. Lewis Harcourt, it was arranged that the

meetings should be held in the Royal Gallery
of the House of Lords. The architect certainly
had never thought of its acoustic properties, and
a temporary sounding-board had to be placed over
the platform ; the decorations were by no means
of a pacific character, for Wellington and Nelson
looked down from the walls upon men who believed
that " Peace hath her victories not less renowned
than war."

What a splendid gathering it was ! The British
representatives present numbered 252 and the
foreign 356, making a grand total of 617. No
less than 22 Parliaments were represented, including even those of Russia, Mexico, and Japan.
What a contrast from the first meeting in Paris,
when in 1889 barely a hundred met, under the
presidency of Jules Simon, and these almost exclusively English and French !

Lord Weardale, who presided, in his opening
address paid a merited tribute to Cremer as the
founder of the Union. As he himself had been
present at the first conference at Paris, and at
all those that followed, he rapidly sketched the
rise and progress of the Union, which included in
its ranks 2,500 members of various Parliaments.
In particular he alluded to the notable meeting at
Buda-Pesth, when they formulated their plans for
the creation of an International Tribunal, from
which sprang the first diplomatic conference at
The Hague. In conclusion, he said : " We have
won an acknowledged place in the world. The

cause of peace is making triumphant progress. It is no longer the subject of public derision or of indifference ; on the contrary, it is gradually imposing its principles on the conscience of humanity. We are resolutely advancing towards a brighter future. With confidence we await the time—to-day no longer distant—when no Government or people will resort to arms without having in the first place made a supreme appeal to conciliation and international justice ; and we foresee as a consequence the progressive reduction of the heavy burden of military and naval expenditure. Our voice is making itself heard. Our purely moral influence asserts itself even in the highest spheres. Illustrious men associate themselves with our efforts. The last conference in Paris was presided over by M. Fallières, now President of the French Republic. In the United States we were received by President Roosevelt, who addressed us in a memorable and historic speech."

The Prime Minister, Sir Henry Campbell-Bannerman, who, like Lord Weardale, spoke in French, gave a hearty welcome to the conference in the name of the British Government and of the nation, and added : " I have the honour to announce to you that I am authorised to welcome you in the name of the King, whose services in the cause of peace are known to you all, and who has expressed a special interest in this historic gathering."

Sir Henry congratulated the conference on the fact that since 1903 no fewer than 38 arbitration treaties had been signed by various Powers—10 of them by Great Britain, thanks to Lord Lansdowne. This country has taken a leading part in the movement, for we owe to the Government of the late Lord Salisbury and to our delegates at the first Hague Congress the initiation of the permanent tribunal of arbitration.

Sir Henry recalled the utterance of M. Fallières, the President of the French Republic, when he occupied the chair of the Union at the Paris Conference in 1900: " Gràce à vous, nous sommes déjà loin de l'epoque où la conception de l'arbitrage était considérée comme un jeu de l'esprit ou une hardiesse condamnée par ce que l'on a coutume d'appeler, partout où se dresse une opposition injustifiée, la ' sagesse des nations.' Aujourdhui, il faut faire le part de l'évidence. Des tentatives que ont abouti sont là démontrer qu'il en est des peuples comme des hommes, et que, pour les prémiers comme pour les seconds, il n'y a pas de résistance qui ne disparaisse, à la longue, devant la toute-puissance d'une idée, quand cette idée puise sa force a la source sainte de la fraternité ! "

In discussing the question of armaments, Sir Henry reminded the conference of the words of the Tzar of Russia in convening the first Hague Congress : " The financial charges consequent on this state of things strike at public prosperity at its very source. The intellectual and physical

strength of the nations, labour, and capital are
diverted from their natural application and unproductively consumed.   Hundreds of millions are
devoted to acquiring terrible engines of destruction,
which, although to-day they are regarded as the
last word of science, are destined to-morrow to lose
all value in consequence of some fresh discovery
in the same field."

Sir Henry said : " Thanks to Lord Lansdowne,
Great Britain has signed with ten other States conventions in virtue of which will be carried before
the permanent Arbitration Court, seated at the
Hague, all legal questions which may arise between
the two contracting Powers, and all questions which
concern the interpretation of treaties and cannot be
settled by diplomacy."

Sir Henry went on to say : " Is it not evident that
a process of simultaneous and progressive arming
defeats its own purpose?   Scare answers to scare,
and force begets force, until at length it comes to
be seen that we are racing one against another
after a phantom security which continually vanishes
as we approach.   If we hold with the late Mr. Hay
that war is the most futile and ferocious of human
follies, what are we to say of the surpassing futility
of expending the strength and substance of nations
on preparations for war, possessing no finality,
amenable to no alliances that statesmanship can
devise, and for ever consuming the reserve on
which a State must ultimately rely, viz., the well-
being and vitality of its people."

In conclusion, Sir Henry gave a special welcome to the seven members of the first Russian Douma, the dissolution of which body had just been announced. Amid a scene of indescribable enthusiasm, the whole audience rising to their feet, Sir Henry said : " New institutions have often a disturbed, if not a stormy, youth. The Douma will revive in one form or another. We can say with all sincerity, ' The Douma is dead : long live the Douma ! "

Professor M. Kovelevsky, the spokesman of the Douma, said in response : " Our first legislative assembly believed itself to be called to express for your work its lively sympathy, and delegated us for this reason to represent it in your conference. Our mission comes abruptly to an end, but we return to our country with the unshakable resolution to continue the great fight for our freedom and for the peace of the world, henceforth inseparable."

On the motion of Count Apponyi (Hungary) the following telegram was sent to King Edward :

"The Interparliamentary Conference now in session has received with profound gratitude his Britannic Majesty's gracious message of welcome and respectfully desires to express an earnest hope that his Majesty may long be spared to promote the welfare of the British people and the cause of international peace."

It would be obviously impossible within the limits of this chapter to give even a summary of the debates at the conference ; a few of the most important points under discussion must suffice.

Freiherr von Plener (Austria) presented the Report of the Commission on a Model Treaty of Arbitration, which was ultimately adopted. Mr. W. J. Bryan (who subsequently stood as the Democratic candidate for the Presidency of the United States) moved the following amendment, which he supported in an eloquent speech : " If a disagreement should occur between the contracting parties which, in the terms of the arbitration treaty, need not be submitted to arbitration, they shall, before declaring war or engaging in any hostilities, submit the question in controversy to the Hague Court or some other impartial international tribunal for investigation and report, each party reserving the right to act independently afterwards." This amendment, in a somewhat modified form, was accepted by the conference.

Baron d'Estournelles de Constant (France), who was present in an official capacity at the first Hague Congress, and who has since rendered distinguished service to the cause of peace in his own country, presented an elaborate Report on the limitation of armaments. It is perhaps worthy of notice that the Baron and Cremer had rather serious differences as to the future organisation of the Interparliamentary Union, but as soon as Cremer's death was announced the Baron sent a letter to the present writer expressing the warmest appreciation of Cremer's energy and devotion. M. d'Estournelles de Constant pleaded strenuously, not so much for a diminution as for an arrest of armaments.

M. Messimy, the reporter of the Naval and Military Budget in the French Chamber of Deputies, followed with a statistical account of the war expenditure of the various Powers. He ended with this remarkable suggestion : " I should like to see a small number of delegates, strong in the support of this great and illustrious assembly, and regularly invested by the political groups which, in each Parliament, have to deal with international arbitration, assemble within a few months in a town which it may please you to specify. The sole object of this meeting would be to discuss the means to be employed in civilised countries—or in Parliamentary countries, it is all the same—for putting an end to the increase of military budgets, and to maintain them within the limits of the figures which they have at present reached."

Mr. John M. Robertson, M.P., moved a resolution urging the Hague Congress to make the arrest of armaments the subject of serious consideration, and it was supported by Professor Eickhoff (Germany). All the world now knows that the British Government took the initiative in this matter and that Germany prevented its discussion.

M. von Plener (Austria) brought up the Report of the commission appointed to draft a model treaty of arbitration. This was constructed more especially for the use of States that were not yet ready to adopt arbitration without any reserve. It should be noted that Denmark and one or two other Powers had adopted arbitration treaties without any

reserve at all. M. Eickhoff (Germany) observed
that substantially the model treaty presented by
the commission followed the lines of that concluded
between Great Britain and Germany in 1904. This
model treaty was unanimously approved. The advantage of such a model is obvious, considering
that there are about sixty independent States, and
if each adopted a different form, more than three
thousand treaties would be required.

The conference was entertained at a *déjeuner*
in Westminster Hall, at which nearly a thousand
guests were present. The Lord Chancellor (Lord
Loreburn) presided, and the vice-chair was occupied by Mr. Emmott, Deputy Speaker of the
House of Commons, the Speaker himself being
absent through domestic bereavement. Lord
Loreburn in his speech said he would express
his sympathy with the purposes expressed by Mr.
Bryan with respect to arbitration. If time and
deliberation could only be secured, the dangers
of war would almost disappear, and he was looking
forward to the time when those who had in
obscurity struggled for that cause would stand,
in the opinion of mankind, alongside the greatest
heroes who had secured victories in time of war.
Count Apponyi, Mr. Bryan, and Baron d'Estournelles de Constant followed. It must have been
a proud moment in Westminster Hall for the
humble carpenter who, thirty-six years before,
had commenced with only a score or two of
workmen around him, and with his own lodgings

for an office ; yet from first to last in the
official record of the proceedings, which was
compiled by himself, his name does not appear
among the speakers. This man was always to the
front when necessary work was to be done, and
was always ready to efface himself when that work
could be done by others.

It only remains to be said that the members of
the conference afterwards visited Windsor Castle
by special invitation of the King. After an inspec-
tion of the multitudinous art treasures, the whole
of the royal apartments being thrown open, the
visitors made their way to the lawn and slopes in
front of the castle, where a military band dis-
coursed sweet music, while an ample supply of
refreshments was served in the orangery.

Lord Weardale and Sir Charles Maclaren gave
receptions to the foreign visitors, a large number
of whom visited Southampton and Portsmouth
Dockyard. The proceedings concluded with a
popular banquet at the Crystal Palace, over which
the Duke of Argyll presided, in the absence of
Mr. Balfour.

It should be added that, at the instance of Sir
Henry Campbell-Bannerman, a sum of £5,000 was
voted by the House of Commons for expenses in
connection with the meeting of the Interparliamentary Union in London, the Union being an
entirely non-party organisation, including members
who sit on both sides of the House.

In 1908 the Government undertook to propose
19

in Parliament an annual grant of £300 in aid of
the expenses of the permanent organisation of the
Union, and it is expected that before long this
example will be followed by the Governments of
some of the other Great Powers.

CHAPTER XXX

SECOND HAGUE CONFERENCE

In the autumn of 1905 the Interparliamentary Union met at Brussels, the Chamber of Deputies having been placed at its disposal, and it was officially received by the King and the Belgium Parliament. M. Beernaert (ex-Prime Minister) presided, and nineteen Members of the British House of Commons were present. For the first time in the history of the Interparliamentary Union the United States occupied a prominent position. At the outset a cablegram was sent to President Roosevelt, thanking him for his good offices in bringing the Russo-Japanese war to a conclusion, and congratulating him upon his success.

One result of the St. Louis conference of the preceding year was to excite greater interest on the part of United States Congressmen. Before that conference the United States had occasionally a solitary representative ; at Brussels the number had increased to eighteen. Until recent years the majority of the people of the United States had taken but a philanthropic interest in questions of arbitration and disarmament ; but the rapid increase of the United States navy, and the rise of the Japanese power in the Pacific has brought about a change. At both Brussels and London the United States Congressmen took a prominent part in the debates. Mr. Richard Bartholdt brought forward a draft of a general treaty of arbitration and also a project for the establishment of an International Legislative Congress. The latter scheme contained somewhat dubious provisions. For example, it proposed that the armed forces of the nations represented at the said congress should be placed at the service of the congress for an enforcement of any decree by the Hague Court according to the treaty of arbitration. These proposals were referred to a commission for examination. The conference further discussed the questions of war loans and of the obligatory nature of arbitrations.

Two events of this year rejoiced the hearts of all the friends of peace. The South American Republics of Chili and Argentina concluded a treaty which was in some respects an advance on anything that had been previously achieved. It provided that all disputes between the two countries should be adjusted by arbitration, unless the Constitution of either country was involved. Yet further a convention was drawn up by which the contracting Powers agreed to desist from acquiring vessels of war that were then being built or from making new ones for a period of five years, notice to be given by either Power of its intention to abrogate the Convention a year and a half beforehand. These two Powers yet further agreed to reduce their fleets, and, what is more remarkable, engaged themselves not to sell any war vessels to countries that had questions of dispute pending.

In December the same year Sir Henry Campbell-Bannerman, who had just become Prime Minister, delivered a great speech at the Albert Hall, London, in which he said :

" I rejoice that the principle of arbitration has made great strides, and that to-day it is no longer counted weakness for any of the Great Powers of the world to submit those issues which would once have been referred to the arbitrament of self-assertion and of passion to a higher tribunal. I hold that the growth of armaments is a great danger to the peace of the world. A policy of huge armaments keeps alive, and stimulates, and feeds the idea that force is the best, if not the only solution of international differences. It is a policy that tends to inflame old sores and to create new sores, and I submit to you that as the principle of pacific arbitration gains ground, it becomes one of the highest tasks of a statesman to adjust those armaments to a newer and happier condition of things. What nobler *rôle* could this great country assume than at the fitting moment to place itself at the head of a League of Peace through whose instrumentality this great work would have been effected? "

Almost on the same day M. Jaurès in the French Chamber expounded the foreign policy of the Socialist Party in France as follows : " That which we maintain with like firmness and force is constantly to increase the action of the proletariat of all countries, in order that, by its collective and combined action, it should anticipate as far as possible the explosion of wars, and if they break out in spite of us, to reduce to impotence, from one end of Europe to the other, the criminal Governments which have let loose the storm ; to reverse an abominable European system of oppression and disorder which holds society under the tyranny of anarchic rivalry and the peoples under the tyranny of war.   As a sign of this new European spirit we demand that the Government of the French Republic shall propose to all nations for the settlement of disputes which may arise between them the systematic and universal practice of international arbitration."

The second Hague Conference met in August, 1907, M. Nelidoff, who represented Russia, presiding. No less than forty-four sovereign States sent delegates to the conference. It was known beforehand that any proposal in regard to the limitation of armaments would have no immediate result ; nevertheless, at the instance of our Government, Sir Edward Fry introduced the question in a powerful speech, and concluded by proposing the following resolution :

"The conference confirms the resolution adopted by the conference of 1889 in regard to the limitation of military charges; and in view of the fact that military charges have considerably increased in almost all countries since that year, the conference declares that it is highly desirable that the Governments should resume the serious study of this question."

This proposal was supported by the representatives of the United States, Spain, Argentina, Chili, and France. M. Bourgeois, who represented France, said : "In the name of the French delegation I declare our support of the proposal formulated by Sir Edward Fry, and upheld by our colleagues of the United States of America. The first delegate of the French Republic, remembering that he was in 1899 the initiator of the desire of the first conference, will perhaps be allowed to express the confident belief that between now and the meeting of the next assembly the study to which the conference invites the Governments in the name of humanity will be resolutely pursued."

MM. Drago and Concha, who had themselves negotiated the treaty of disarmament between Argentina and Chili five years previously, supported the British proposal, as did also M. Nelidoff, the president, who represented Russia, and the resolution was then carried without a dissentient voice.

The friends of peace had hoped for something more substantial than this academic resolution. As all the world knows, it was Germany that stood in the way. This is not the place to argue the question whether her reasons were justifiable ; it is sufficient to record the fact, and to acknowledge that under the circumstances it was impossible for our Government to proceed farther. As Sir Henry Campbell-Bannerman said at the Lord Mayor's banquet :

" Our delegates did all in their power, and if greater results were not obtained, it must be borne in mind that all progress in these matters depends on general consent, and that any attempt to force the pace beyond the general goodwill of nations is bound to have a negative result, and may even lead to friction, which is a good deal worse than the negative result."

In other respects the second Hague Conference was by no means fruitless. In regard to arbitration the following addition was made : " In case of dispute between two Powers, either of them is empowered to address to the International Bureau at The Hague a declaration that it is prepared to submit the dispute to arbitration." It was also agreed not to have recourse to armed force for the recovery of contract debt, claimed from the Government of one country by the Government of another country, on behalf of private creditors, unless arbitration had been refused, or an arbitration award had not been submitted to.

A number of conventions were drawn up with the object of limiting the rights of belligerents, into which it is unnecessary to enter in detail. Suffice it to say that by these conventions the use of submarine mines and torpedoes was limited, the bombardment of undefended places was forbidden, as also the discharge of projectiles and explosives from balloons ; and arrangements were made for the re-creation of an International Prize Court.

In addition to the conventions, the final conclusions of the conference contained the following paragraphs :

" The conference is unanimous—

" 1. In admitting the principle of compulsory arbitration.

" 2. In declaring that certain disputes, in particular those relating to the interpretation and application of international agreements, should be submitted to compulsory arbitration without any restriction."

It is greatly to be regretted that the Powers represented at the second Hague Conference did not come to an unanimous decision to abolish the seizure of private property at sea by a belligerent. Here Great Britain stands in the way. So long as private property is liable to capture, every Power which has an expanding trade and growing colonial interests must be expected to maintain a large navy in order to protect its commerce. In the judgment of not a few high authorities who have studied this question the key of the present unfortunate situation is to be found here. Our possible gain in the event of war is far counterbalanced by the loss which we constantly sustain through the long years of peace.

CHAPTER XXXI

THE FINAL EFFORT

At a meeting of the Council of the League in March, 1908, Mr. F. Maddison proposed that a fraternal address to the workers of Germany should be prepared and should be presented by a deputation. In May Cremer reported progress. The address was drawn up, and was signed by some three thousand officers of working men's societies, as well as the whole of the forty-eight labour M.P.'s. Although old age and enfeebled health were visibly telling upon him, Cremer threw himself into this movement with renewed energy. To collect the adhesion of so large a number of representative men in a brief time was obviously no easy task, but Cremer had an efficient assistant in Mr. Edward G. Smith.

Hitherto in this biography very sparing use has been made of documents issued by the League, partly because the ordinary reader is apt to skip over such matter, partly because most of these documents were the joint work of Cremer and the present writer. The German address, however, was entirely Cremer's own work, and was, indeed, the last thing to which he put his pen. It is therefore given *in extenso*.

"THE WORKERS OF BRITAIN TO THE WORKERS OF GERMANY.

"BROTHERS,—In the past, wars were generally caused by the dynastic quarrels of monarchs, the intrigues and wrangling of statesmen, religious bickerings and persecutions, or racial prejudices. Some of these, indeed, still remain as potent causes of mischief, but to-day the most powerful agency for evil is that portion of the Press which is owned and controlled by unprincipled capitalists, and we are pained at the frequent attempts of these journals to create strife between your country and ours ; but we assure you that these sinister attempts are neither prompted nor endorsed by the workers of Britain. For many years the same evil agencies were successfully employed in creating dissension between the workers of France and ourselves, the people of both countries being taught to hate each other and waste their resources by rivalling each other in militarism and armaments, the almost incalculable cost of which had to be defrayed by the British and French peoples. Not only were these wasted millions extracted from the toilers, but for generations the people of both countries fought and killed each other like savages, the only persons who profited by the carnage being the usurers and personally interested classes. The masses paid and fought ; the interested classes reaped the fruits of their insensate folly. At last, however, after long years of persistent efforts, peace has been secured by a treaty of arbitration being concluded between the two countries. That treaty is a triumph for the workers of Britain and France, for it was they who, thirty-seven years, ago, amidst obloquy and scorn, pioneered it, and ultimately secured its adoption. The treaty was speedily followed by a convention appointed by the British and French Governments, which easily discovered a way of settling all the outstanding differences between this country and France. The Report of that convention was ratified by the French and British Parliaments, with the result that the dread of invasion entertained in both countries no longer exists, to the disadvantage of Stock Exchange gamblers and panic-mongers, but to the ultimate advantage of the industrial classes generally. What is there to prevent the workers of Germany and Britain from doing what France and Britain have done? You and we have no quarrel, or cause of quarrel, with each other. It is not only our desire, but our interest, that harmony between us should be unbroken, and yet it frequently happens that a number of journals in both countries deliberately invent and circulate malicious statements concerning the ill-will of Germans towards us and our ill-will towards you. That feeling may be entertained by bellicose journalists and other interested persons, but it is not shared by the workers, who extend the hand of friendship to you, the workers of Germany.

" Those who come to you with this fraternal message, and all whose names are appended, while rejoicing at the progress which has been made in systematising arbitration and so providing an alternative method of settling disputes, are sincerely anxious that the same amicable relations shall be established between Germany and Britain that now exist between this country and France. In this spirit and with this hope we approach you. Differing, as many of us do, in our political, social, and religious opinions, we are united in believing that peace is not only the breath of life, but the first and indispensable condition of progress. Strong in that belief, we desire to forge another link in the chain of human brotherhood, and to make the chain binding together the peoples of Germany and Britain so strong that the united powers of evil shall be unable to break it asunder.

" But all our hopes and aspirations, however important they may be, are subsidiary to the mighty problem of how to reduce the crushing burden imposed by militarism and costly armaments.

" We believe that, with some exceptions, monarchs and statesmen really are desirous of avoiding war, although some of them have peculiar views as to the best means of preserving peace ; but, whatever may be the views of rulers, the producers of wealth have every reason for settling disputes without fighting each other. The quarrels of nations are not of their making, but they have to pay the cost of war and shed their blood.

" We have no mandate to speak for the workers of France, but from our knowledge of them we venture to express the belief that the *entente* they have concluded with us they would be rejoiced to extend to you ; and with the workers of Britain, France, and Germany united in demanding that arbitration shall be substituted for war, the pernicious influence of the exploiters and panic-mongers and their journals would be weakened, the peace of Europe would be less likely to be broken, and millions of money wasted on armaments would cease to be extracted from the pockets of the toilers.

" We shall be glad to exchange communications with you or receive a return visit from you."

Past experience had taught us the absolute necessity of making preparations beforehand on the spot when a foreign capital was to be visited. As Cremer was the only man who was well acquainted with some of the labour leaders in Berlin, he was requested by the council to pay an early visit to that city, and in spite of growing weakness he was already preparing to do so, when he was attacked by a sickness which soon proved to be fatal. To the last his heart was in his work. Only a few days before his death, when he was almost speechless, the present writer spoke to him of an approaching council meeting, at which final preparations were to be made for the presentation of the Berlin address. To the question," Shall I tell them to go forward? " he nodded assent, and then murmured, "But I want to be there." Alas! it was not to be.

Cremer, however, had the consolation that he had made all possible preparations for the continuance and enlargement of the work of the League. His gift of the Nobél prize and of a large part of his own savings had delivered it from the poverty by which it had been so often crippled, and his own successor had been already chosen.

Some years previously, in the agony of an attack which seemed likely to be fatal, Cremer discussed with the present writer who should be chosen as the next secretary. We both fixed on Maddison, who was not then in the House of Commons. Cremer recovered,, and for some years continued his work. But as age advanced he more than once expressed a wish to retire, and as the council urged him to remain he insisted that at any rate his successor should be appointed. The Emergency Committee (a sort of cabinet of the League), after conference with both Cremer and Maddison, recommended the council to choose Maddison, and this was ratified by a unanimous vote. Here it may be as well to say that when the vacancy did actually arise, Maddison left the council absolutely to choose whom they would, but again the vote was unanimous. It was no small comfort to Cremer on his dying bed that the banner of arbitration as it fell from his palsied grasp was raised again by so stalwart an arm.

CHAPTER XXXII

IN MEMORIAM

OF Cremer's fatal illness there is little to be said. Early in the second week of July, 1908, some of his friends in the House of Commons noticed that he seemed to be ailing. He remained at home for a day or two, and when his doctor was called in he pronounced it to be a case of pneumonia and ordered the patient's removal to a nursing home, where he was treated with constant solicitude. A large number of Members of Parliament and other friends called upon him, but as he was practically speechless, only a few of the most intimate, such as Lord Weardale, Mr. J. G. Weir, M.P., Mr. Maddison, Mr. Edward G. Smith, and the present writer could be admitted to the sick-chamber. Almost at the last moment Cremer rallied, but on the morning of July 22nd all was over.

By his will the executors, being his friends John Morgan, George Procter, and Howard Evans, were directed that his body should be cremated, and the ashes buried in the grave of his second wife, Lucy, at Hampstead Cemetery, and that not more than

£100 should be expended on a memorial-stone. Certain decorations, medals, &c., were left as heirlooms to the League, and a small pecuniary legacy and some ornaments to a nephew. The residue of his small property was to be handed over to the League, but with an important reservation.

Cremer had for some time conceived the idea of erecting four almshouses at Fareham in memory of his mother, but he died before he could fully carry out his intentions. He left, however, a memorandum to his executors, in which, without fettering their freedom, he expressed the desire that they would complete the work he had begun. The executors have already taken steps to comply with the wishes of the testator, and the cottages are now ready for occupation.

On the announcement of Cremer's death his nearest friends at first contemplated a funeral service at St. Margaret's, the Church of the House of Commons. Archdeacon Wilberforce, the Chaplain of the House, was consulted, but as he was confident that no eulogistic speeches would be allowed, and as Cremer's friends regarded these as indispensable, arrangements were made that the service should be held at Whitefield's, Tottenham Court Road, from whose platform Cremer had again and again advocated the cause of peace.

The funeral *cortège* started from Lincoln's Inn Fields, the hearse being literally covered with beautiful floral tributes, some of them " cabled " by American friends, and one sent by Baron

d'Estournelles on behalf of the French group. The
mourners included Mrs. Pyle (sister), and Mr.
Pyle, Mr. Wilson (brother-in-law), Mr. W. Cremer
(nephew), and Mr. Tutte (cousin), also the
Cremer trustees, the executors, and nearly all the
members of the council.

At the church there was a large assembly.
Among those present were the Prime Minister,
Archdeacon Wilberforce (Chaplain of the House of
Commons), the Right Hon. Thomas Burt, M.P.,
and many other members of Parliament.

The Union of Peace Societies, the Peace Society,
the International Arbitration and Peace Society,
the American Peace Society, the Liverpool, Bristol,
and Birmingham Peace Societies, the Haggerston
Liberal and Radical Association, and many other
bodies were also represented.

The service commenced with a hymn, " O God,
our help in ages past." Then Mr. Silvester Horne
read appropriate passages of Scripture and offered
a touching prayer, after which the following brief
addresses were delivered :

Mr. Howard Evans said that in the early days
of the movement they were regarded as fanatical
dreamers, but their objects had so far been realised
that nobody laughed now. He continued : " I have
no time to dwell upon the work that our friend
Cremer accomplished, to refer to his repeated
missions to the United States, where the work of
the unofficial ambassador of the democracy was
warmly welcomed by statesmen and diplomatists.

I pass over those great peace demonstrations in Paris which our friend organised, the greatest being on the morrow of Fashoda, when three thousand French workmen assembled in the Bourse du Travail and M. Jaurès was the chief speaker, uttering words of true fraternity. I pass over also that memorable scene when after our friend had received, and deservedly received, the Nobel prize, he handed it over to myself and fellow-trustees, subsequently adding to his gift £1,000, and it was only a day or two before he was struck down that he had arranged with me to meet him in order to hand over a further sum. I come to the creation of the Interparliamentary Union in 1889, when Jules Simon presided over some ninety-nine French and British Deputies and Members in Paris. Year by year, as you know, that gathering, increasing in strength, met in various capitals ; and, as we have reason to believe, a perusal of the proceedings at Buda-Pesth led the Tzar of Russia to issue the first call for the conference at The Hague. Two years ago, by permission of King Edward the Peace-maker, over six hundred Members of various Parliaments in all parts of the civilised world met in the Royal Gallery of the House of Lords, and were addressed by Sir Henry Campbell-Bannerman, while the great Sacrament of Peace was celebrated in Westminster Hall, the Lord Chancellor presiding. Our Lord Jesus Christ, as we have been reminded, bestowed His blessing on the peace-makers. I think that the best way in which to

study ancient prophecies is to strive for their fulfil-
ment.   It is written of the reign of the Prince of
Peace : ' They shall beat their swords into plough-
shares, and their spears into pruning-hooks, neither
shall they learn war any more.'   Whatever doubts
disturbed the mind of our departed brother, he had
faith to believe this.   Is this life worth living?
Who can doubt it, with such a record as our friend
and brother has left behind?   Let the record of
his eighty years inspire you who are yet in the
morning of life."

Lord Weardale said : " I have been asked, as an
old friend and comrade of Sir William Randal
Cremer, to say some few words to-day at this sad
ceremony on behalf of the British Interparliamentary Group, of which he was for so many years
the honoured secretary, and of the Interparliamentary Union, of which he was the founder.   Our
friend lived, as we all know, a long and laborious
life.   He has passed away in the plenitude of
years, but those years have been a period of continuous effort, and they have not been wasted.
Of the seed which he has sown we can see some
fruit already upon the tree ; but another generation
will see, I think, a glorious harvest, for he has
preached the gospel of the future, the gospel which
teaches us that international quarrels as well as
private ones should not be decided by the sword,
but by the principle of international law.   The
dawn of that era is close at hand.   In every
country witness is borne to its truth.   I have been

asked to day, on behalf of the French Parliamentary Group, and in the name of Baron d'Estournelles de Constant, to lay a wreath upon the coffin of his friend, and I have also received a telegraphic message from the German Group of Interparliamentary Union and also from the President of the Italian Group, as well as many telegrams from elsewhere, all testifying to the fact that the fame and the work of our friend are not confined to this land, but have spread all over the world ; and in saying farewell to him to-day we say, it is true, farewell to his mortal remains, but his life teaching and example will be imperishable records in the world."

Mr. F. Maddison, M.P., said : " In such a solemn moment as this silence seems more fitting than the sound even of the most friendly voices, and I think it seems more appropriate, for our dead leader was a pathetically lonely man. He lived in an upper room, solitary and alone, and he died in a nursing home, where, I am delighted to know, he was faithfully ministered to. On such an occasion as this there is no room for sadness. With regard to his life open before us only joy can predominate. It is a guarantee of the progress of the race. Born in poverty, he enriched humanity. He was a practical reformer. He saw in this latter day of civilisation and of Christianity that war still scourged the world. He examined it in his simple way, and came to the conclusion, which the world is yet going to ratify, that it was

absolutely unnecessary. But he did more. He
pointed the better way—the way of reason, the way
of progress, the way of truth. His memory will be
an abiding inspiration, and his example a continuous
stimulus. His earthly task is over, his life's work
is ended ; but, standing here before that coffin,
I should be false to myself if I did not say that
I do not believe that that life is done. It came
from God and has gone to God by the same
eternal law which causes the river to find the sea.
We sorrow not as those who have no hope. At
this moment, as generations before us have
done, we peer into that mysterious future which
superstition has peopled with terrors, gloom, and
darkness, but which rational religion radiates with
everlasting hope. We say with Lewis Morris :

> "'Somewhere he is, though where we cannot tell,
> But wheresoe'er he is God hides him well.'"

Mr. Horne then gave out the concluding hymn,
" It came upon the midnight clear," the last verse
of which was sung with great fervour :

> "For lo ! the days are hastening on,
>   By prophet-bards foretold,
> When with the ever-circling years
>   Comes round the age of gold ;
> When peace shall over all the earth
>   Its ancient splendours bring,
> And the whole world send back the song
>   Which now the angels sing."

After the Benediction the Dead March in " Saul " was played, the great congregation remaining standing till the coffin was removed.

The following messages were received amongst many others :

FROM MR. ANDREW CARNEGIE.

" DEAR LORD WEARDALE,—I only received Mr. Evans's wire last evening, too late to attend the memorial service of our dear lamented friend, which I wished very much to do.

" Only now I realise at its value my intercourse with that noble character ; how poor seem the ordinary lives of men compared to his—self-seekers after fame or riches, his the noble pursuit of making earth, this life, more worthy of the heaven which he sought to establish among his fellows.

" Mr. Evans, or some one equally conversant with our friend's long life, should devote himself to producing a memorial volume for general circulation as the ideal of a twentieth century hero ; the hero of civilisation as contrasted with that of the barbarous past—the man who devotes his life to ' serve or save his fellows,' in contrast to him who kills or maims him. Truly I know of no finer, more heroic life than that of Cremer. It should be held up for the imitation of men."

FROM PROFESSOR EICKHOFF, PRESIDENT OF THE
    GERMAN GROUP OF THE INTERPARLIAMEN-
    TARY UNION.

" Please receive expression of the sincere grief
of the German Group at the death of their distinguished friend, Sir William Cremer.

                              " EICKHOFF."

FROM M. AUGUSTE BEERNAERT, EX-PREMIER OF
    BELGIUM AND PRESIDENT OF THE BELGIAN
    GROUP.

" We hear with the greatest surprise of the death
of Sir Randal Cremer. As I am unacquainted
with his relatives, I address to you the regrets and
sympathy of all the members of the Belgian Group.
I beg you to make this known to your colleagues.

                          " A. BEERNAERT."

FROM THE BARON D'ESTOURNELLES DES
                CONSTANT.

" We beg you to express at Cremer's funeral
our profound regret. As a pioneer of arbitration
his memory will remain imperishably with us as
will also his accomplished work."

FROM THE DANISH GROUP OF THE INTERPARLIA-
MENTARY UNION.

" In the name of the Danish Interparliamentary
Group we send you our sincere condolences on the
death of Sir William Randal Cremer, the founder
of the Interparliamentary Conference.

" N. NEERGAARD, President.

" FREDERIC BAJER, Secretary."

A memorial meeting was held at the Memorial
Hall on October 23rd, when a large number of
Cremer's friends assembled. Appreciative letters
were read from absent friends, including the Bishop
of Hereford, the Dean of Durham, Archdeacon
Wilberforce, and Miss Peckover. Sir Samuel
Evans, the Solicitor-General, wrote : " I have the
greatest admiration and affection for Cremer. He
did noble work, quietly and unobtrusively, and his
memory deserves to be kept alive." Mr. Geo.
Cadbury wrote : " A generation hence Sir Randal
Cremer will be looked upon as infinitely nobler
than the men who have risen to a reputation by the
slaughter of their fellows."

Lord Weardale presided, and in a sympathetic
speech proposed a resolution recording the high
appreciation of the long and eminent services that
Cremer rendered to the cause of international
peace.

Among other speakers who followed was Lord
Kinnaird, who said : " The more one learned of

Sir Randal the more one learned to respect him. He was a man of strong convictions and was not ashamed of sticking to them and of letting people know that he had them." Sir Brampton Gurdon, M.P., said : " Their friend was always ready to work and never spared himself. He always kept modestly in the background, but always gave unstinted labour for the cause he loved. At the Interparliamentary Conference held in London he almost excelled himself. That gathering would ever remain a monument of administrative skill. It marked a very successful and definite step towards the foundation of universal peace." The Rev. W. Cuff, of whose tabernacle many of Cremer's constituents were members, said that he had been behind the scenes at parliamentary elections and he knew something about temptations that came to the man who was going to fight a constituency, but he never knew Sir Randal do a tricky thing. He went straight, acted straight, and everywhere won confidence and respect. Mr. H. J. Wilson, M.P., said : " There was a kind of splendid audacity in the thought that Cremer originated long years ago, and he educated the world to a very large extent up to his ideas. There was one thing which fitted him exactly, and that was the account of a boy who was asked why, when Daniel was put in the lions' den, the lions did not eat him. The boy replied : ' Because half of him was backbone and the other half grit.' That appeared to have been very much the case with

CREMER COTTAGES AT FAREHAM.

To face p. 314.]

Cremer." Those were qualities which were very much wanted in England to-day.

Brief eulogistic addresses were also delivered by Sir Wm. Collins, M.P., Mr. Pirie, M.P., Mr. John Wilson, M.P., Mr. Idris, M.P., Mr. Bowerman, M.P., Mr. A. King, M.P., Mr. Walter Hazel, Mr. J. Argyle, and Mr. Howard Evans.

CHAPTER XXXIII

" HE BEING DEAD, YET SPEAKETH "

THE presentation of the fraternal address to
German workmen surpassed all Cremer's previous
triumphs. It was preceded a few days before by
a meeting of the Interparliamentary Conference in
Berlin, at which no less than twenty-one countries
were represented, including Austria-Hungary,
Great Britain, France, Germany, Italy, Belgium,
Holland, Denmark, Russia, Japan, Norway,
Sweden, Portugal, Roumania, Switzerland, Spain,
Canada, and the United States. The British group
was represented by about sixty members, headed
by Lord Weardale. Prince von Bülow, the
Imperial Chancellor, in opening the proceedings,
was supported by the chief Ministers of State,
including those of War and Marine, and the Crown
Prince received a number of the leading representatives on behalf of the Emperor. In addition, there
were receptions in the Reichstag, by the Berlin
Chamber of Commerce, and a garden party given
by the Chancellor, at which over a thousand guests
were present.

After Prince Schoenaich-Carolath, the President, had opened the Conference, Prince Bülow delivered an address.

The Imperial Chancellor commended the increased participation of German Deputies in the movement which organisations like the Interparliamentary Union had initiated, and he claimed that the love of peace to which this growth of interest testified was in itself an act of patriotism, since the labours of the Congress would help to remove the obstacles which obstructed humanity upon its march towards the common goal of all ages and peoples.

Count Albert Apponyi, Hungarian Minister of Public Instruction, in the course of the proceedings, delivered an eloquent eulogy on Cremer's life and work, in the course of which he said : " We have lost Randal Cremer ; this upright intelligence, this quiet and concentrated enthusiasm, this great soul of a good man and one devoted to good works is no longer amongst us in order to inspire us ; this heart of pure gold which was all aglow in working for his fellow-men has ceased to beat. Will history rise to allow him a place in her annals ? I do not know ; he took no pains to write his name there, but he wished to perpetuate his ideas ; he planted a tree beneath whose shade later generations will find a rest and an assured place ; that has been his work. His work is not of stone or bronze, it cannot be finished with one stroke ; it is organic and grows slowly ; when it blossoms it ceases to be personal. In his magnanimous simplicity, Randal Cremer seems to have been appointed by Destiny to work which promised more useful results, more inward satisfaction, than noisy success. In any event, it is our duty to set forth the traits of this noble man, and to preserve and extend his memory : for such an example must not be withheld from poor humanity. Gentlemen, I request you to express to our British friends the deep sympathy which we feel in the loss which touches us all, but which, in the first place, touches them. May we continue the work of Randal Cremer with an energy which is equal to the admiration we feel for his virtues."

Following the meeting of the Interparliamentary Union, on Sunday, September 20th, the fraternal address to the German workmen was presented by eleven Labour M.P.'s and nine other Labour leaders and members of the council of the League. Berlin, and, indeed, no other European capital, has witnessed the like of the peace demonstrations which took place on that day. Two demonstrations were held, viz., that of the Social Democrats, and that of the Hirsch-Duncker trade unionists. At the first meeting the vast hall was packed hours beforehand with a crowd of five thousand persons, while eighteen thousand more in the gardens outside waited in vain for admission.

Herr Legien, the Chairman, in opening the meeting, extended a hearty welcome to the English Labour leaders. He declared that the decision as to peace and war now lay in the hands of the working classes, and if the working classes were once united the power of the Chauvinists would be broken for ever.

Mr. F. Maddison, M.P., who was received with a vast roar of welcome, presented the address. He said : " It falls to my lot, as Secretary of the International Arbitration League, to present to this great meeting, and to you, sir, an address of goodwill from representative British workers to their brothers and sisters in Germany. In order to save time, we have had the address printed in German, and therefore it will not be necessary for me to read it. In the course of translation changes in phrases have been made, and in several instances they have altered the sense as expressed in the English text, which, of course, is the reliable medium for conveying our meaning. But these defects in the German translation do not in any way affect the message of the address, which is solely concerned with the question of international peace and concord, matters of economics and party politics being outside its scope. We seek in it to represent peace as the vested interest of all engaged in legitimate trade and commerce.

" This address is the outcome of a pressing need, created by the poisonous output of a section of our press, which, we regret to know, is not without its counterpart in Germany. The Council of the International Arbitration League, led by my revered predecessor, William Randal Cremer, conceived the idea of a declaration of Anglo-German friendship, conveying the assurance of goodwill from representative trade unionists, co-operators, and friendly society men.

" Thus the object of the address is a simple one. It is to tell you, in this magnificent gathering of German workers, that the masses of the people of the United Kingdom repudiate the scaremongers of whatever party they belong to, that they attribute to the German nation no hostile designs, and that the overwhelming majority of the industrial and trading classes entertain only the friendliest of feelings towards Germany.

" Of the character of the address little need be said. It bears some three thousand representative names, which might easily have been doubled had time permitted. With two or three exceptions, all the Labour members of both sections have signed it, and amongst the signatures will be found those of many of the most prominent working-class leaders. But the address is much more than a mere official one. The bulk of the names are those of the men and women who influence opinion in their different localities, and are, therefore, in the closest touch with the rank and file.

" It is this address, Mr. Chairman, which it is my honour, on behalf of the signatories, my colleagues of the deputation, and of the International Arbitration League, to present to you, and through you, to the great German people. Our mission is not the result of any fear on our part of the power of Germany, for fear has never been a characteristic of your race or ours, but of a desire to express our fraternal regard for you and the nation of which you form a part. We do not come as politicians to politicians, but as Englishmen to Germans. As such, we scout the thought of war between the two countries, and denounce as enemies of mankind whoever by word or deed fosters the idea of so terrible a calamity, as unnecessary as it would be wicked. We want to trade with each other, not to fight, and we rejoice that we buy and sell so largely of each other's products. It is to the free exchange of the things that we each require, un-hampered by artificial restrictions, that we look for the progress of civilisation. Labour has a vested interest in peace. War only means to the toilers privation and death. It is not on the field of battle that we look for glory, but in human service. In both our countries we are burdened by excessive expenditure on armaments, and we feel that the time has more than come when we should rid ourselves of much of this ruinous waste, so that the money now devoted to non-productive purposes may be used for peaceful industry and social amelioration.

" It is in the confident belief that an Anglo-German understanding is well within the domain of statesmanship, and would be a permanent foun-dation for the world's peace, that we ask you, Mr. Chairman, to accept this address in a spirit of fra-

ternity, and, offering you the right hand of fellow-
ship, we pledge ourselves to work unceasingly for
the triumph of reason over force by the settlement
of all international disputes by arbitration."

Herr Fischer, who eulogised the liberty of
British institutions, moved a resolution, the terms of
which are given later.

Mr. Shackleton, M.P. (Chairman of the Trade
Union Congress), spoke next, expressing his pleasure at being able to convey a message of peace
from over two million organised British workers.
The workmen's feelings, he was glad to say, were
shared by the Government.

Mr. W. A. Appleton (secretary of the General
Federation of Trade Unions) and Mr. T. A. Allen
(president of the Co-operative Congress) also delivered addresses, assuring the great assembly of
the determination of the workers of Great Britain
to strive for permanent peace between the two
countries and all other nations.

At this stage the vast meeting adjourned to the
gardens outside, where brief speeches were made
by Mr. John Ward, M.P., Mr. G. D. Kelley, M.P.,
and Mr. Charles Freak. The crowds were
enormous, and the enthusiasm literally terrific.
The demonstration reached its climax when, from
the stage of the open-air theatre, Herr Legien put
this resolution :

" The working classes of Berlin organised in the
free trade unions and the Social Democratic Party
most cordially salute the delegates of the British

working classes and receive the address they have brought as an expression of fraternal solidarity.

" The dangerous and criminal agitation of certain sections directed to incite two such civilised peoples as the German and the British people against each other and to goad them on to war serves only the most narrow-minded and most shortsighted interests of the exploiting and governing classes.

" This agitation is altogether opposed to the sentiment of international brotherhood of the exploited masses of all the nations united by the closest solidarity of interests.

" In the face of the sacrifices in goods and blood which every war in the first instance imposes on the working masses, and of the enormous injury in regard to wealth and culture it inflicts on the people as a whole ; in the face of our manifold international, economical, and political connections in consequence of which each conflict between two of the civilised nations carries the danger of an international conflagration :

" The workers assembled to-day, in accordance with the resolution of the Stuttgart International Congress of 1907, pledge themselves to exert, hand in hand with the British working classes, all the appropriate means to destroy the jingoistic spirit and to safeguard peace."

When the chairman called for three cheers for the English visitors the effect was overwhelming. From the great sea of people, extended on all sides, burst a deep-throated roar of " *Hoch*," while thousands of hats were waved in the air.

The gathering of the Hirsch-Duncker trade unionists, though smaller, was equally enthusiastic. Herr Hartmann, General Secretary of the Engineers, who presided, said :

" We rejoice with you that the treaty of arbitration has been successfully concluded between France and Britain, and hear with great satisfaction from you that the enmity which had existed for so many years between these two nations has now given place to esteem and friendship. We also see therein a triumph for the workers of Britain and France, who have helped in spite of all obstacles to secure the adoption of this treaty. Nothing can prevent the workers of Germany from striving for the same goal for England and Germany."

The speeches of the English delegates were repeated at this meeting, and Herr Goldschmidt, in accepting the address, said :

" BROTHERS,—We extend to you our most cordial greeting of welcome, and desire to thank you sincerely for the statements you have just uttered. We feel ourselves in unison with you in the thought that war is detestable. Like yourselves, we also condemn the malicious attempts of a certain class of journals to sow discord between your nation and ours. Like our brothers in the great British Empire, so are we German workmen earnest defenders of peace. The German workmen know no enmity towards the workers of other civilised nations, least of all towards the English, and we are convinced that the entire German people are in unison with us in this sentiment."

One cannot but regret that the heroes of so many peace campaigns in both the Old World and the New, who in past years had found Germany somewhat stony and thorny ground, but who nevertheless had scattered the good seed therein far and wide, should not have lived to reap this magnificent harvest of fraternity and goodwill. But it will long be remembered that it was he who planned the beneficent Berlin campaign and who penned the splendid fraternal address which received so enthusiastic a welcome.

CHAPTER XXXIV

REPORTING PROGRESS

THE adoption of treaties of arbitration between
different nations, and the introduction of an arbitration clause in treaties is of course no new thing,
but the signing of an arbitration treaty between
Great Britain and France in 1903 marks a new
departure, seeing that in that treaty direct reference is made to the Hague Tribunal, and that
that treaty, the text of which was given in a
previous chapter, is the model on which most
subsequent treaties have since been formed. The
progress has indeed been remarkable, as is shown
by a chart issued by the French Ministry for
Foreign Affairs in April, 1908. This document
states that the recommendation contained in
Article 19 of the Hague Convention on Arbitration remained practically a dead letter until the
rapprochement between France and Great Britain
in October, 1903. The number of treaties has
increased every year. There were 2 in 1903,
they had grown to 27 in 1904, to 48 in 1905, to
49 in 1906, to 53 in 1907, and to 60 up to April,

To face p. 326.]

1908. Great Britain leads the way with twelve such treaties, Portugal and Switzerland follow with 10 ; Spain, France, Italy, and Norway with 9 ; Belgium, Denmark, Sweden, with 8 ; the United States with 7 ; and eleven other Powers with a smaller number. This document of the French Foreign office goes on to say :

" The second conference at the Hague in 1907 sought to extend and unify these results by means of an engagement which would have included all the 44 States there represented. The general formula which was proposed was adopted at a sitting on October 5, 1907, by the delegates of 35 countries, who declared themselves ready to establish amongst themselves, under certain reserves, a common obligation to have recourse to arbitration."

The whole of the arbitration proposal, which contained, in addition to the general formula, provisions according to which obligatory arbitration was in certain cases applicable without reserve, was voted by 32 States.

Although, owing to a want of unanimity, this vote could not be transformed into a resolution of the conference itself, it constitutes none the less an important fact, and a noteworthy advance on the results of the first conference.

It is worthy of mention that at this time no arbitration treaty was in existence between Russia and Great Britain ; nevertheless, the peaceful settlement of the differences between Great Britain and Russia over the unfortunate Dogger Bank incident was a signal triumph for the course adopted by statesmen and diplomatists who assembled at the first Hague Conference. For a week or two in this country a large part of the Press was clamorous for immediate hostilities, and but for the good sense of both Governments and the provision made at The Hague for such contingencies the quarrel might easily have led to war. It is true that the dispute was not referred to the Hague Court, but it is also true that it was settled in conformity with Article 9 of the Hague Convention. This Article runs as follows :

" In differences of an international nature involving neither honour nor vital interests, and arising from a difference of opinion on points of fact, the Signatory Powers recommend that the parties who have not been able to come to an agreement by means of diplomacy should, as far as circumstances allow, institute an International Commission of Inquiry, to facilitate a solution of these differences by elucidating the facts by means of an impartial and conscientious investigation."

Throughout the whole of its history the League has constantly combated the sinister efforts of the military party, who have from time to time endeavoured to introduce conscription into this country.

As far back as 1875 an address on the subject was issued to working men, in which the following passages occur :

" Conscription means that a large number of young men in the flower of their age shall be taken by force from their occupations to become private soldiers. Think of the loss of wages, the loss of liberty, the loss of higher education, and the loss of home influences. Think of the immorality of barrack life, the liability to foreign service in deadly climates, the slavish subordination of the soldier to his officer, the possibility of being called on to fight in quarrels in which you have no interest whatever. Fathers and mothers, do you wish your sons to be torn from you? Young men, do you wish to be dragged from useful occupations at the very time when you are beginning to make your way in the world?

" What has conscription done for France? It placed an immense army at the disposal of Napoleon III., which was used to stifle liberty. It crippled industry, it swelled taxation, it fed the vanity of the rulers, it provoked war, it led to a great national catastrophe, and instead of extending the boundaries of France, or even protecting them, it left her at the end of the war despoiled of two of her fairest provinces. At the present hour it burdens her with a crushing weight of taxation, and a constant dread of fresh attack from her old enemy.

" What has the more general, and therefore more odious, form of conscription done for Germany? It made Germany the master of France for the moment, but it has also made militarism the master of German liberty for at least a generation. What conquests, however splendid, can compensate the people for the loss of freedom? The conqueror needs pity almost as much as the conquered. Today the military system of Germany is so grievous in its drain of both men and money that thousands are emigrating to freer lands, and the whole population groans beneath the burden it has to sustain, both nations looking with dread to a renewal of the bloody strife that is still fresh in our memory."

CHAPTER XXXV

CHARACTERISTICS, BENEFACTIONS, HONOURS

CREMER had a reputation of being the most pugnacious of all pacificists, and not altogether without reason. His intolerance to those who differed from him increased with advancing years. This tendency was more especially manifested during the South African War, when not a few ministers of religion, like the Rev. Hugh Price Hughes, who had hitherto been sincere supporters of the arbitration movement, fell out of the ranks and were swept away by the current of popular feeling. For such men Cremer could find no excuse, and he attacked them with language of unmeasured severity. On this account, too, he was estranged from some of his own relatives, though they were quiet people who had never taken any public action in the matter. Some allowance, however, must be made for his bitter disappointment at the formidable obstacle suddenly raised by the outbreak of the war against the great cause which he had at heart. Hitherto this country had taken the lead in the arbitration movement, but our comrades throughout Europe deplored and denounced the action of Great

Britain, and Cremer himself keenly felt their re-
proaches although he had done his utmost in the
way of protest. To him the future of the Transvaal
was a matter of small importance compared with
the vast issues that hung upon the future success
of international arbitration. It was said of Cecil
Rhodes that he was a man who thought in continents ; Cremer's thought was for the world at
large.

Though Cremer allied himself with the Liberal-
Labour Party his sympathies were largely in a
socialistic direction. He was a strenuous advocate
of land nationalisation, of old age pensions, and
what is generally understood by municipal social-
ism. In the great cause to which his life was
devoted he welcomed the co-operation of pronounced Socialists like Mr. Herbert Burrows and
Mr. George Barnes. Indeed, the League was, as
far as he could make it, independent of party, and
numbered among its supporters Conservatives like
the late Marquis of Bristol, the late Sir Howard
Vincent, Mr. Agg-Gardner, and Lord Avebury.
The one bond of union was belief in arbitration as
a substitute for war. That was enough. He was
ready to enrol in the cause men as far apart as
Crispi of Italy, the ex-Garibaldian, and Beernaert,
the Catholic ex-Premier of Belgium ; he would
have enrolled the Pope himself if that had been
possible.

For some years Cremer was an active member
of the Kitchen Committee of the House of

Commons, and took an honest pride in his work thereon, for it is largely due to the reforms which he introduced that a Labour Member is now able to dine inside the House of Commons as cheaply as outside. He also caused something like a revolution in the wine list. A distinguished authority in the wine trade used to say that beyond a certain figure all the people paid for was a label. Cremer held the same view, and protested against the exorbitant prices which are so often charged in this country for claret and other light wines. He took so much trouble in this matter that he once introduced into the cellar of the House of Commons a hogshead of white wine direct from the vineyard of one of the most distinguished of French Pacificists, and connoisseurs declared that its bouquet was as admirable as its cheapness.

Among his peculiarities was his dislike to the tip system by which waiters were paid, which he regarded as degrading and demoralising to the recipients. Of course, he did not object to a fair wage for any class of men, but he held that the employer should pay his own servants. More than once when arranging a social function he stipulated for the payment of a fixed sum to waiters, and nothing roused his resentment more than to find the men who had been thus paid already cadging for further payment by the guests. This view of the relation of customers to waiters has been adopted by Messrs. Lyons & Co. and other large catering firms ; but before their time Cremer had endeavoured to bring it into force in the House of Commons.

Few political men have lived so lonely a life as Cremer in his later years. His large office was in reality his sleeping chamber. At the back of a bookcase was a turn-down bed, which apparently he made himself ; a small gas-stove enabled him to prepare his own breakfast. For the rest of the day he obtained his meals at the House of Commons or elsewhere. This, however, was by no means an unpleasant hermitage. Lincoln's Inn Fields is a veritable *rus in urbe*. The rich foliage of the extensive gardens altogether hid the houses on the opposite side of the square. Only from his third floor front was it possible to get a glimpse of the dome of St. Paul's, and the graceful *flêche* of the Law Courts in the Strand.

Cremer was all the more lonely because he had a horror of bores, who often are very interesting persons when you come to know them. On the landing leading to his office, he had fixed a small iron gate which he always kept locked. A casual caller had to ring for the clerk, and if the clerk happened to be out, the caller had to depart as he came ; for Cremer had a peephole which enabled him to determine whether or no he wished to receive the visitor. A few of us had the *open sesame*, and always found a warm welcome, for never was a man more accessible and companionable to his own friends.

Until he had grown old, Cremer was · a great

lover of the beauties of Nature. In the lifetime of his second wife he frequently spoke with enthusiasm of his country rambles in her company. In later years he was more interested in great cities, and seemed sometimes annoyed because the pressure of journalistic work prevented me from accompanying him on foreign expeditions. I had, however, to look after the work of the office in his absence.

It has been said that Cremer was not easy to work with, and certainly I shall not deny the fact. During his long and varied career he had not a few quarrels, some of them with men quite as honourable as himself, some with provocation, some without. His differences with George Howell, the secretary of the Reform League, always seemed trivial to the friends of both ; but they lasted for some years. It was with a chuckle of satisfaction that some of us saw the two men flung together on a common platform in Shoreditch Town Hall as Radical candidates for Haggerston and North-East Bethnal Green. At one time a serious dispute arose in the Amalgamated Society of Carpenters ; Mr. Robert Applegarth, the secretary, was supported by most of the country branches ; Cremer took an active part on the opposite side, and I fear was not justified in his action. The mention of certain other disputes, especially in the earlier parts of his career, had better be buried in oblivion.

Sometimes it was difficult for others to work in harness with him ; but the council of the

League usually gave him a free hand, and he could always rely on their cordial co-operation. Occasionally he was out-voted ; but he was content to let the adverse majority have their way, though protesting to the last that he was right.

Always his work was characterised by a steady persistence and even a splendid audacity. When once resolved upon a course of action no obstacles could daunt him, and he had the happy faculty of getting all sorts and conditions of men to do what he wanted. It was sometimes amazing to find how he laid hold of the most unlikely persons and induced them to co-operate.

On one occasion a certain financier who professed Liberal opinions and who was anxious to secure a seat in Parliament cast envious eyes upon Haggerston, and even went so far as to secure some following among the electors, to Cremer's great annoyance. The financier in question intimated that he was very desirous of entering the House of Commons, and that he considered that Haggerston was exactly the kind of constituency that would suit him. He thought that it might be possible to enter into an amicable arrangement. A man with Cremer's political reputation would find little difficulty in securing a seat elsewhere, though of course that would be attended with a certain amount of expense, and under these circumstances he would be quite willing to pay Cremer £1,000.

Of all sorts and conditions of men who seek

to enter Parliament the moneymonger was to
Cremer far more obnoxious than even the aristo-
crat or the plutocrat. I well remember that some
years before Cremer had a hand in introducing
Mr. Keir Hardie to the Radicals of West Ham
in order to spoil the game of a person of this
kind, who afterwards committed suicide. The
audacious proposal that he should sell his constituents in this manner filled him with fierce
indignation. His only answer to the man who
made this insulting suggestion was " Thy money
perish with thee."

Of Cremer's kind-heartedness to people in distress it would be easy to give instances, but it will
be sufficient to cite the following passage from a
letter written by Mr. Henry Morris, of Dalston, one
of his prominent supporters. He says : " I have
enclosed, as promised, some of the many communications I have received from Sir Randal, whose
almoner I was for his constituency. He had a
soft place for numerous appeals which I know he
personally attended to. He must have been frugal
in his own living to enable him to assist so many.
As you know, Haggerston is extremely poor, and
always has its share of out-of-works. I, as one of
the Shoreditch trustees, painfully know this by
experience. He was so well understood here that
many have denied themselves of possible help
rather than appeal to him, feeling proud of being
represented by a poor ex-working man. He contributed to our funds, but in the main the expenses of

22

the association were covered by the members' subscriptions and the grant from headquarters. However, he was a power in our midst, and many is the time that he has by his personal influence changed the whole aspect of what seemed certain collapse. Though I have at times asked him to lie low, knowing the workings of prospective changes that seemed best to his supporters, still somehow it seemed that he generally brought about what he personally thought best. Our association had much labour to keep him in his position."

Though he lived to a great age Cremer was repeatedly attacked by serious illnesses. At one time he was an inmate of the London Temperance Hospital, under the care of Sir William Collins. At another time he was carried almost lifeless to Westminster Hospital ; more than once he had to be taken to a nursing home, and it was in a nursing home that he died.

As to Cremer's views on matters of religion I incline to think that he had something more than that *nachschein* of Christianity which is often found among those who have received a Christian training in their youth, but have subsequently drifted away from all organised Christian churches. Never for a moment, even in the familiarity of friendly intercourse, did I hear Cremer utter a word, even in jest, that could be offensive to those possessing strong religious convictions. Possibly he was a doubter, but of that type that " cleaves ever to the sunnier side of doubt." My view is confirmed by one who was closely associated with him in the last few years of his life. This man, himself a secularist, said : I should reckon Cremer a very broad-minded Christian.

When Cremer lost his seat for Haggerston in 1895, Miss Frances Willard, the President of the World's Women's Christian Temperance Union, sent a resolution to Cremer from that body thanking him for his exertions in the cause of international peace. This was accompanied by a personal note in which the writer said : " I do not know of a calamity connected with the recent election that seems to me more lamentable than that you are not returned. If women had had the ballot I believe you would have had an overwhelming majority."

Cremer was probably of a different opinion. Throughout his parliamentary life Cremer was a resolute opponent of the woman suffrage movement ; indeed, he might be described as an Anti-Woman Suffrage Society in himself. He issued a tract with the title " Shall Men or Women Rule the World? " which gave thirty-three reasons against Woman Suffrage. He contended strongly that so far from women being treated unjustly by the laws of this country, privileges were conferred upon them in preference to men, and he widely circulated a leaflet entitled " Some of the Legal Privileges of Women," which ran as follows :

" That Man-made law, is, on the whole, more favourable to Women than Men is proved by the fact that Women are immune from many legal obligations, which are imposed upon Men. To prove this assertion the following illustrations and instances will suffice :—

"A Woman, however wealthy, is not legally bound to contribute to the support of her parents, however necessitous they may be, but a Man, however poor he may be, is legally responsible.

"A Man is legally responsible for any debts his Wife may incur, even without his knowledge, but a Wife is not responsible for any debts of her Husband, although she may be a wealthy Woman.

"A married Man may, by a County Court Judge, be imprisoned for Contempt of Court, if it is proved that he has the means of paying and will not do so, either his own or his Wife's debts, but no such punishment can be inflicted on a married Woman, however wealthy she may be.

"If a married Woman incurs debts, she cannot be made personally liable by being committed to prison for Contempt of Court if she fails to pay ; nor can her property be seized in order to satisfy her creditors if that property has been settled on her in the usual way. She is thus in a unique and privileged position. No similar right is allowed to a Married Man.

"A bankruptcy order can be served against a married Man, but not against a married Woman, however much wealth she may possess, unless she is carrying on a trade separately from her Husband.

"A Wife may leave her Husband without any risk, and he cannot compel her to return to him ; but if the Husband leaves his Wife, she can summon him for desertion and obtain an order for his return and support.

"A Wife may leave her Husband, occupy a separate residence, refuse to let him in, and he has no remedy ; but if he leaves her, his Wife *has* a remedy. She can support herself on his credit and obtain an order for restitution of conjugal rights and maintenance, which he disobeys at his peril.

"If a man's Wife who has a separate estate of her own slanders another Woman, and the slandered Woman is awarded damages, the Husband of the slanderer, although he knew nothing about or disapproved of what his Wife had done, is liable to pay the costs of the trial and damages, while his wealthy Wife escapes with impunity.

"If a Man has a Wife who spends his wages in drink, sells his furniture and breaks up his home to obtain drink, deserts him and his children, leaving them without food, he has no remedy, and cannot leave her without risk of being punished for desertion ; but if a Man behaves in such a manner towards his wife, she can obtain a judicial separation and an order compelling him to maintain her.

"All these laws, exempting Women from obligations which Men are compelled to perform, were made by what Suffragists refer to as "Mere Men." If the Suffragists, instead of denouncing those who differ from them as "brutes, tyrants," etc., etc., would prove that Women suffer any real injustice, and state what their grievances are, they would be respectfully listened to and redressed."

Twice Cremer spoke in the House of Commons against woman suffrage, and he declared that several Members who had voted in its favour came to him afterwards and congratulated him upon his courageous opposition. He republished and widely distributed these speeches, because some of the suffragettes charged him with having shamefully slandered women. Cremer contended that if any women should be enfranchised all women should be enfranchised, and that thereby the male population of the country would be swamped, seeing that the female population outnumbers the men by nearly a million. He urged also that the ultimate object of the leaders of the movement was to secure admission for themselves into the House of Commons, and that but for this hope the movement would speedily collapse. Yet further he insisted that women were largely under the influence of priests and of pseudo-philanthropists, who were only masked politicians. He further protested that women were unfitted by their physical nature to exercise political power, and he firmly believed that the majority of them had no desire to obtain it.

It required no small amount of courage for Cremer to resist a demand in opposition to the majority of his own political friends. The feeling on both sides was decidedly bitter. Occasionally some of the militant suffragettes appeared at meetings at which Cremer was to speak on the arbitration question. On one occasion when he had to address a large P.S.A. meeting at Camberwell a number of these ladies attended, some of whom mounted the platform and delivered an ineffectual protest, which was not at all relished by the majority of the audience. On another occasion when Cremer was announced to speak at a peace meeting in Manchester Mrs. Philip Snowden refused to appear on the platform with him. Still more recently Cremer bitterly complained that a cabal was formed by some of his Haggerston constituents and certain leaders of the Metropolitan Liberal Association to drive him from his seat. Reasonable advocates of woman suffrage will certainly not question Cremer's honesty and courage.

Some years before his death Cremer had expressed to me his intention to erect a few almshouses at Fareham, his birthplace. He had a double motive. He wished to pay a tribute of filial piety to the memory of his mother, of whom he said in a speech in the House of Commons on the woman suffrage question that he proudly acknowledged whatever he was and had were due to her devotion. He desired also to do something toward helping those who had fought the battle of life more or less unsuccessfully in their declining days. For many years it had been the policy of those who had the administration of endowed charities to alienate as far as possible what they called " doles " to educational purposes, not unfrequently to the education of the children of the middle classes. Cremer held that this policy was unjust. Happily of late there has been a healthy reaction in favour of old age pensions.

So large a proportion of Cremer's means had been already devoted to the cause in which he had so long laboured that he was only able to carry out his wishes in regard to the almshouses on a very modest scale. He purchased a plot of land at the cost of about £350, on which four almshouses were to be built, and in which the occupants were to live rent free. Next he invested £200 in Hampshire County Council stock in order to provide for rates and repairs. Had he lived but a few months longer all the necessary materials would have been purchased by himself and the houses erected under his personal supervision ; but his design remained uncompleted at his death.

Like his old friend Lord Hobhouse, he did not believe in the " dead hand," and he left his executors entirely unfettered, as will be seen by the following extract from his will : " Upon trust that my executors, or so many of them as shall prove this my will, shall retain for their use jointly and absolutely, the sum of nine hundred pounds (free of legacy duty) provided that (but nevertheless without imposing upon them any legal or equitable obligation, trust, or election whatsoever, or interfering with their full and absolute beneficial right or property in that sum) I declare it to be my wish that as soon after my death as may be they shall, in so far as they think proper, pay and apply the same for the benefit of the charitable objects mentioned in the signed letter and memorandum left by me and deposited with this my will and headed ' Cottages at Fareham,' and I hope that it may be possible for them to carry out the wishes expressed in the said letter and memorandum."

As far back as 1890 M. Carnot, the President of the French Republic, conferred upon Cremer the Cross of the Legion of Honour, which makes the recipient a " Chevalier " of the Legion. Cremer's exertions in promoting the *entente cordiale* had been unremitting for some years previously ; but as the distinction was conferred only a few months after the meeting of the first interparliamentary conference at Paris, it was regarded as a mark of sympathy on the part of the French Government with the work so well begun. Times have indeed changed since Napoleon Bonaparte founded this Order, which, by the way, is partly military and partly civilian. The honour has not unfrequently been conferred upon British subjects, but except in the case of Mr. Hodgson Pratt, I remember no instance in which the decoration was conferred directly for promoting concord between the two nations. On this account Cremer was proud of the distinction and often wore its ribbon.

After the Nobel Prize was awarded to Cremer he was made a Commander of the Norwegian Order of Saint Olav. This Order bears the name of that ancient King of Norway who sought to convert its people to Christianity by fire and sword. The name at once recalls Longfellow's poem in " Tales of a Wayside Inn," where he represents the Abbess of Drontheim listening to the voice of St. John the beloved disciple.

> " It is accepted
> The angry defiance,
> The challenge of battle !
> It is accepted,
> But not with the weapons
> Of war that thou wieldest !

Cross against corselet,
Love against hatred,
Peace-cry for war-cry,
Patience is wonderful ;
He that o'ercometh
Hath power o'er the nations.

Stronger than steel
Is the sword of the Spirit ;
Swifter than arrows
The light of the truth is ;
Greater than anger
Is love, and subdueth."

It is a rule of the Order of St. Olav that on the death of a Commander his " star " has to be returned, otherwise we should have been glad to have retained it among the heirlooms of the League.

Shortly after Sir Henry Campbell-Bannerman became Prime Minister he offered Cremer the honour of knighthood. Cremer was doubtful whether he should accept it, and consulted two or three of his intimate friends. We were all dubious about such titular distinction, and therefore Cremer declined the honour. But Sir Henry made the offer a second time and it had to be reconsidered. Cremer, of course, did not care a straw for titles ; as I happen to know from his private papers the one honour he cherished most was that he had been five times elected Member for Haggerston. There was, however, no hereditary nonsense about a knighthood. In former days

every knight was a warrior, and usually won his
spurs on the field of battle ; but in recent times
explorers, scientists, artists, musicians, and in-
ventors have received such a distinction.   Why
should a representative of labour be compelled to
stand aside?   In the diplomatic service of the
country similar and even larger honours are often
awarded to men who have done nothing more than
perform a round of official duty ; why should not
" the fountain of honour " recognise the unofficial
services of a man who had for long years been
the representative of a nation rather than of a
Court, and the value of whose work had been
freely recognised by statesmen and diplomatists?
Cremer's main reason for acceptance was that the
offer was an indirect recognition in the highest
quarters of the value of the work of the League.

CHAPTER XXXVI

THE ULTIMATE GOAL

THE dreams of democracy often become the statesmanship of the future. More than a century ago France led the way, inscribing on her banner, "Liberty, Equality, Fraternity!" The international coalition of monarchs and aristocrats drove the people of France to madness, and made them the victims of a military adventurer, from the consequences of whose cruel ambition Europe has not fully recovered even now. But all the while the peoples have been steadily pressing forward to the realisation of a noble ideal, in spite of the reaction caused by the great war of 1870. The international coalition of monarchs and aristocrats, which is dying or dead, has been replaced by a new international coalition of the democracy, whose watchword is, "A bas les frontières." Slowly, but surely, the solidarity of labour is becoming an accomplished fact. Through long centuries the pride and greed of priestcraft and the alliance of the Christian Church with the secular power have thwarted the Divine idea of Jesus.

The professed servants of the Master, who knew their Lord's will and did it not, are being replaced by those unconscious instruments who know not their Lord's will but unconsciously do it ; and happily, there is now a growing disposition on the part of modern official representatives of Christianity to cherish broader and deeper conceptions of patriotism, not only in the Free Churches, which have usually borne witness for peace, but in the English Established Church itself.

To what does all this lead? To the fact that war panics are visionary and ephemeral. Yet, further, to the fact that in spite of occasional backward eddies the stream of progress is ever onward. Who can doubt that

" Through the ages one increasing purpose runs,
  And the thoughts of men are widened with the progress of
      the suns " ?

With deliberate purpose I have largely used names of eminent men and quotations from their utterances in this biography. Less than half a century ago those who contended against militarism were regarded, not only by the governing class, but even by democrats as amiable enthusiasts whose ideas were altogether outside the domain of practical politics. Who would dare to affirm this now?

Largely by the efforts of the man whose life-story is here told, a strong international peace party has been created, whose spokesmen have their representatives in every Parliament of the civilised world. We have friends and helpers in almost every cabinet and in almost every embassy. The foremost leaders in religion are aroused to their duty as they never were before, and labour in its solidarity is rapidly becoming strong enough to confront militarism in every country.

This book is written at a time when the most desperate efforts are being made to create another war panic. The stage, the music-hall, the studio, and the gutter press are all freely used by the scaremongers. The leaders of the Conservative Party, though Lord Lansdowne and Mr. Balfour have, to their credit, contributed to the cause of international peace, seem only too ready to foster the dread of invasion in the hope that it may facilitate their return to power. It is not the first time that the champions of class privileges and class interests have sought to delude the people by setting up a phantom enemy. But the devices of mendacity which were so successfully used at the outset of the Boer War have been too recently exposed to produce much effect now. Against the nefarious wickedness of those who, either in Britain or Germany, sow the dragon's teeth of distrust and hatred, we must oppose the resolute determination of all men of goodwill and clear judgment. Britain and Germany, who have never fought each other in the past, have no cause of quarrel now ; their quarrel is with those disseminators of discord who are the common enemies of humanity. Happily, not only

moral but economic forces are ranging themselves
on our side. The mischief-makers in all countries
are unwittingly aiding our efforts, for the revolt
against the monstrous burden of war expenditure
is rapidly extending to the very classes who have
hitherto been the promoters of panics.

The champion of peace whose biography is here
written had lived through half a dozen war scares,
and had been unmoved through them all. He
had seen British blood and treasure wantonly
wasted in the abortive effort to maintain the barbarous rule of the Sultan throughout the Balkan
peninsula ; he had heard the stupid clamour for
war between France and England, on both sides
of the Channel, when Napoleon III. was in
power ; he had seen the Guards dispatched to
Canada when the United States cruiser seized the
Confederate envoys ; he had resisted the cry for
war when the Russians were almost at the gates
of Constantinople, and again when the Russian
fleet fired by mistake on English fishermen ; he
had made a happy use of the Fashoda *contretemps*
to bring about an *entente cordiale* between the
British and the French democracies. What sane
man to-day would dare to stand up and say that
he was wrong?

We, who mourn our lost leader, shall continue
his work. We are practical politicians. While
the apparent necessity lasts we do not oppose
adequate measures of national defence ; but it
is the imperative duty of the international peace

party, now fully organised, to destroy such necessity—first, by means of international arbitration, and, second, by a mutual and simultaneous reduction of armaments. The former object is already more than half accomplished, and this success should impel us to renewed efforts on behalf of the latter. The substitution of arbitration for war must in the end produce a revolt against wasteful, ruinous war preparations. We know that we can only advance step by step, but the goal before us is the total abolition of war, and to that end we press forward with resolute courage and unfaltering faith.

INDEX

ALVERSTONE, Lord, 73, 183
American Civil War, 26, 29
Anglo-French Treaty, 228
Apponyi, Count Albert, 176, 317
Arbitration, Progress of, 327
Arbitration Treaty, Abortive, 167, 185, 187
Arbitration Treaty in French Chamber, 170
Arbitration with the United States, 150
Avebury, Lord (Sir John Lubbock), 152

BARTHOLDT, Hon. Richard, 260, 292
Basili, M., 178, 180
Beales, Edmond, 42, 86
Behring Sea Arbitration, 156, 164
Berlin Demonstration, 318
Berry, Dr. Charles, 186
Blaine, James G., 132
Boer War, 206, 216
Bourgeois, M., 194
Bourse du Travail Demonstration, 208, 212

Bright, John, Letter of, 28
Brunner, Sir John, 232
Bryce, Mr. James, 264
Builders' Lock-out, 25
Burritt, Elihu, 59
Burt, Rt. Hon. Thomas, 86, 111, 270

CAMPBELL-BANNERMAN, Sir H., 282, 293, 346
Carnegie, Mr. Andrew, 123, 125, 132, 276, 277, 311
Chamberlain, Mr., and Lord Weardale, 220
Chartists, 21
Chili and Argentina, 166, 292
Clemenceau, M., 112
Cleveland, President, 127, 161, 164
Cluseret's Revolutionary Project, 45
Corn Law Days, 20
Cremer, Sir Randal, Birth and Parentage, 19; early Poverty, 21; goes to Work, 23; apprenticed, 23; migrates to London, 24; Nine Hours'

Movement, ·25 ; American Civil War, 27 ; the International, 31 ; Garibaldi in London, 40 ; Reform League, 42 ; Warwick Elections, 49 ; St. Pancras Vestry, 54 ; Workmen's Peace Committee, 82 ; W. P. Association, 83 ; Pioneer Work in Paris, 88 ; the Eastern Crisis, 97 ; Anti - war Demonstrations, 100 ; South African Affairs, 106 ; Egypt, 107 ; in Paris again, 109 ; Haggerston Elections, 114 ; Death of second Wife, 119 ; first Visit to Washington, 123 ; first Parliamentary Memorial, 126 ; Pan-American Conference, 132 ; Birth of the Interparliamentary Union, 135 (for its conferences see separate heading) ; Dispute with Portugal, 143 ; Arbitration Resolution in House of Commons, 150 ; second Visit to Washington, 158 ; second Parliamentary Memorial, 160 ; Defeat and Petition at Haggerston, 172 ; Labour Memorial to the United States, 182 ; third Visit to Washington, 182 ; the Tsar's Rescript, 189 ; first Hague Conference, 194 ; Nobel Peace Prize, 201, 259 ; Address to French Workmen, 208 ; at the Bourse du Travail, 210 ; French

Workers Visit London, 213 ; Boer War, 216 ; returned again for Haggerston, 221 ; French Parliamentary Visit to London, 225 ; British Parliamentary Visit to France, 235 ; fourth Visit to Washington, 260 ; the Nobel Dinner, 267 ; Interparliamentary Union at Westminster, 281 ; second Hague Conference, 294 ; the Final Effort, 298 ; last Illness and Death, 304 ; Will, 304 ; Funeral Service, 305 ; Count Albert Apponyi's Eulogy, 317 ; Berlin Labour Demonstrations, 313 ; Characteristics, 331 ; Benefactions, 337 ; Female Suffrage, 339 ; Fareham Cottages, 343 ; Legion of Honour, 344 ; Cross of St. Olav, 345 ; Knighthood, 346

Cremer's Trustees, 275
Crimean War, 63
Criterion Dinner to Labour M.P.'s, 118

Davitt, Michael, 185
De Profundis, 119
Derby, Lord, Deputation to, 98
D'Estournelles de Constant, Baron, 225, 227, 286
Descamps, Baron, 177

Eastern Crisis, 98 ; Peace Manifesto, 98

Eastern Peace Demonstration, 100

"Edward the Peacemaker," 225

Egypt, 107

FALLIÈRES, M., 206

Fareham, 19 ; Cottages, 343

Female Suffrage, 339

Field, David Dudley, 71, 142

Forewords, 11

French Labour Visit to London, 213

French Parliamentary Visit to London, 224

Fry, Sir Edward, 294

GARIBALDI in London, 14

Geneva Arbitration, 74 ; Consequential Damages, 77 ; these withdrawn, 79 ; Judgment, 79

German Workmen, Address to, 299

Gladstone, Mr., 69, 101, 105, 107, 141, 152

Goal, Ultimate, 348

Grant from British Government, 290

Gresham, Mr. Secretary, 158, 161, 163

HAGGERSTON Elections, 114, 117, 118, 173, 221

Haggerston Petition, 174

Haggerston Testimonial, 279

Hague Conferences, The, 194, 291

Harcourt, Sir W., 154, 222, 269

Hereford, Bishop of, 279

Herschell, Lord, 142

INTERNATIONAL Arbitration League (see Workmen's Peace Association and Cremer).

International, The, 31; Balancesheet, 35

International Geneva Conference, 35 ; Collapse, 38

International Law Association, 70

Inter - Parliamentary Union, Projected, 134 ; Birth, 135 ; Conferences, 138, 146, 169, 171, 174, 198, 199, 203, 230, 260, 281, 291, 317

JOFFRIN, M., 110

LABOUR Conferences, Official, 33

Longuet, M., 37, 212

Lund, John, 199

McKINLEY, President, 188

Maddison, F., 278, 298, 303, 309, 319

Maret, M. Henri, 110

Memorial Meeting, 313

Morgan, Senator, 185

NINE Hours' Movement, 25

Nobel Dinner, 267

Nobel Peace Prize, 201, 259, 266

OLNEY, Mr. Secretary, 167

PAN-AMERICAN Conference, 131

Paris Exhibition, 203

Paris, Meetings in, 88, 93, 94, 109, 208, 212

Paris, Treaty of, 65

Parliamentary Memorial, First, 126 ; Second, 160

Parliamentary Visit to France, 235

Passy, M. Frederic, 170

Pauncefote, Sir Julian, 158, 162, 194, 196

Peace Conference, First, 60

Peace Society, 56, 63

Portugal, Dispute with, 143

Pratt, Hodgson, 73

REFORM League, Birth, 42 ; Trafalgar Square, 43 ; Hyde Park, 44, 67 ; Dissolved, 48

Richard, Henry, 57, 65, 69, 70

Rogers, Dr. Guinness, 165

Roosevelt, President, 262

Root, Mr. Secretary, 264

Rosebery, Lord, 194

Russians at Westminster, 285

ST. PANCRAS Vestry, 54

Salisbury, Lord, 145, 179, 183, 184

Scarborough Riots, 218

School Board Contests, 53

Sherman, Senator, 140, 162

Simon, Jules, 137

Smith, Mr. E. G., 299

Stead, W. T., 179, 200

Sturge, Joseph, 58

Times, The, on Hague Conference, 196

Tolain, Senator, 31, 37

Transvaal Troubles, 106

Trarieux, M., 171

Tsar's Rescript, 189

VENEZUELA Dispute, 164

WAR Scares, 66

Warwick Elections, 49

Washington, Visits to, 123, 161, 182, 260

Weardale, Lord, 169, 198, 220, 281, 308

Westminster Hall Banquet, 288

Whittier, John G., 133

Workmen's Peace Committee, 82 ; Association, 83 ; Programme, 84 ; Manifesto, 85

YELLOW Press, 208, 217

ZULU War, 105

UNWIN BROTHERS, LIMITED, THE GRESHAM PRESS, WOKING AND LONDON.